YALE ORIENTAL SERIES · RESEARCHES · VOLUME XV

NABONIDUS AND BELSHAZZAR

A STUDY OF THE CLOSING EVENTS OF THE NEO-BABYLONIAN EMPIRE

BY

RAYMOND PHILIP DOUGHERTY

William M. Laffan Professor of Assyriology and Babylonian Literature and Curator of the Babylonian Collection, Yale University

LVX ET VERITAS

NEW HAVEN

YALE UNIVERSITY PRESS

LONDON · HUMPHREY MILFORD · OXFORD UNIVERSITY PRESS

MDCCCCXXIX

1929

Printed in the United States of America

To My Father and Mother
IN GRATEFUL REMEMBRANCE

PREFACE

The impulse to prepare this monograph originated a little more than ten years ago from the study of Neo-Babylonian contract tablets under the direction of Professor A. T. Clay, whose inspiring instruction and contagious enthusiasm engendered a liking for the field of Assyriological research. Afterwards the privilege of devoting personal attention to the decipherment of Nabonidus texts in the Yale Babylonian Collection led to an investigation of all available Neo-Babylonian source material for the purpose of discovering Belshazzar's rôle in history. Publication of cuneiform tablets of the same reign belonging to Goucher College widened the range of pertinent data and contributed an important clue to the political situation which was a prelude to the close of the Neo-Babylonian empire.

Special mention should be made of the practical help rendered by Doctor E. M. Grice, who exhibited deep interest in the questions discussed in this monograph and was ready at all times to aid in the solution of textual and interpretative problems. The incentive and assistance obtained from Professor Clay and Doctor Grice are acknowledged with grateful appreciation. That it was necessary for them to give up their labors in the midst of strenuous achievement will ever be regarded as an irreparable loss to the science of Assyriology.

Helpful suggestions and valuable information were furnished by the following: Professors C. C. Torrey, E. H. Sturtevant, J. A. Montgomery, W. F. Albright, A. H. Sayce, T. G. Pinches, and S. Langdon. In addition the author is indebted to Doctor H. R. Hall for the opportunity of studying tablets in the British Museum, and to Messrs. Sidney Smith and C. J. Gadd for kind assistance.

Sincere gratitude is expressed to all who coöperated in any way in the production of this volume.

RAYMOND PHILIP DOUGHERTY.

New Haven, Conn.,
September 22, 1928

CONTENTS

ILLUSTRATIONS

ABBREVIATIONS

AENN	Dougherty, *Archives from Erech, Time of Nebuchadrezzar and Nabonidus, GCCI* I.
AJSL	*American Journal of Semitic Languages and Literatures.*
B	Brünnow, *A Classified List of all Simple and Compound Cuneiform Ideographs.*
BA	*Beiträge zur Assyriologie.*
Bar	Barton, *The Origin and Development of Babylonian Writing, BA* IX.
BE	*The Babylonian Expedition of the University of Pennsylvania, Series A: Cuneiform Texts.*
BHT	Smith, *Babylonian Historical Texts.*
BIN	*Babylonian Inscriptions in the Collection of J. B. Nies.*
CAH	*The Cambridge Ancient History.*
CB	Aucher, *Eusebii Pamphilii Caesariensis Episcopi Chronicon Bipartitum*, Pars I, MDCCCXVIII.
CD	Muss-Arnoldt, *A Concise Dictionary of the Assyrian Language.*
CLP	Schoene, *Eusebii Chronicorum Liber Prior.*
ContCL	Contenau, *Contrats et Lettres d'Assyrie et de Babylonie, Musée du Louvre—Département des Antiquités Orientales, Textes Cunéiformes*, IX.
ContCN	Contenau, *Contrats Néo-Babyloniens, Musée du Louvre—Département des Antiquités Orientales, Textes Cunéiformes*, XII.
CT	*Cuneiform Texts from Babylonian Tablets, etc., in the British Museum.*
DlSGl	Delitzsch, *Sumerisches Glossar.*
EMNL	Evetts, *Inscriptions of the Reigns of Evil-Merodach, Neriglissar, and Laborosoarchod.*
GCCI	*Goucher College Cuneiform Inscriptions.*
Euseb. Praep.	Eusebius, *Praeparatio Evangelica.*
HRETA	Nies and Keiser, *Historical, Religious, and Economic Texts and Antiquities, BIN* II.
Hwb	Delitzsch, *Assyrisches Handwörterbuch.*
JADD	Johns, *Assyrian Deeds and Documents.*
JAOS	*Journal of the American Oriental Society.*
JRAS	*Journal of the Royal Asiatic Society.*
K	*Kouyunjik Collection of the British Museum.*

KA	Weissbach, *Die Keilinschriften der Achämeniden, VAB* III.
*KAT*³	Schrader, *Die Keilinschriften und das Alte Testament,* 3te Aufl.
KB	Schrader, *Keilinschriftliche Bibliothek.*
LCE	Keiser, *Letters and Contracts from Erech, BIN* I.
LSS	*Leipziger Semitistische Studien.*
M	Meissner, *Seltene assyrische Ideogramme.*
MI	Clay, *Miscellaneous Inscriptions in the Yale Babylonian Collection, YBT* I.
NKI	Langdon, *Die Neubabylonische Königsinschriften, VAB* IV.
NLE	Clay, *Neo-Babylonian Letters from Erech, YBT* III.
OLZ	*Orientalistische Literaturzeitung.*
PgnIS	Pognon, *Inscriptions Sémitiques de la Syrie, de la Mésopotamie et de la Région de Mossoul.*
PSBA	*Proceedings of the Society of Biblical Archaeology.*
R	Rawlinson, *The Cuneiform Inscriptions of Western Asia.*
RA	*Revue d'Assyriologie et d'Archéologie Orientale.*
RB	*Revue Biblique Internationale.*
RECC	Tremayne, *Records from Erech, Time of Cyrus and Cambyses, YBT* VII.
REN	Dougherty, *Records from Erech, Time of Nabonidus, YBT* VI.
SBD	Dougherty, *The Shirkûtu of Babylonian Deities, YOR* V-2.
StrCamb	Strassmaier, *Inschriften von Cambyses.*
StrCyr	Strassmaier, *Inschriften von Cyrus.*
StrDar	Strassmaier, *Inschriften von Darius.*
StrNbk	Strassmaier, *Inschriften von Nabuchodonosor.*
StrNbn	Strassmaier, *Inschriften von Nabonidus.*
TSBA	*Transactions of the Society of Biblical Archaeology.*
VAB	*Vorderasiatische Bibliothek.*
VS	*Vorderasiatische Schriftdenkmäler.*
YBT	*Yale Oriental Series, Babylonian Texts.*
YOR	*Yale Oriental Series, Researches.*
ZA	*Zeitschrift für Assyriologie.*
ZDMG	*Zeitschrift der Deutschen Morgenländischen Gesellschaft.*

I

INTRODUCTION

Southwestern Asia witnessed the enactment of a notable historical drama during the eight decades which preceded the fall of Babylon in 539 B. C. Assyria, on account of Elamite aggression, had been able to impose only partial domination upon Babylonia for little more than a century following the Ninth Babylonian Dynasty which ended in 732 B. C. Its own military excesses and Scythian invasion of the land caused Nineveh to suffer serious decline, and hence the imperial city yielded to the united onslaught of Medes, Scythians, and Babylonians in 612 B. C.[1] This event signalized the beginning of a renaissance of Babylonian political power which produced the Neo-Babylonian empire, known formerly as the Chaldaean empire, whose sovereigns were Nabopolassar, Nebuchadrezzar II, Amêl-Marduk, Neriglissar, Lâbâshi-Marduk, and Nabonidus in conjunction with his son Belshazzar. During this epoch of sturdy Babylonian national and cultural life there was opportunity for an intense development of society in the southern part of the Tigris-Euphrates valley. At the same time more energetic expansion of Babylonian political influence beyond the limits of the kingdom became feasible. Attractive as all the movements and events of Neo-Babylonian history are, no inclusive and detailed discussion of them is possible in this monograph, as the aim is to give specific attention to the period in which Nabonidus and Belshazzar were the controlling personalities. Copious quotations and translations of original sources will enable the reader to judge for himself as to the amount of light thrown upon this interesting era.

During three quarters of a century of advance in cuneiform decipherment the contents of numerous inscriptions dated in the reign of Nabonidus have been made available to the world. More than five hundred tablets of this type have been published in the last decade.[2] This accumulation of records contemporaneous with the

[1] See Gadd, *The Fall of Nineveh*, pp. 13–20.

[2] Most of the new texts appear in *LCE*, *HRETA*, *REN*, *AENN*, and *ContCL*.

closing years of the Neo-Babylonian empire is of inestimable value to the philologist, the archaeologist, and the historian. Certain documents coming from the time of Cyrus belong to the source material which should be studied. All these texts furnish linguistic, social, industrial, commercial, legal, and religious data the authenticity and veracity of which cannot be questioned. Since inscriptions of actual historical significance are supplemented by various kinds of contract literature, the true course of events is indicated both directly and indirectly. Each text represents some phase of the life of the period. A single record, though revealing nothing more than an ordinary transaction, may provide a clue of the utmost importance.

When the initial translation of a cuneiform document or the review of a well-known record suggests a more accurate basis of exposition, much may be gained by a careful examination of related inscriptions. Interpretation in the field of Assyriology, due to the fact that new discoveries may shed light over a wide range of texts, is subject to periodic revision. The consequent need for a fresh orientation of ideas and conclusions concerning the past should be welcomed by all interested in the study of history, the decipherer of Babylonian tablets included. With these principles in mind, the general situation during the last reign of the Neo-Babylonian empire will be considered. An attempt will be made to determine more accurately the rôles played by the dominant national leaders of the time, viz., *Nabû-nâ'id,* known commonly as Nabonidus, the last native king of Babylon, and *Bêl-šar-uṣur,* his son, the Biblical Belshazzar. The fascination of this study springs from the work of comparing and elucidating numerous documents which will now be classified.

DOCUMENTARY SOURCES

Primary and secondary sources of information, representing different periods of composition and contrasting types of literature, are at hand for the investigation which has been outlined in the foregoing statements. A fresh inquiry into the character of the last Neo-Babylonian reign possesses unusual significance on account of interesting extant writings which were impressed upon clay at the time when the human activities described by them took place. With very little exception the origin of these documents synchronizes with the date of their contents. The works of later historians, separated by centuries from the events recorded by them and dependent in the main upon tradition, are less accurate in details. Nevertheless they contain assertions and intimations which are valuable reflections of ancient times, for which reason their pages may often be appraised with corroborative results in the light of cuneiform data.

1. Cuneiform Sources

Original cuneiform texts in the Babylonian language, dealing with the last part of the Neo-Babylonian régime and the first part of the Persian era, have come down to us from the sixth century B. C. Those which furnish data concerning Nabonidus and Belshazzar may be summarized as follows:

(1) *Building Inscriptions of Nabonidus.* These texts describe the restoration of temples at Ḫarrân, Sippar, Larsa, and Ur.[3]

(2) *Nabonidus Chronicle,* also called *Cyrus-Nabonidus Chronicle, Nabonidus-Cyrus Chronicle,* and *The Annalistic Tablet of Cyrus.* This inscription of Cyrus depicts the main events of the reign of Nabonidus year by year and describes the fall of Babylon.[4]

(3) *Persian Verse Account of Nabonidus.* This is a further interpretation of the occurrences which took place in the reign of Nabonidus.[5]

(4) *Cyrus Cylinder,* or *Cylinder Inscription of Cyrus.* The capture of Babylon by Cyrus and his accession to the rulership of an extensive kingdom are recorded in this historical inscription.[6]

(5) *Eski-Ḫarrân Inscription.* This text has been interpreted as an inscription of the father or the mother of Nabonidus.[7]

[3] Nos. 1–8 of Nabonidus inscriptions, *NKI* pp. 46–57, 218–289; *KB* III, 2, pp. 80–119. For the sake of uniformity Roman numerals are used in referring to the volumes of publications.

[4] *TSBA* VII, pp. 139–176; *KB* III, 2, pp. 128ff; *BA* II, pp. 214–225; 235–257; *BHT* pp. 98–123, pls. XI–XIV.

[5] *BHT* pp. 27–97, pls. VI–X. Albright styles the inscription *The Neo-Babylonian Panegyric of Cyrus.* See *JRAS* April, 1925, p. 293.

[6] *KA* pp. 2–9; *KB* III, 2, pp. 120–127; *BA* II, pp. 208ff.

[7] *PgnIS* pp. 1–14; *RB* V, pp. 130–135; *NKI* pp. 57f; 288–294.

(6) *Business Documents.* These texts consist of legal records, commercial accounts, and official letters from temple archives.[8]

2. Greek Sources

Certain historians using the Greek language, ranging from the fifth century B. C. to the third century A. D., have recorded interesting facts concerning Neo-Babylonian kings and the fall of Babylon. In chronological order these historians are as follows:

(1) *Herodotus* (484–425 B. C.), recognized as "The Father of History." He claims to have made extended travels and investigations in the lands concerning which he wrote.[9]

(2) *Xenophon* (431–355 B. C.). The *Cyropaedia* is his most important work from the standpoint of information concerning the fall of Babylon.[10]

(3) *Megasthenes*, of the time of Seleucus Nicator (312–280 B. C.). The fragment of his work quoted by Eusebius comes from Abydenus.[11] A further quotation is given by Annius.[12]

(4) *Berossus* (c. 250 B. C.), a Babylonian priest of Bêl. He wrote a history of his people in the Greek language with the help of cuneiform sources. His works have perished, but fragments have been preserved by Josephus and Eusebius.[13]

(5) *Alexander Polyhistor*, of the first century B. C. He is called Polyhistor because of his voluminous historical writings, fragments of which are quoted by Josephus and Eusebius.[14]

(6) *Claudius Ptolemy*, a versatile writer of the second century A. D. He wrote on such subjects as mathematics, astronomy, geography, etc. His κανὼν βασιλέων, quoted generally as the *Canon of Ptolemy*,

[8] *StrNbn*, *MI*, *NLE*, *REN*, *AENN*, *VS*, and *ContCL* contain the most important references to Nabonidus and Belshazzar in published Neo-Babylonian contract tablets and letters.

[9] Herodotus I, 188–191.

[10] *Cyropaedia* IV, 6; VII, 5.

[11] *CB* pp. 29f; *CLP* cols. 41ff.

[12] *TSBA* I, pp. 247 and 262.

[13] Josephus, *Contra Apionem* I, 20. See Schnabel, *Berossus und die babylonisch-hellenistische Literatur*, pp. 273–275; Richter, *Berosi Chaldaeorum Historiae.*

[14] *CB* p. 22; *CLP* col. 27f.

contains tables of the reigns of Assyrian, Babylonian, Persian, and Greek kings.[15]

(7) *Abydenus,* a Greek historian, probably of Semitic origin, who wrote in the second or third century A. D. A fragment of his work is quoted by Eusebius.[16]

3. Jewish Sources

That certain references to Neo-Babylonian history should appear in Jewish writings is not surprising. The following sources exist:

(1) *Canonical Source, i.e. The Fifth Chapter of Daniel,* a portion of the Hagiographa of the Jews. This source is an ancient document in the Aramaic language containing the traditional Jewish account of the closing scene in Neo-Babylonian history.[17]

(2) *Deutero-Canonical Source, i.e. The Book of Baruch,* classed among the Apocrypha. Its historical introduction (1:1–15) is regarded by some as having been written originally in the Hebrew language.[18]

(3) *Non-Canonical Source, i.e. The Works of Flavius Josephus,* written in the Greek language by a Jewish historian of the first century A. D. Important quotations from Megasthenes, Berossus and Alexander Polyhistor are preserved in his extensive historical writings.[19]

4. Ecclesiastical Sources

The works of early church historians have chronicled important events and preserved valuable information recorded in older sources. These church historians are as follows:

[15] Halma, *Table Chronologique des Règnes,* 1819, Seconde Partie, p. 3; Cory, *Ancient Fragments of the Phoenician, Chaldaean, Egyptian, Tyrian, Carthaginian, Indian, Persian and Other Writers,* 1832, p. 83f; Kugler, *Sternkunde und Sterndienst in Babel,* 1924, II, 2, 2, p. 391.

[16] *CB* p. 27; *CLP* cols. 31ff; *Euseb. Praep.* IX, 41.

[17] For an exhaustive study of the fifth chapter of Daniel see Prince, *Mene, Mene, Tekel, Upharsin.* It should be remembered, however, that this volume was written before the most recently discovered cuneiform references to Belshazzar came into the possession of scholars.

[18] See *The Apocrypha, According to the Authorized Version;* Swete, *The Old Testament in Greek,* III, p. 351f; Charles, *Apocrypha and Pseudepigrapha of the Old Testament,* I, p. 571f; Schaff's *Critical, Doctrinal, and Homiletical Commentary,* XV, pp. 410–419.

[19] See Niese, *Flavii Josephi Opera,* Dindorfius, *Flavii Josephi Opera,* and Whiston's translation entitled *The Works of Flavius Josephus,* for *Antiq. Jud.,* and *Contra Apionem.*

(1) *Eusebius Pamphilius*, known as *Eusebius*, a bishop at Caesarea and a prominent historian. He was born between 260 and 265 A. D. and died in 339 or 340 A. D. His main work was a *Chronicle*[20] in the Greek language consisting of two parts, the first giving an epitome of history, the second containing chronological tables. Armenian,[21] Syriac,[22] and Latin[23] versions of this *Chronicle* have been preserved.

(2) *Eusebius Sophronius Hieronymus*, known as *Saint Jerome*, belonging to the period extending from about 340 to 420 A. D. His great work was the Vulgate translation of the Bible. He also translated the *Chronicle of Eusebius* into Latin and wrote commentaries on various prophetical books, including Daniel, which he defended against Porphyry.[24]

(3) *Georgius Syncellus*, of the last part of the eighth century A. D. He wrote a *Chronicle*[25] in the Greek language recording events from the time of Adam to Diocletian (285 A. D.). This *Chronicle* is valuable because it preserves fragments of ancient writings, *e.g.* much of the original text of the *Canon of Ptolemy* and the *Chronicle of Eusebius*.

[20] The two prominent editions of this *Chronicle* are those of Aucher and Schoene referred to in this discussion as *CB* and *CLP*.

[21] *CB* is based upon the Armenian text. The author describes his work as *nunc primum ex Armeniaco textu in Latinum conversum adnotationibus auctum Graecis fragmentis exornatum*. *CLP* makes use of the Armenian text also.

[22] In *CLP* app. III, pp. 53–57, and vol. II of the same work by Schoene, pp. 203–219, Syriac fragments occur under the title *Epitome Syria*.

[23] See *The Bodleian Manuscript of Jerome's Version of the Chronicle of Eusebius*, Oxford, 1905.

[24] Porphyry is described as *acerrimus Christianorum hostis*. His anti-Christian activity is indicated by the following statement: *Adversus autem Christianos quindecim evomuit volumina, quorum decimustertius contra Danielis prophetiam contexebatur*. See *Operum D. Hieronymi*, Romae, MDLXXII, index, vol. IX, under Porphyrius. Cf. also *Epistolarum D. Hieronymi Stridoniensis*, Romae, MDLXV, III, p. 21, where, in *Hieronymi in Danielem Praefatio*, occurs a reference to the fact that Porphyry exerted his influence *contra hunc librum*.

[25] See *Georgius Syncellus et Nicephorus Cp. ex recensione Guilielmi Dindorfii*, Bonnae, 1829, pp. 388ff. The Latin title of the work is *Chronographiae ab Adamo usque ad Diocletianum, auctore Georgio Monacho, Tarasii Patriarchae Constantinopolitani quondam Syncello, concinne digesta collectio*.

II

LISTS OF NEO-BABYLONIAN KINGS

The cuneiform sources which deal with the activities of Nabonidus and Belshazzar have become available as deciphered texts within the past seventy-five years. Before the recovery and translation of records upon clay knowledge concerning the deeds and accomplishments of Neo-Babylonian kings was meager. Since Herodotus and Xenophon give few exact details, Megasthenes, Berossus, Alexander Polyhistor, Claudius Ptolemy, Saint Jerome, and Syncellus are the main non-cuneiform sources of information.[26] A scientific procedure demands the consideration of general chronological data before more particular cuneiform evidence is introduced. The following tabulation enables a comparison of the different Neo-Babylonian king-lists which are known at the present time. For the sake of logical arrangement the Babylonian chronicle, although of comparatively recent discovery, is presented first.

1. Neo-Babylonian Kings according to Cuneiform Texts[27]

Nabû-apal-uṣur	21 years	626/625–605 B. C.
Nabû-kudurri-uṣur[28]	43 years	605–562 B. C.
Amêl-Marduk	2 years	562–560 B. C.
Nergal-šar-uṣur	4 years	560–556 B. C.
Lâbâši-Marduk	A few months	556 B. C.
Nabû-nâ'id	17 years	556–539 B. C.

[26] Josephus, *Antiq. Jud.*, X, 11, 2, gives the following inaccurate chronology with no reference to the length of Nebuchadrezzar's reign: Evil-Merodach, eighteen years; Niglissar, forty years; Labosordachus, nine months; Baltasar, also called Naboandelus, seventeen years. In *Contra Apionem* I, 20, Josephus quotes the chronology of Berossus.

[27] This list is based upon cuneiform historical texts and upon dated contract tablets of the Neo-Babylonian period. See references in notes 2 and 8. These Babylonian documents furnish evidence that *Nabû-apal-uṣur* (Nabopolassar) was the father of *Nabû-kudurri-uṣur* (Nebuchadrezzar), and that *Amêl-Marduk* (Evil-Merodach) was the son of Nebuchadrezzar. According to Berossus (Josephus, *Contra Apionem* I, 20; *CLP* cols. 49, 50), *Nergal-šar-uṣur* (Neriglissar) was the son-in-law of Nebuchadrezzar. *Lâbâši-Marduk* (Laborosoarchod) is referred to in cuneiform texts as the son of Neriglissar. *Nabû-nâ'id* (Nabonidus) is not mentioned as being related to any Neo-Babylonian king. This is no final criterion, however, as the available cuneiform records are silent also as to Neriglissar's relationship by marriage to Nebuchadrezzar. For the

2. *Neo-Babylonian Kings according to Megasthenes*[29]

Ναβουκοδρόσορος	*Nabucodrossorus*
Εὐιλμαλούρουχος	*Amilmarodocus*
Νηριγλισάρης	*Niglissaris*
Λαβασσοάρασκος	*Labossoracus*
Ναβαννίδοχος	*Nabonedochus*

3. *Neo-Babylonian Kings according to Berossus*[30]

Ναβοπαλάσσαρος	*Nabupalsarus*	21 years
Ναβουχοδονόσορος	*Nabucodrosorus*	43 years
Εὐειλμαράδουχος	*Evilumarudochus*	2 years
Νηριγλισσόορος	*Neriglasarus*	4 years
Λαβοροσοάρχοδος	*Labesorachus*	9 months
Ναβόννηδος	*Nabonnedus*	17 years

4. *Neo-Babylonian Kings according to Polyhistor*[31]

	Nabupalsar	21 years
	Nabucodrossorus	43 years

---

most recent discussions of the chronology of the Neo-Babylonian period see Kugler, *Sternkunde und Sterndienst in Babel* II, 2, 2, noting particularly p. 391 of the general article on *Eingehende Untersuchung der babylonischen Chronologie der letzten sechs Jahrhunderte v. Chr.*, pp. 383–463; Weissbach, *Über einige neuere Arbeiten zur babylonisch-persischen Chronologie*, *ZDMG* LV, pp. 195–220; Weissbach, *Zur neubabylonischen Chronologie*, in *Studia Orientalia, Societas Orientalis Fennica*, Helsingforsiae, 1925, pp. 358–369.

[28] This king is in reality Nebuchadrezzar II, or Nebuchadrezzar the Great, but from the standpoint of a general discussion of the Neo-Babylonian period it is convenient to refer to him as Nebuchadrezzar. The forms *Nebuchadrezzar* and *Nebuchadnezzar* occur in the Bible (Jeremiah 21: 2, 7; 22: 25, etc. 2 Chronicles 36: 6, etc.), but the former corresponds more closely to the Babylonian consonants of the king's name. The spelling *Nebuchadrezzar* is used in this monograph except in quotations from non-Biblical works in which *Nebuchadnezzar* occurs.

[29] *CB* pp. 29f; *CLP* cols. 41, 42. In these passages Abydenus quotes Megasthenes, who does not mention the lengths of the reigns of Neo-Babylonian kings.

[30] The Greek forms of the names are from Josephus, *Contra Apionem* I, 19, 20. The Latin forms are from the Latin translation of *CB* based upon the Armenian version. The forms of the names vary as follows in *CLP:* Ναβοπαλάσαρος = *Nabupalsarus;* Ναβουκδρόσορος = *Nabukodrosorus;* Εὐιλμαρούδουχος = *Evilumarudokhus;* Νηριγλίσαρος = *Neriglasarus;* Λαβαεσσοαρᾶχος = *Labesorakhus;* Ναβόννιδος = *Nabonedus.* Cf. *CLP* cols. 49, 50. See references in note 13.

[31] *CB* p. 22; *CLP* col. 29. No Greek text has been preserved of Alexander Polyhistor's statement. The Latin names of the Neo-Babylonian kings in his list go back to the Armenian version.

	Amilmarudochus	12 years
	(Ilmarodochus)	
	Neglisarus	4 years
	Nabodenus	17 years

5. Neo-Babylonian Kings according to Ptolemy[32]

Ναβοπολλασσάρου	*Nabopollassar*	21 years
Ναβοκολασσάρου	*Nabocolassar*	43 years
Ἰλλοαρουδάμου	*Iloaroudam*	2 years
Νηρικασολασσάρου	*Nericasolassar*	4 years
Ναβοναδίου	*Nabonad*	17 years

6. Neo-Babylonian Kings according to Saint Jerome[33]

Nabuchodonosor	43 years
Evilmerodach	
Neglisar	
Labosordach	
Baltasar	

7. Neo-Babylonian Kings according to Syncellus

(1) Juxta regulam astronomicam[34]

Ναβοπαλασσάρου, πατρὸς Ναβουχοδονόσορ	*Nabopalassari, patris Nabuchodonosor*	21 years
Ναβουπαλασάρου, τοῦ καὶ Ναβουχοδονόσορ	*Nabupalasari, qui et Nabuchodonosor*	43 years
Ἰλλουαρουδάμου	*Illuarudami*	3 years
Νηρηγασολασάρου	*Nerogasolasari*	5 years
Ναβοναδιόν, τοῦ καὶ Ἀστυάγους	*Nabonadii, qui et Astyages*	34 years

[32] See references in note 15. In the Greek text the names occur in the genitive case.

[33] Jerome's statement in his commentary on Daniel (see *Operum D. Hieronymi, Tomus Quartus*, p. 674) is based upon Josephus' quotation from Berossus, *Contra Apionem* I, 20.

[34] See Goar, *Chronographia ab Adamo usque ad Diocletianum*, 1829, I, p. 391. Cf. note 25. In both the Greek and Latin texts the names occur in the genitive case.

(2) *Juxta ecclesiasticum computum*[35]

Ναβοπαλάσαρος	*Nabopalasarus*	21 years
Ναβουχοδονόσωρ, υἵος	*Nabuchodonosor, filius ejus*	43 years
'Εβιδὰν Μεροδάχ	*Ebidan Merodach*	5 years
Νιρηγλήσαρος, ὁ καὶ Βαλτάσαρ	*Nireglesarus, qui et Baltasar*	3 years
Ναβονάδιος, ὁ καὶ 'Αστυάγης Δαρεῖος, 'Ασσουήρου καὶ 'Αρταξέρξης	*Nabonadius, qui et Astyages, Darius, Assuerus, et Artaxerxes*	17 years

Of the above Neo-Babylonian king-lists the first is based upon more than two thousand dated cuneiform documents. It must therefore be accepted as the ultimate criterion in the determination of Neo-Babylonian chronological questions, the majority of which are connected with events which took place in the sixth century B. C. Judged by this unimpeachable standard, the writings of Herodotus of the fifth century B. C. and those of Xenophon of the first part of the fourth century B. C. are lacking in true historical perspective so far as an orderly enumeration of Neo-Babylonian kings is concerned. The record of Megasthenes, next in point of time, is defective inasmuch as he makes no mention of Nabopolassar, the founder of the dynasty, and gives no information as to how long each king reigned. It is not until the third century B. C. that the Berossus list, with a real Babylonian background and therefore of appreciable accuracy, appears. Polyhistor of the first century B. C. names all the kings except Lâbâshi-Marduk and states accurately how long each king reigned, barring the period assigned to Amêl-Marduk. Ptolemy of the second century A. D. differs from Polyhistor only in giving the correct number of years for Amêl-Marduk's reign. Saint Jerome, who belongs mainly to the fourth century A. D., excludes Nabopolassar from his list and registers the Biblical tradition concerning Belshazzar. In actual chronology he is wanting, as he mentions the length of no reign except that of Nebuchadrezzar. Syncellus of the eighth century A. D. pays special attention to the Neo-Babylonian period in his historical investigation which is based upon astronomical and ecclesiastical data. Like Polyhistor and Ptolemy he omits the name of Lâbâshi-Marduk in both his lists. In stating the length of reigns he ascribes varying periods to Amêl-Marduk, Neriglissar, and Nabonidus.

[35] See Goar, *ibid.*, I, p. 393.

III

NABONIDUS AND BELSHAZZAR IN NON-CUNEIFORM LITERATURE

1. Summary of Ancient Non-Cuneiform Allusions to Nabonidus and Belshazzar

Although given proper recognition in the lists of Neo-Babylonian kings derived from classical sources, Nabonidus takes a secondary place in other records and in some cases drops out of the scene altogether. Similarly Belshazzar, who is described as king in the books of Daniel and Baruch, receives only scant mention in post-Babylonian lists of Neo-Babylonian kings.[36] Even Berossus, who is equal to the cuneiform record in chronological accuracy, fails to state anything about him. This paucity of references to Belshazzar in ancient non-cuneiform and extra-Biblical literature is striking. To summarize, in some documents the father obscures the son; in others the son eclipses the father. No one can doubt the strangeness of this historical phenomenon, the details of which may be presented as follows:

(1) Herodotus calls the final Neo-Babylonian king Labynetus, the son of a former Labynetus and Nitocris.[37] Cyrus is regarded as the next king of Babylon.[38]

(2) Xenophon does not mention the last native king of Babylon by name. He describes him as the impious son of a noble-minded king, also not named.[39] The successor to the throne is Cyrus.[40]

(3) Megasthenes, quoted by Abydenus as recorded by Eusebius, states that Nabonedochus became the last Neo-Babylonian king, although he was no kin of Neriglissar by direct blood relationship.[41] Nabonedochus was followed by Cyrus, the conqueror of Babylon.[42]

[36] See Josephus, *Antiq. Jud.*, X, 11, 2. See note 58.

[37] Herodotus I, 188.

[38] Herodotus I, 191.

[39] Xenophon, *Cyropaedia* IV, 6. The last Neo-Babylonian king is designated ὁ ἀνόσιος. *Ibid.*, IV, 6, 4.

[40] *Ibid.*, VII, 4 and 5.

[41] *CB* p. 30; *CLP* cols. 41, 42. See pp. 74–78 of this monograph.

[42] See references in the preceding note.

(4) Berossus states that Nabonnedus, who came to the throne as the result of an insurrection, was king of Babylon when the city was captured in the seventeenth year of his reign by Cyrus who succeeded him.[43]

(5) Alexander Polyhistor states that Nabodenus reigned seventeen years as the last Neo-Babylonian king and was succeeded by Cyrus.[44]

(6) Claudius Ptolemy refers to Nabonadius as the last Neo-Babylonian king. Cyrus is mentioned as the next king.[45]

(7) The information preserved by Abydenus is contained in the above statement of Megasthenes quoted by him.[46]

(8) The fifth chapter of Daniel refers to Belshazzar as the last Neo-Babylonian king.[47] Nebuchadrezzar is mentioned as the father of Belshazzar.[48] There is no reference to Nabonidus. Darius the Mede is regarded as the successor of Belshazzar.[49]

(9) The book of Baruch refers to Nabuchodonosor as king of Babylon and to Balthasar as his son.[50] There is no allusion to Nabonidus.

(10) Josephus states that Baltasar was called Naboandelus by the Babylonians and that he reigned seventeen years.[51] He was followed by Darius, king of Media, who helped Cyrus to capture Babylon.[52]

(11) The information contained in the quotations of Eusebius from ancient authorities has already been given. He adds little information of his own.[53]

(12) According to Saint Jerome the last Neo-Babylonian king was Baltasar, whom he regards as the son of Labosordach. Baltasar was put to death by Darius, king of the Medes, and the Chaldaean empire was destroyed by Cyrus.[54]

[43] See Josephus, *Contra Apionem* I, 20.

[44] The record of Alexander Polyhistor comes to us from the Armenian version of the Chronicle of Eusebius, with Latin translations in *CB* p. 22 and *CLP* col. 29.

[45] See references in note 15.

[46] Cf. note 41.

[47] Daniel 5: 1, 9, 30.

[48] Daniel 5: 2, 11, 18, 22. The form *Nebuchadnezzar* occurs in these passages.

[49] Daniel 6: 1, according to the Hebrew verse notation.

[50] Baruch 1: 11, 12.

[51] Josephus, *Antiq. Jud.*, X, 11, 2.

[52] Josephus, *ibid.*, X, 11, 4.

[53] For a brief interpretation of the historical situation see note 58.

[54] See note 33.

(13) Syncellus refers to Nabonadius as the last Neo-Babylonian king. He identifies Baltasar with Nireglesarus. Cyrus is mentioned as the next king of Babylon.[55]

2. Attempts at Harmonizing Non-Cuneiform Data concerning Nabonidus and Belshazzar

Before the discovery and decipherment of cuneiform documents mentioning Nabonidus and Belshazzar scholars endeavored to explain the above non-cuneiform references to them in various ways, the general tendency being to leave undisturbed the position of Nabonidus as the last Neo-Babylonian king. Hence it was natural that divergence of critical theory should arise from attempts to provide a suitable historical rôle for Belshazzar. The following suppositions have been advanced:

(1) The name Belshazzar was a pure invention on the part of the writer of the fifth chapter of Daniel.[56]

(2) Belshazzar was Evil-Merodach (*Amêl-Marduk*), and hence a son of Nebuchadrezzar.[57]

(3) Belshazzar was a brother of Evil-Merodach, and hence a son of Nebuchadrezzar.[58]

(4) Belshazzar was a son of Evil-Merodach, and hence a grandson of Nebuchadrezzar.[59]

[55] See notes 34 and 35.

[56] This view was advanced before the discovery of the name *Bêl-šar-uṣur* in cuneiform literature. See commentaries on Daniel by Von Lengerke, p. 204, and Hitzig, p. 75.

[57] This identification is supported by Zöckler in his commentary on Daniel, p. 34, Schaff's *Critical, Doctrinal and Homiletical Commentary*, XIII, where he enumerates a number of authorities in its favor, of whom Kranichfeld, Marsham, Niebuhr, Oehler, Röckerath and Zündel may be mentioned.

[58] See Sulpitius Severus, *Hist.* II, p. 6. Cf. Schoene, *Eusebii Chronicorum Libri Duo*, p. 95, for the following statement made by Eusebius: *Mortuo Nabochodonosor Babyloniorum rege suscepit imperium Euilmarodach cui successit frater eius Balthasar sub quo Daniel eam scribturam quae in pariete apparuerat interpretatus est significantem imperium Chaldaeorum in Medos et Persas transferendum.*

[59] See Quatremère in *Annales de la philosophie chrétienne*, (*Dict. de la Bible* II, p. 30, note), as quoted by Prince in *Mene, Mene, Tekel, Upharsin.* Quatremère advanced his hypothesis as an interpretation of Jeremiah 27: 7. Cf. Annius Viterbensis in *Antiquitatum Variarum Volumina XVII*, published in 1498, as quoted in *TSBA* I, p. 247 and p. 262, for the following list of Neo-Babylonian kings: *Nabugdonosor, annis 45; Amilinus Evilmerodach, annis 30; Filius hujus primus Ragassar, annis 3; Secundus Lab-Assardoch,*

(5) Belshazzar was Neriglissar (*Nergal-šar-uṣur*), and hence a son-in-law of Nebuchadrezzar.[60]

(6) Belshazzar was Laborosoarchod (*Lâbâši-Marduk*), and hence a grandson of Nebuchadrezzar.[61]

(7) Belshazzar and Nabonidus were two different names of the last Neo-Babylonian king.[62]

(8) Nabonidus was a son-in-law of Nebuchadrezzar. Therefore his son Belshazzar was a grandson of Nebuchadrezzar.[63]

3. *Scope of the Present Inquiry*

The most tenable of the foregoing hypotheses will be revealed as the discussion proceeds. Fortunately we are dependent no longer upon pure supposition in dealing with the problem. There is now available a rich and valuable accumulation of Babylonian texts making specific reference to Nabonidus and Belshazzar. These new contemporaneous sources of information have thrown so much light upon the period under investigation that it is necessary to revise former critical and historical conclusions. It is now possible to prove

---

annis 6; Tertius Baltassar, annis 5. According to the theory of Annius, *Nergal-šar-uṣur*, *Lâbâši-Marduk*, and *Bêl-šar-uṣur* were the first, second, and third sons of *Amêl-Marduk*.

[60] See Boscawen in *TSBA* VI, pp. 28, 29, 43, where the attempt is made to connect Belshazzar with *Marduk-šar-uṣur*, misread for *Nergal-šar-uṣur*. Syncellus associated Belshazzar with Neriglissar in his list of Neo-Babylonian kings *juxta ecclesiasticum computum*. See p. 10.

[61] See Scaliger, *Isagogicorum chronologiae canonum libri tres* III, p. 190; Ebrard, *Comm. zur Offenbarung Johannis*, p. 45; Hofmann, *Die 70 Jahre*, p. 44. Prince, *op. cit.*, quotes these references.

[62] As has already been indicated in note 26, Josephus thought that Baltasar (Belshazzar) and Naboandelus (Nabonidus) were the same person. Some commentators accepted this view of Josephus, *e.g.* Bertholdt, Bleek, Browne, Ewald, Hävernick, Hengstenberg, Herzfeld, Kirms, and Michaelis. See Prince, *op. cit.*, p. 29, for references.

[63] George Rawlinson in his work entitled *Herodotus* I, p. 424, advanced this view, which may be summarized as follows: Nabonidus when he came to the throne would naturally want to make his position secure by allying himself with the family of Nebuchadrezzar. "He may have taken to wife Neriglissar's widow, or he may have married some other daughter of Nebuchadnezzar. Belshazzar may thus have been the grandson of Nebuchadnezzar on the mother's side." Rawlinson believed in the probability of such an alliance of Nabonidus with the house of Nebuchadrezzar because of the indications that Nabonidus had a son named after Nebuchadrezzar. See *KA* pp. 23ff and p. 55.

the verity of certain facts and episodes in the careers of Nabonidus and Belshazzar with considerable finality. Even where the premises will not permit assured inferences, great probability exists. The following topics indicate the scope of the inquiry which will be pursued:

(1) The exalted and noble ancestry of Nabonidus.
(2) The high position of Nabonidus before he came to the throne.
(3) The prominence of Belshazzar before his father became king.
(4) The manner of Nabonidus' accession to the throne.
(5) The character of Belshazzar as a man of affairs.
(6) The devotion of Belshazzar to the worship of the gods.
(7) The association of Belshazzar with Nabonidus in the kingship.
(8) The administrative power of Belshazzar in Babylonia during Nabonidus' absence in Arabia.
(9) The events which took place in connection with the fall of Babylon.
(10) The meaning of non-cuneiform allusions to Belshazzar.

IV

THE EXALTED ANCESTRY OF NABONIDUS

In seeking to evaluate the personal character and imperial record of Nabonidus one reverts naturally to indications as to his ancestral background. The parentage of the man whose lot it was to become the final regal representative of the dynasty of Nabopolassar and Nebuchadrezzar and whose firstborn son gained a position of unique authority as an associate on the throne is of no little historical importance. Whatever light can be thrown upon the early paternal and maternal influence experienced by Nabonidus will aid greatly in the appraisal of many phases of his later life. Happily such an investigation with regard to the father and mother of the last Neo-Babylonian king is not futile. Documents are at hand which show with clearness the heritage of princely nobility and religious piety with which Nabonidus was endowed.

1. The Father of Nabonidus

Until very recently the general belief had been that Nabonidus came to the kingship with little to commend him from the standpoint of family or station aside from the fact that he was of the priestly class. The following cuneiform passages indicate that he was a man of no mean parentage:[64]

(1) [1] *^{d}Nabû-na-'-id šar Bâbili^{ki}* [2]*ni-bi-it ^{d}Na-bi-um ù ^{d}Marduk* [3]*apil ^{d}Nabû-balâṭ-su-iq-bi rubû im-ga a-na-ku.*[65]

[64] In the *Cyrus Cylinder*, *KA* p. 2f, line 3, occurs the following statement: *Ma-ṭu-ú iš-šak-na a-na e-nu-tu ma-ti-šu,* 'A weakling was appointed to the priesthood of his land.' The word *e-nu-tu* has been translated 'lordship' as well as 'priesthood.' The passage is interpreted to mean that Nabonidus came to the throne as a nobody. The obscureness of the language and the extreme prejudice of the inscription towards Nabonidus must be taken into account. It is true that Nabonidus could not claim royal ancestry, at any rate so far as his parents were concerned, but he was not a mere upstart. Cf. *Zeitschrift für die alttestamentliche Wissenschaft*, XLIV, p. 45, for Baumgartner's argument for 'Herrschaft' instead of 'Priesteramt' as the meaning of *enûtu* in the above passage of the *Cyrus Cylinder* which is interpreted as referring to Nabonidus.

[65] *NKI* p. 294, no. 10.

[1]Nabonidus, the king of Babylon, [2]the appointed one of Nabû and Marduk, [3]the son of Nabû-balâṭsu-iqbi, the wise prince, am I.

(2) [1] *^{d}Na-bi-um-na-'-id šar Bâbili^{ki}* [2]*za-nin Ê-sag-ila ù Ê-zi-da e-piš damqâti^{meš}* [3]*apil ^{d}Nabû-balâṭ-su-iq-bi rubû git-ma-lu ana-k*[*u*].[66]

[1]Nabonidus, the king of Babylon, [2]the preserver of Êsagila and Êzida, the performer of pious deeds, [3]the son of Nabû-balâṭsu-iqbi, the perfect prince, am I.

(3) [1]*A-na-ku ^{d}Na-bi-um-na-'-id šarru ra-bu-ú šarru dan-nu* [2]*šar kiš-ša-ti šar Bâbili^{ki} šar kib-ra-a-ti ir-bit-ti* [3]*za-ni-in Ê-sag-ila ù Ê-zi-da* [4]*ša ^{d}Sin ù ^{d}Nin-gal i-na lib um-mi-šu* [5]*a-na ši-ma-at šarru-ú-tu i-ši-mu ši-ma-at-su* [6]*mâr ^{d}Nabû-balâṭ-su-iq-bi rubû e-im-qu pa-li-iḫ ilâni rabûti*[67] [7]*a-na-ku.*[68]

[1]I am Nabonidus, the great king, the mighty king, [2]the king of totality, the king of Babylon, the king of the four quarters, [3]the preserver of Êsagila and Êzida, [4]whose destiny Sin and Ningal while he was in his mother's womb [5]decreed for the lot of royalty; [6]the son of Nabû-balâṭsu-iqbi, the wise prince, the reverer of the great gods, [7]am I.

(4) [1] *^{d}Na-bi-um-na-'-id šar Bâbili^{ki} id-lam ki-nim ša a-na ṭe-me ilâni^{meš} pu-ú-qu* [2]*áš-ri ka-an-šú pa-li-iḫ ilâni^{meš} rabûti^{meš}* [3]*rubû e-im-ga ḫa-sis mimma šum-šú pa-te-si(išakku) ṣi-i-ri mu-ud-di-iš kal ma-ḫa-zu* [4]*ma-al-ku it-pi-šú mu-šak-lil eš-ri-e-ti mu-daḫ-ḫi-id sat-tuk-ku* [5]*rê'û ni-ši rapšâti^{meš} ra-'-im mi-ša-ri mu-kin kit-ti* [6]*lu-li-mu šú-pu-ú e-til-lu šarrâni^{meš} bi-nu-tu ga-at ša ^{d}Nabû u ^{d}Marduk* [7]*mu-uṣ-ṣir ú-ṣu-ra-a-ti bîtâti^{meš} ilâni^{meš} mu-šar-šid ^{iş}ḫar-ri* [8]*na-aš-pa-ri ḫa-an-ṭu ša ilâni^{meš} rabûti^{meš} mu-šal-lim kal šip-ri mu-ṭi-ib lib-bi-šu-un* [9]*mâr ^{d}Nabû-balâṭ-su-iq-bi GAN-NITAḪ qit-ru-du pa-li-iḫ ilâni(AN-AN) u ^{d}ištarâti$^{[meš]}$ a-na-ku.*[69]

[1]Nabonidus, the king of Babylon, the faithful lord, who heeds the decrees of the gods, [2]the humble one, the submissive one, the reverer of the great gods, [3]the wise prince, the one who is mindful of whatever exists, the exalted princely priest, the renewer of all cities, [4]the prudent prince, the one who causes temples to be finished, the increaser of offerings, [5]the shepherd of numerous peoples, the lover of righteousness, the establisher of truth, [6]the magnificent leader, the ruler of kings, the creature of the hand of Nabû

[66] *NKI* p. 294, no. 12.
[67] *AN-GAL-GAL.*
[68] *NKI* p. 218, no. 1, col. I, lines 1–7.
[69] *NKI* p. 252, no. 6, col. I, lines 1–9.

and Marduk, [7]the protector of the inclosures of the temples of the gods, the establisher of the plan [8]of the swift messenger of the great gods, the executor of every command, the one who gladdens their hearts, [9]the son of Nabû-balâṭsu-iqbi, the courageous minister, the reverer of the gods and goddesses, am I.

The remaining Nabonidus inscriptions of similar import need not be quoted.[70] The above passages indicate many of the titles assumed by Nabonidus and in a sense reveal the Babylonian idea of true kingship. The descriptive titles applied to Nabû-balâṭsu-iqbi follow his name in the inscriptions which have been quoted. These appellations throw light upon the station and dignity of Nabonidus' father. They may be summarized as follows:

Rubû imga.	'Wise prince.'
Rubû gitmalu.	'Perfect prince.'
GAN-NITAḪ qitrudu.	'Courageous minister.'
Pâliḫ ilâni rabûti.	'Reverer of the great gods.'
Pâliḫ ilâni u ^{d}ištarâti.	'Reverer of the gods and goddesses.'

Such titles justify us in assuming that Nabû-balâṭsu-iqbi, the father of Nabonidus, had noble connection, political importance, and religious piety.

2. *The Mother of Nabonidus*

Evidence which may be regarded as confirming the exalted ancestry of Nabonidus is furnished by a somewhat mutilated ancient record from Eski-Ḫarrân, located a short distance east of Ḫarrân. This valuable cuneiform document was discovered by Pognon in 1906. Inasmuch as he could not carry away the inscribed stone, it is fortunate that he was able to take an impression of the writing. He published a copy and an interpretation of the text in 1907.[71] Dhorme

[70] *NKI* pp. 230–235, no. 2; pp. 234–243, no. 3; pp. 242–251, no. 4; pp. 250–253, no. 5; pp. 262–271, no. 7; pp. 270–289, no. 8; pp. 294–297, nos. 11, 13, 14, 15. The longest inscriptions contain interesting accounts of Nabonidus' building operations. References will be made to important sections of these inscriptions, which as a whole bear clear evidence of the religious zeal and devotion of Nabonidus. His fervent prayers and his interest in the repair of temple structures show that he was thoroughly imbued with the spirit of his Assyrian and Babylonian predecessors.

[71] *PgnIS* pp. 1–14; pls. XII, XIII.

wrote an appreciation of this work in 1908 and threw further light upon the real nature of the inscription.[72] Langdon transliterated and translated it in 1912.[73] Smith expressed his views concerning the document in 1924[74] and Genouillac discussed the bearing of its contents in 1925.[75]

A brief summary of the lines which remain in the three columns of the Eski-Ḫarrân inscription will reveal their significance. Column I, column II, and lines 1–19a of column III are written in the first person and represent the words of a religious devotee dwelling at Ḫarrân. Lines 19b–32 of column III are written in the third person. Column I begins with an assertion of extreme piety on the part of the one commemorated by the inscription. This is followed by a review of priestly service, presumably at Ḫarrân, from the time of Ashurbanipal to the reign of Nabonidus, the names of Ashurbanipal, Ashur-etil-ilâni, Nabopolassar, Nebuchadrezzar, Neriglissar, and Nabonidus appearing in the text. The names of Amêl-Marduk and Lâbâshi-Marduk may be supplied, as there are breaks in the inscription which favor such a restoration. The column closes with an allusion to the cult of the moon god at Ḫarrân. Column II extols the pious deeds of Nabonidus who is described as the son of the devout personage referred to in column I. The temple Êḫulḫul is rebuilt at Ḫarrân and the city is made more complete than before. Sin, Ningal, Nusku, and Sadarnunna are brought from Babylon and established in Êḫulḫul. Column II closes with a vivid depiction of the attainment of unimpaired old age by the above-mentioned parent of Nabonidus. The main event recorded in column III is the death of this parent of Nabonidus in the ninth year of his reign.

Differing opinions are on record as to the identity of the individual in whose honor the Eski-Ḫarrân monument was inscribed. Pognon advances the view that this notable person was an aged high priest of the temple of Sin at Ḫarrân, who, while not the actual father of Nabonidus, nevertheless called him son as an expression of gratitude and friendship.[76] Dhorme with keen insight interprets the text as

[72] *RB* V, pp. 130–135. The line numbers of *RB* V follow those of *PgnIS*.

[73] *NKI* pp. 288–295, no. 9. The line numbers of *NKI* differ from those of *PgnIS*.

[74] *BHT* pp. 36–38.

[75] *RA* XXII, no. 2, p. 74.

[76] *PgnIS* p. 10.

referring to the mother of Nabonidus,[77] whereas Langdon asserts as positively that the inscription deals with the father of Nabonidus.[78] Smith evaluates the real difficulties which exist on account of the fragmentary condition of the text and therefore arrives at no definite conclusion, although he seems at times to incline to Langdon's verdict.[79] Genouillac, on the other hand, favors Dhorme's exposition.[80]

Some idea of the problems involved in an interpretation of the text may be gained by a consideration of internal evidence. This critical investigation will be presented briefly.

(1) The possible occurrence of the name of that parent of Nabonidus whose memory is preserved in the Eski-Ḫarrân inscription should be noted. In column I, line 20, there are cuneiform signs which Pognon, followed by Langdon, reads *šal-mu-u-a dam-qa*, Pognon's translation being 'ma tranquillité vertueuse.'[81] Dhorme believes that these signs represent a feminine personal name, *i.e.* ^{f}*Šumu-u-a-dam-qa*. This suggests a possible restoration at the commencement of column I, the first line of which is illegible. Line 2 according to Pognon, again followed by Langdon, begins as follows: *a-na . . . . u a-da-an-nim*,[82] but Pognon's copy[83] indicates the remnant of a *ku* after *a-na* and a nearly complete *mu* before *u* after the break. The reading *nim* for the last sign of the expression is doubtful. What has survived appears more like *qa*. On the basis of ^{f}*Šumu-u-a-dam-qa* in line 20, Dhorme restores the first part of line 2 thus: *A-na-ku* $^{[f]}$*Šumu-u-a-da-an-qa*, 'I am Shumûa-danqa.'[84] The form *danqa* is a legitimate variant of *damqa*.[85] A coincidence which should not be overlooked is the fact that Šhumûa-damqa, 'My name is gracious,' accords with the following statement in column II, line 23, *šuma ṭâba ina mâti iš-ku-na-an-ni*,

[77] *RB* V, p. 131.

[78] *NKI* p. 57f; p. 293, note 1.

[79] *BHT* p. 37f.

[80] *RA* XXII, no. 2, p. 74. Thureau-Dangin, *RA* IX, p. 84, and Streck, *Assurbanipal*, I, p. ccvii, note 2, also agree with Dhorme.

[81] *PgnIS* pp. 2, 5, 7; *NKI* p. 290, line 19. Langdon translates "mein freundliches Wohlergehen." See *ibid.*, p. 291.

[82] *PgnIS* p. 5; *NKI* p. 288.

[83] *PgnIS* pl. XII.

[84] *RB* V, p. 132.

[85] Cf. *dumqu*, *dunqu*, *Hwb* p. 222, *CD* p. 255.

'he (the god Sin) established for me a good name in the land.'[86] This adds greatly to the plausibility of Dhorme's suggestion and intimates very strongly that the main personage of the text was a high priestess of the god Sin at Ḫarrân.[87]

(2) The above view as to the character of the religious dignitary mentioned prominently in the Eski-Ḫarrân inscription gathers weight from two brief statements which appear in the text. In column III, line 4, the following words occur: *Ki-ma mârti ṣi-it lib-bi-šu-*[*nu*], 'Like a daughter, the offspring of their heart.' After a break in the column which extends over line 5 and the first part of line 6, the sentence begun in line 4 ends thus: *ul-lu-ú ri-ši-ia*, 'they lifted my head.' It is inconceivable that a man would use the expression "like a daughter" when referring to himself. The only rational explanation of the passage is that the words are those of a woman. In column III, line 23, the death of Nabonidus' parent having been recorded, the zeal of Nabonidus in performing proper obsequies is ascribed significantly to the fact that he was *na-ra-am ummi-šu*, 'beloved of his mother.' This phrase would be inexplicable if the rest of the inscription referred with absolute certainty to the father of Nabonidus. Such a dilemma is imaginary, however, as has already been shown.

(3) A crux of the problem is the employment of masculine possessive pronouns in the account of the death and funeral rites of Nabonidus' parent. Langdon[88] considers this feature of the text definite proof that the inscription deals with the father of Nabonidus, but Dhorme[89] and Genouillac[90] are able to overcome the grammatical difficulty, and their viewpoint in this respect is accepted by Smith.[91] Linguistic freedom, especially in Neo-Babylonian times, allowed the use of mascu-

[86] *PgnIS* pp. 5, 8; *NKI* p. 290f, line 22; *RB* V, p. 133f.

[87] Attention should be called to a brief assertion in column III, line 3, of the text. *PgnIS* p. 6, transliterates *choumiya ouchannima* and translates, p. 8, 'je changeai mon nom,' or 'il changea mon nom.' *NKI* p. 292f, varies as follows: *šuma-a unakkiruma*, 'Meinen Namen änderten sie.' *RB* V, p. 133, takes into account the succeeding words and construes thus: *šumi-a kur-ba-nu-ú ina pâni-šu-nu iš-*[*kun-ma*], translating as follows on p. 135: 'En mon nom [il plaça] des présents devant eux [et].' The full significance of the passage remains uncertain.

[88] *NKI* p. 293f, note 1.

[89] *RB* V, p. 131.

[90] *RA* XXII, no. 2, p. 74.

[91] *BHT* p. 36.

line pronominal suffixes where feminine forms would be expected.[92] All the passages in the Eski-Ḫarrân text where this principle applies are in column III. The high priestess at Ḫarrân states that she continued performing the duties of her office long after those who had elevated her had passed away. With this assertion of ceaseless piety the part of the inscription written in the first person ends. Immediately following, in lines 19–21, are the words: *Ina šatti 9^kam^ ^md^Nabû-nâ'id šar Bâbili^ki^ ši-im-[tu] ra-am-ni-šu ú-bil-šu-má,* 'In the ninth year of Nabonidus, the king of Babylon, fate carried her herself off.' In lines 22, 23a is the passage: *^md^Nabû-nâ'id šar Bâbili^ki^ mâru ṣi-[it] lib-bi-šu,* 'Nabonidus, the king of Babylon, the son (and) offspring of her heart.' Finally in the record of the burial ceremony there occurs in line 28 the expression *šal-mat-su,* 'her body.' It would be natural under ordinary circumstances to ascribe the meaning 'his' to *šu* (or *su*), when construed as in the above passages, but since there is strong evidence that the feminine possessive is intended it should be translated 'her.'

(4) In the words ascribed by the Eski-Ḫarrân inscription to the one who was evidently the mother of Nabonidus, the latter is characterized twice (column II, lines 5 and 28) as *mâru ṣi-it lib-bi-iá,* 'the son (and) offspring of my heart,' or 'the son (who is) the offspring of my heart.' In the impersonal part of the text the expression is *mâru ṣi-[it] lib-bi-šu,* as quoted in the preceding paragraph. There has been some discussion as to the interpretative value of the idiom represented by these passages.[93] It was common for a king, either Assyrian or Babylonian, to refer to his son as *mâru ṣit libbîa.*[94] Was it a term which was confined strictly to such usage, or could it be attributed with equal propriety by a mother to her son, perhaps with metaphorical force? That there was some deviation in the employment of the words is indicated by the fact that Nabonidus calls his daughter Bêl-shalṭi-Nannar *mârtu ṣit libbîa.*[95] This instance of latitude in the use of the idiom suggests that it may have been somewhat elastic

[92] See Delitzsch, *Assyrische Grammatik,* 2nd edition, pp. 142, 144.

[93] *RB* V, p. 131.

[94] Dhorme in *RB* V, p. 131, note 1, calls attention to the instances of this use recorded in *Hwb* p. 367 and *CD* p. 898.

[95] *MI* 45, col. I, lines 20, 24. See *ibid.* pp. 70, 73.

in its application. Hence no good reason exists why the occurrences of the expression in the Eski-Ḫarrân inscription should be regarded as pointing to the father rather than to the mother of Nabonidus.

(5) More positive evidence is provided by those sections of the Eski-Ḫarrân inscription which show paramount devotion to the god Sin. It is not necessary to quote all passages of this character. A typical assertion is the following from column II, lines 18b–23:

[18b] *Ša ul-tu pa-na-ma* [19] *[d]Sin šar ilâni[meš] lâ i-pu-šú-ma* [20]*a-na man-ma lâ id-di-nu ina na-ra-mi-iá* [21]*ša ilu-ú-tú-šú ap-la-ḫu susikta-šu* [22]*aṣ-ba-tum [d]Sin šar ilâni[meš] ri-ši-ia* [23]*ul-li-ma šuma ṭâba ina mâti iš-ku-na-an-ni.*

[18b] That which formerly [19]Sin, the king of the gods, did not do and [20]to no one gave, out of love for me, [21]who revered his divinity (and) his garment [22]grasped, Sin, the king of the gods, my head [23]lifted up and established for me a good name in the land.

Careful weighing of the above statement and others[96] like it leads to the conclusion that the parent of Nabonidus referred to in the Eski-Ḫarrân inscription was interested in the cult of a single god, with little tendency towards the worship of Babylonian deities in general.[97] One should compare with this the fact that Nabonidus states definitely that his father was 'a reverer of the great gods,' 'a reverer of the gods and goddesses,' with no intimation that Sin was a favorite.[98] A real distinction seems to be made between the cult of Nabonidus' father and that of his parent mentioned in the Eski-Ḫarrân inscription. This may be taken as further proof that Pognon's text records words which were ascribed to the mother of Nabonidus.

(6) A most interesting passage of the Eski-Ḫarrân inscription reveals the great length of life attained by the one who appears now to be identified as the mother of Nabonidus. Column II, lines 24–30 may be quoted in full:

[24]*Ū-mu ár-qi-tú šanâti[meš] ṭu-ub lib-bi* [25]*uṣ-ṣi-pa-am-ma ul-tu pa-ni* [26] *[md]Aššur-bâni-aplu šar [mât]Aš-šur a-di-i* [27]*šatti 9[kam] [d]Nabû-nâ'id šar Bâbili[ki]* [28]*mâr*

[96] See col. I, lines 3–7, 27.

[97] The deities Ningal, Nusku, and Sadarnunna are also mentioned in the inscription. See col. II, lines 6, 7, 14. Ningal was the consort of Sin. Nusku was the god of fire and Sadarnunna was his consort. Nusku cannot be regarded as a rival of Sin.

[98] See p. 17f.

ṣi-it lib-bi-iá 104 šanâti^{meš} ^{29}*damqâti*^{meš} *ina pu-ú-ti ša* ^{d}*Sin šar ilâni*^{meš} ^{30}*ina lib-bi-ia iš-ku-nu-ma ú-bal-li-ṭ-an-ni.*

^{24}A distant day, years of goodness of heart ^{25}he (the god Sin) added and from the time of ^{26}Ashurbanipal, the king of Assyria, until ^{27}the ninth year of Nabonidus, the king of Babylon, ^{28,29}the son (and) offspring of my heart, one hundred and four propitious years in the presence of Sin, the king of the gods, ^{30}unto me he established and caused me to live.

The text continues with a statement that impairment of eyesight, deterioration of mental acuteness, and decline of bodily health were not the lot of the aged high priestess of the god Sin at Ḫarrân. On the basis of the interpretation which has been made, two facts of unusual importance in the career of Nabonidus' maternal ancestor should be noted, viz., that the early part of her life fell in the reign of Ashurbanipal and that she was connected intimately with the cult of the moon god whose temple Êḫulḫul at Ḫarrân was a celebrated religious center. Ashurbanipal himself was interested in the exaltation of moon worship at this shrine. Evidence of this is furnished by the following words from one of his texts: *Aššur-etil-šamê-irṣitim-uballiṭ-su aḫi-ia ṣiḫru ana* ^{amêl}*urigallûtu ina pâni* ^{d}*Sin âšib* ^{al}*Ḫarrâni uktallul,*[99] 'I appointed Ashur-etil-shamê-irṣitim-uballiṭsu, my younger brother, as high priest to the god Sin dwelling in Ḫarrân.' The references to Ashurbanipal in the inscriptions of Nabonidus indicate that the last great Assyrian king was revered to the very end of the Neo-Babylonian empire.[100] At any rate Nabonidus, who was devoted to the patron deity of Ḫarrân, recognized Ashurbanipal's renown and influence in no uncertain way. Hence there may be factors in the reign of Nabonidus which are survivals of Ashurbanipal's policy at Ḫarrân.[101]

(7) A question which has been debated is the date given by the Eski-Ḫarrân inscription for the death of the one indicated as the mother of Nabonidus by the weighty considerations which have been presented. The year of Nabonidus' reign in which this event occurred

[99] *K* 891 obv. 17 (= I *R* 8). Professor Langdon has called the writer's attention to the fact that Ashurbanipal's grandfather received a revelation at Ḫarrân. See Harper, *Assyrian and Babylonian Letters* IX, no. 923, p. 996.

[100] *NKI* p. 220, line 47; p. 222, line 3; p. 224, line 44; p. 286, line 34.

[101] For a discussion of the Ḫarrân background of Nabonidus see *NKI* p. 57f; *BHT* pp. 36–68.

is recorded in column II, line 27, and in column III, line 19. A study of Pognon's copy of the text[102] shows that the date has been preserved only partially in each instance, but enough remains to make it clear that the scribe wrote the cuneiform equivalent of the numeral '9' in both places, and this is the translation of Pognon and Dhorme.[103] Genouillac accepts their view,[104] while Langdon is inclined to the reading '6.'[105] The unquestioned testimony of the *Nabonidus Chronicle* is that Nabonidus' mother died in the ninth year of his reign.[106] This corroborative evidence is helpful, but it must be insisted that neither instance of the record of the year in Pognon's copy lends the slightest weight to the view that the Babylonian scribe meant to state that the event under discussion took place in the sixth year of Nabonidus' reign. This fact may be accepted, therefore, as additional proof that the text refers to the mother of Nabonidus.[107]

(8) The *Nabonidus Chronicle* states that the mother of Nabonidus died at 'Dûr-Karâshu on the bank of the Euphrates above Sippar.'[108] There is no positive affirmation in the Eski-Ḫarrân inscription as to where her death occurred. Its simple assertion is that the parent of Nabonidus to whom reference is made completed long years of service in the presence of the god Sin. Smith on this account expresses doubt as to the finality of the conclusion that the Eski-Ḫarrân inscription refers to the mother of Nabonidus.[109] However, since the text does not make an unequivocal statement, there is some opportunity for reconciling it with the *Nabonidus Chronicle*. This harmonization should be attempted with all pertinent facts in mind. Considering the positive evidence which exists in favor of the opinion that the Eski-Ḫarrân inscription refers to the mother of Nabonidus, passages of uncertain meaning should be interpreted accordingly. The testimony of the *Nabonidus Chronicle* cannot be ignored. One is driven to the

[102] *PgnIS* pls. XII, XIII.

[103] *Ibid.*, pp. 8, 9; *RB* V, pp. 134, 135.

[104] *RA* XXII, no. 2, p. 74.

[105] *NKI* p. 293, note 1.

[106] *TSBA* VII, p. 158; *BA* II, p. 218; *BHT* p. 112.

[107] The *possibility* that the father and mother of Nabonidus died in the same year must be granted, but it is *improbable* that this was the case.

[108] See references given in note 106.

[109] *BHT* p. 38.

conclusion that the mother of Nabonidus was a priestess of the god Sin at Ḫarrân and that she died while visiting Babylonia.[110]

(9) An apparent quandary arises from the comparison of other data furnished by the cuneiform records which are related to this question. The full evidence concerning Nabonidus' stay at Têmâ in Arabia will be considered later, but mention should be made now that available texts indicate that he was not in Babylonia in the ninth year of his reign,[111] when, according to the facts which have been summarized above, the death of his mother occurred at Dûr-Karâshu near Sippar. The intimation of the *Nabonidus Chronicle* is that he took part neither in the three-day period of mourning which was observed by Belshazzar and the army immediately after her death on the fifth day of Nisan nor in the general mourning during the month Sivan of the same year. On the other hand the Eski-Ḫarrân inscription, column III, lines 19b–32, attributes to Nabonidus the performance of the extensive burial rites which were common in antiquity.[112] The body of his mother was honored with the finest drapery, precious stones, and anointing oil. Animals were sacrificed as a part of the solemn ceremony. The last fragmentary line of the text indicates that the people of Babylon and Borsippa were assembled by Nabonidus, presumably that they might participate in the respect paid to his departed parent. How can all these strands of information be coordinated? It should be noted, first of all, that the records deal with two entirely different aspects of the situation, viz., official mourning for the king's dead mother and ceremonial reverence shown by the king himself. Considerable significance may be attached to the fact that two periods of mourning were observed, with an interval of seven and one-half weeks between them.[113] A plausible explanation may be suggested. Nabonidus was at Têmâ in Arabia when his mother's death occurred. Immediate grief was expressed by Belshazzar and his soldiers, but royal proclamation of a period of universal mourning

[110] The cult of Sin was more or less general in Babylonia. Hence Nabonidus' mother, as a high functionary of this deity at Ḫarrân, could have found opportunity for the expression of her devotion even when she was at a distance from the local shrine in which she was interested.

[111] *TSBA* VII, p. 157; *BA* II, p. 218; *BHT* p. 112.

[112] *PgnIS* pp. 6, 9; *RB* V, pp. 133, 135; *NKI* p. 294f.

[113] See p. 113f.

could be issued in Babylonia only after the absent king had been apprised of his bereavement and after a messenger from him had returned. It is probable that this accounts for the delay in appointing a time of general weeping. There is no indication that Nabonidus returned to take part in it, but he gave orders doubtless that all appropriate rites should be performed in his name. A record of the fulfilment of these commands, after they had been received or in anticipation of their arrival, may be preserved by the Eski-Ḫarrân inscription. Anything done at the behest of a distant sovereign was credited to him as positively as if he had been present at the execution of his decree. It is also probable that acts according to law and usage could be performed in behalf of a king who was elsewhere, even without his expressed sanction, if necessity required. More urgency would arise with regard to the ceremonial of burial, unless some form of the art of temporary embalming was practiced, than with regard to a period of official mourning in the nation, for in this respect deference would naturally be shown to the wish of the absent king.

3. Summary of Data

The character of the immediate ancestry of Nabonidus may now be estimated. Nabû-balâṭsu-iqbi, his father, ranked as a prince known for his wisdom and excellent attainments. In religion he did not attach himself exclusively to the cult of one deity, but seems to have worshipped all the gods and goddesses with equal devotion. His mother, if available cuneiform evidence may be regarded as final testimony, was Shumûa-damqa. As a woman of unusual personality and influence her piety and loyalty were expended upon the moon god at Ḫarrân, where she performed faithful service as a famed high priestess in the temple which became one of the beneficiaries of the religious zeal of her son. Living to the advanced age of one hundred and four years she was venerated and honored throughout the land.[114]

A summarization of data shows that the heritage of Nabonidus from his father was a prestige derived from princely nobility, while that from his mother was a religious proclivity which surrendered itself largely to the cult of the moon god. These two influences were important

[114] Cf. Streck, *Assurbanipal* I, p. ccxxviii.

factors in the molding of his character and in the shaping of his career. To the former he owed the privilege of access to the throne of Babylon, for it is hardly credible that a man with no patrician eligibility would have been chosen to rule the Neo-Babylonian nation. To the latter must be ascribed his ardent interest in the shrines located at Ur[115] and Ḫarrân,[116] at both of which Sin was glorified as the divinity preëminently worthy of adoration.

Nothing is known concerning the more remote ancestry of Nabonidus. If records giving his descent through a number of generations exist, they remain to be discovered. In the absence of such a genealogical table one hesitates to make a categorical statement, but it is altogether likely that Nabonidus could look back upon a long line of distinguished forbears. However that may be, it can be asserted with assurance that the advantages of rank and the qualities of personality which were bequeathed to him by his father and mother prepared him for the unique position which he filled as the last Neo-Babylonian king.

[115] *NKI* p. 250f, no. 5.

[116] *NKI* pp. 220–223, col. I, 44, to col. II, 24; pp. 284–287, col. X, 12–51; *BHT* pp. 84, 88, col. II, 4–17.

V

THE EARLY PROMINENCE OF NABONIDUS AND BELSHAZZAR

The high rank and positive character inherited by Nabonidus suggest that he was not inactive in political matters during the period of his mature life which preceded his accession to the throne. There is every indication that Babylonia in the sixth century B. C. offered considerable scope for self-expression to men of energy and ability. Society was highly organized and avenues for public service were exceedingly diverse. Positions of authority, affording opportunity for the exercise of capacities of leadership, were numerous. Every city provided an arena for the pursuit of official careers both in civic and religious affairs. In addition, the broad range of interrelations between nations presented a field for ambitious achievements. Cuneiform inscriptions furnish ample proof that Assyrian and Babylonian kings were in constant need of capable subordinates and dependable emissaries.

It is conceivable, therefore, that Nabonidus, with distinguished ancestry to commend him and with definite parental example to inspire him, grouped himself, as soon as he could assert his individuality, with the influential elements of the empire. That he gained wide experience in posts of importance may be regarded as extremely likely. Furthermore, the early elevation of Belshazzar, his firstborn son, to a position of responsibility must be viewed as possible. The ultimate rôles played by Nabonidus and Belshazzar presuppose executive caliber of a type which would be derived from actual acquaintance with governmental tasks. Babylonian and Greek data which add very much to the soundness of these inferences will now be discussed.

1. Nabonidus' Prominence before He Became King

(1) Babylonian Data

A cuneiform text, dated in the eighth year of the reign of Nebuchadrezzar, is attested by a number of witnesses, the first in the list being Nabû-nâ'id.[117] Duplicate records of this text are available. In one Nabû-nâ'id, the witness, is described with the phrase *ša eli âli*, 'who is over the city.' In the other he is designated *apil amêl šarri*, 'the son of a man of the king,' or possibly *apil amêl šarrûti* [-*ti*], 'the son of a man of royalty.' The following considerations suggest the high rank of the Nabû-nâ'id of these duplicate texts and indicate the probability that he is to be identified with Nabonidus.

A. Prominence of Nabû-nâ'id, the Witness

Not a little weight should be attached to the fact that the parentage of the Nabû-nâ'id under consideration is not recorded. It was the custom of Neo-Babylonian scribes to write the names of very high officials without a statement as to ancestry.[118] A person of ordinary rank had to be distinguished from other persons of the same name by the mention of his father, and even his grandfather in most cases. It was not necessary to do this when referring to an individual occupying an influential position. In all likelihood the immediate subordinates of Babylonian kings were as well known as the sovereigns themselves, and hence the mere citation of their names together with their titles was sufficient. That there was a man called Nabû-nâ'id in the eighth year of Nebuchadrezzar's reign of such prominence that his status as a witness was fixed without the naming of his father and grandfather is significant. This fact alone warrants a comparison between him and the Nabonidus who became king.

[117] *StrNbk* 70: 9. The document records the fact that Adi'ilu and Ḫulti, his wife, sold their son to Shulâ. The import of the text is discussed in *BA* IV, p. 40, *RA* XII, p. 86, and Koschaker, *Babylonisch-assyrisches Bürgschaftsrecht*, p. 47, n. 14. The duplicate of the inscription exhibits striking peculiarities. Thus in line 3 *ma-ra* occurs instead of *TUR* for 'son.' The name *Mar-duk-a* is represented by *Duk-mar-a* in line 11 and by *Duk-mar* in line 13. This leads Édouard Cuq in *RA* XII, p. 86, to suggest that the inscription originated among a people who were accustomed to a method of writing 'inverse de celle des Babyloniens, ce qui est le cas des Araméens.' Furthermore, he cites *Adi'ilu* (variant *Iadi'ilu*), *Ḫulti* (variant *Ḫulîti*), *Agar'u*, and *Marduka* as good Aramaean names, and concludes that Shulâ engaged in the business of purchasing slaves in an Aramaean colony. If these inferences are valid, an Aramaean background of Nabû-nâ'id, the witness, is suggested and this is in harmony with what is known concerning the early racial environment of the Nabonidus who became king.

[118] *E.g. Nabû-šar-uṣur*, a chief officer of the king during Nabonidus' reign. See references in *REN* p. 30.

B. Political Influence of Nabû-nâ'id, the Witness

The phrase *ša eli âli*, 'who is over the city,' *i.e.* 'the one in charge of the city's affairs,' may be regarded as a title reflecting the administrative service of the man by the name of Nabû-nâ'id who rose above the rank and file of Babylonians not many years after Nebuchadrezzar ascended the throne.[119] The meaning and force of this official designation may be compared with Hebrew אשר על העיר[120] 'the one who is over the city,' *i.e.* the governor or commander. There can be no doubt that the person whose position could be described with the words *ša eli âli* was some sort of a municipal overseer or prefect. The text contains no indication as to the particular city which was under the direction of Nabû-nâ'id. Of 460 Strassmaier texts dated in the reign of Nebuchadrezzar, 138 were written in the city of Babylon. This is certain because the city of Babylon is mentioned in the documents.[121] Of the remaining 322 texts 83 are assigned to 37 different cities, the best known of which are Borsippa, Erech, Larsa, Kish, and Sippar. Thus more than one-half of the Strassmaier Nebuchadrezzar texts, the duplicate records under discussion being examples, furnish no clue as to where they were written. It is supposable that some of the documents which supply no intimation as to their provenance may have been part of the archives of the city of Babylon. Many texts reputed to have come from Erech do not mention the name of that city. However, since pure supposition in attempting to solve this phase of the problem should be avoided, no definite conclusion can be reached as to the scene of the local political activity of Nabû-nâ'id during the first part of the reign of Nebuchadrezzar. It may be asserted, on the other hand, that this does not weaken the position which he occupied. At any rate there need be no hesitancy in believing it possible that the Nabû-nâ'id who was prominent as a city administrator in the eighth year of Nebuchadrezzar was afterwards made king of Babylon.

[119] For *amêlu ša eli âli* see *JADD* I, 237: R. 7; 285: 5; II p. 83f. In the Amarna letters the king of a city often calls himself the *amêlu* of the city. See Knudtzon, *Die El-Amarna-Tafeln* I, 299: 4; 314: 4; 315: 3; 319: 5; 320: 5, 6; 321: 5, 6; 328: 5; 329: 6.

[120] II Kings 10: 5.

[121] *StrNbk* p. 18.

C. Princely Connection of Nabû-nâ'id, the Witness

A third aid in estimating the character of the witness Nabû-nâ'id is furnished by a fortunate deviation of the Babylonian copyist. The duplicate text has a variant for *ša eli âli* ending with the ideogram for 'king,' followed in Strassmaier's transcript by what may be adjudged to be either a scribal erasure or the fragment of a mutilated sign. If the former is true, this part of the inscription reads *mdNabû-nâ'id apil amêl šarri*, 'Nabû-nâ'id, the son of a man of the king.' The term *amêl šarri*, 'a man of the king,' *i.e.* 'a man of princely rank,' is unusual in cuneiform writing. There is a corresponding Hebrew term, viz., איש שׂר, 'prince,' or 'chief.'[122] It is evident, therefore, that the words *amêl šarri* denote connection with royalty with resultant princely rank. This being the case, the Nabû-nâ'id mentioned as a witness in the eighth year of the reign of Nebuchadrezzar was the son of a prince. The phrase *apil amêl šarri* indicates this. On the other hand, if the original expression in the text was *apil amêl šarrûti*—this is the only alternative which suggests itself—the above inference is strengthened rather than weakened by the abstract force of the word *šarrûti*, as the words may be translated 'the son of a man of royalty,' or 'the son of a man of princely dignity.' There can be no doubt that the scribe wished to state in emphatic language that the father of Nabû-nâ'id belonged to the aristocratic class in Babylonia. The purport of this fact becomes clear when it is remembered that Nabû-balâṭsu-iqbi, the father of Nabonidus, ranked as a *rubû*, 'prince,' according to the testimony of Nabonidus himself.[123] Hence it is difficult to escape the conclusion that the Nabû-nâ'id of these duplicate texts and the Nabonidus of history were one and the same person.

There is nothing forced in the above interpretation, based, as it is, upon unambiguous and definite phraseology and attested, as is evident, by a background of practical confirmation. That Nabonidus was interested in local affairs of government forty-one years before he became king is not incomprehensible. In all probability he was advanced in years when he ascended the throne.[124] The extreme age

[122] Exodus 2: 14.

[123] See pp. 16–18.

[124] *CAH* III, p. 219.

attained by his mother indicates that longevity with physical and mental abilities unweakened existed among his ancestors. This time element in the career of Nabonidus should be given material weight in the reconstruction of the events of his life. From what we know of his exalted ancestry and the important rôle which he played as the last Neo-Babylonian ruler, it would be surprising if no cuneiform proof of his early prominence had been preserved. We may accept with considerable certainty, therefore, the view that Nabonidus exercised some measure of political influence as early as the eighth year of Nebuchadrezzar's reign.

(2) *Greek Data*

Seven years after the date of the duplicate cuneiform tablets which have just been discussed the Median allies of Nebuchadrezzar, while fighting westward on his right flank, found themselves in conflict with the warlike Lydians of Asia Minor.[125] The latter exhibited such strong defensive powers at the Halys river that five years elapsed without a decisive issue. Finally in 585 B. C.,[126] in the twentieth year of Nebuchadrezzar's reign, a truce was declared for the purpose of settling the dispute by mediation. According to Herodotus two persons were selected as treaty-makers. One was the Syennesis of Cilicia and the other was Labynetus the Babylonian.[127] The negotiations were so successful that an alliance was formed which was symbolized by the marriage of the daughter of Alyattes the Lydian to Astyages the Mede.

A. *Herodotus' References to Labynetus*

It is generally recognized that the strange form Labynetus is Herodotus' preservation of the name Nabonidus, but this has not prevented speculation as to the identity of the Babylonian who helped to make peace between the Lydians and the Medes. A favorite explanation is that the record is a weak reflection of the fact that Nebu-

[125] *Ibid.* III, pp. 214f, 512f.

[126] This date is determined by the occurrence of an eclipse as recorded by Herodotus I, 74.

[127] Herodotus I, 74.

chadrezzar himself was the arbitrator.[128] Since the writings of Herodotus do not actually mention the name of the greatest Neo-Babylonian king, it has been easy to conclude that Labynetus really stands for Nebuchadrezzar in the narrative describing the cessation of hostilities between the Lydians and the Medes. This readiness to admit confusion in the Greek historian's account springs from a tendency to regard his information as inaccurate when it cannot be harmonized completely with interpretations which are often based upon mere suppositions. The question under discussion is a case in point. It is assumed that the Babylonian king represented his empire at the council which brought the warring groups to friendly terms, and on the basis of this hypothesis Herodotus is charged with an erroneous statement. The following discussion shows that this reasoning has no foundation in fact.

In the first place, there are no known circumstances which furnish a vantage ground for the conclusion that one of the mediators between the Lydians and the Medes was Nebuchadrezzar himself. The words of Herodotus provide no clue in justification of this inference. It must be admitted, however, that up to the present there has been little realization of the possibility that Nabonidus, from the standpoint of age, skill, and experience, was capable of acting as a prominent Babylonian emissary in 585 B. C. This has made it difficult to accept the statement of Herodotus at its face value. In other words, his historical accuracy has been discounted due to a lack of data warranting the belief that Nabonidus could perform international service as early as the twentieth year of Nebuchadrezzar's reign. However, additional information and a re-appraisal of ancient records have removed this drawback. Nabonidus now stands before us as the offspring of noble lineage and the inheritor of strong traits of character from his

[128] *E.g.* Sayce, *The Ancient Empires of the East, Herodotus I–III*, p. 44, note 9; Hall, *The Ancient History of the Near East*, 2nd edition, p. 551f, and note 2, p. 552; King, *A History of Babylon*, p. 279, note 2; Evetts, *New Light on the Bible and the Holy Land*, pp. 300ff; Montgomery, *A Critical and Exegetical Commentary on the Book of Daniel*, p. 71. Sidney Smith in *BHT* p. 43 intimates in one paragraph that Labynetus I was Nebuchadrezzar and in another assumes that he was Nabonidus. Genouillac in *RA* XXII, no. 2, p. 74f, regards Nabonidus as 'le fils d'une favorite de Nabukodonosor.' Hölscher in *Theologische Studien und Kritiken* XCII, p. 114, calls Nitocris 'die durch Klugheit berühmte Gemahlin Nebukadnezars.'

immediate ancestors. Cuneiform sources give definite intimation that he was old enough in the eighth year of Nebuchadrezzar's reign to be the chief official of a Babylonian city. Twelve years spent in efficient political activity would increase his prestige. Hence there is no reason why Nabonidus could not have acted as a representative of Nebuchadrezzar in 585 B. C. That Nabonidus, as a man of princely extraction, was with the Babylonian forces during the campaign among Mediterranean lands in the second decade of the sixth century B. C. is altogether probable.[129] It may even be that some sort of promotion had taken him from the scene of local municipal administration and introduced him to wider fields of action and opportunity. The attention which he bestowed upon the Westland after he became king might have some explanation in the fact that he acquired interest in it during prior contact with its physical allurements and military problems. Under the influence of its climate, coupled with the drama of ever-recurring political crises, he may have developed a penchant for adventure in Syria and this may have led him far south into Arabia. Be this as it may, there is no longer any occasion for doubting that he stepped upon the stage of history in 585 B. C. prepared for the rôle which Herodotus ascribes to him. That he and the Syennesis of Cilicia performed their duties well is indicated by the treaty which was affected between the Lydians and the Medes.[130]

The situation may be discussed from another angle. There is no suggestion in records which are available that the Babylonian forces under Nebuchadrezzar entered Asia Minor. His objective was Syria, including Palestine and Phoenicia, and, so far as is known, he confined his operations to this sector of the Westland during the period of his reign with which this inquiry is concerned.[131] If Nebuchadrezzar took a personal part in carrying out his military program, he was with his own troops. It is hardly likely that he left their area of occupation and proceeded on a distant mission which he could have easily entrusted to a capable subordinate. Furthermore, it is safe to

[129] The presence of Neriglissar, a son-in-law of Nebuchadrezzar, at Jerusalem in 586 B. C., should be kept in mind. See Jeremiah 39: 3.

[130] Herodotus I, 74.

[131] *CAH* III, pp. 212–215. See II Kings 25; II Chronicles 36: 11–21; Jeremiah 39: 1–10; 52: 4–30.

assume that the Babylonian king would not have advanced far into Asia Minor unaccompanied by his army or a large part of it. Two considerations make it improbable that such a movement of troops occurred. The subjugation of Jerusalem[132] was too recent and the siege of Tyre[133] was too exacting to warrant much depletion of the garrisons. In the second place, it is conceivable that the arrival of Babylonian reënforcements at the Halys river would have turned the tide against the Lydians and made a compromise settlement unnecessary. No credible circumstance is in favor of the view that Nebuchadrezzar was present in person at the peace conference between the Lydians and the Medes.[134]

When the references of Herodotus to Labynetus are subjected to careful scrutiny, striking corroboration of the above conclusion is obtained. So illuminating are the Greek historian's statements that all doubt that he has Nabonidus in mind vanishes. In the passage dealing with the termination of war between the Lydians and the Medes in 585 B. C. Herodotus says, *οἱ δὲ συμβιβάσαντες αὐτοὺς ἦσαν οἵδε, Συέννεσίς τε ὁ Κίλιξ καὶ Λαβύνητος ὁ Βαβυλώνιος.*[135] It is now believed that Συέννεσις was not an ordinary personal name, but a royal title in Cilicia,[136] and this indicates the high standing of the Cilician participant in the parley. The envoy representing Babylonia was Λαβύνητος ὁ Βαβυλώνιος, the simple interpretation of which is 'Labynetus the Babylonian,' *i.e.* 'Nabonidus the Babylonian.' There is no indication in this phraseology that Herodotus meant to convey the idea that a Babylonian sovereign was associated with the Syennesis of Cilicia in the Medo-Lydian pact which was negotiated in 585 B. C. His words, taken as they stand, are not ambiguous. Nabonidus was present at the council in Asia Minor as a Babylonian citizen, prominent to be sure, but not as a ruler, for he did not become king until

[132] See references in note 131. Jerusalem fell in 586 B. C. and Nebuchadrezzar immediately began the investment of Tyre.

[133] *CAH* III, p. 214. Tyre was besieged by Nebuchadrezzar for thirteen years, 586–573 B. C. Ezekiel 29: 18 indicates the arduousness of the task of reducing Tyre to submission.

[134] It does not seem probable that the parley was held in Cilicia or Syria at a great distance from the warring factions.

[135] Herodotus I, 74.

[136] See Hall, *op. cit.*, p. 552, note 2.

556 B. C. Herodotus in his first allusion to Nabonidus is not at variance with known facts. The same can be said of his second reference to Nabonidus. If an examination be made of the passage which narrates how Croesus after the battle of Pteria in 547 B. C.,[137] the ninth year of Nabonidus' reign, bethought himself of allies, it will be noted that the Babylonians were not overlooked. Herodotus presents the reason for this in the following words: *καὶ γὰρ πρὸς τούτους αὐτῷ ἐπεποίητο συμμαχίη, ἐτυράννευε δὲ τὸν χρόνον τοῦτον τῶν Βαβυλωνίων Λαβύνητος.*[138] There are two assertions in this parenthetical explanation, viz., (*a*) one which refers to the general alliance which had been made with the Babylonians, and (*b*) one which records the fact that Nabonidus was at that time their ruler. The words *τὸν χρόνον τοῦτον* imply a contrast with a former time, mentioned in the narrative, when Nabonidus was not king, and this is borne out by the facts. He was king when Croesus was able to secure the Babylonians as allies, but he was not king in 585 B. C., when Nebuchadrezzar sent him into Asia Minor as a peace ambassador. The meaning of Herodotus' statements is so unmistakable that it is impossible to believe that he confused Nabonidus with Nebuchadrezzar and hence is to be adjudged in error.

One may venture a more far-reaching conclusion. Since the assertion that Croesus made an alliance with the Babylonians is followed by a statement that Nabonidus was the Babylonian ruler at the time, it is not improbable that Herodotus sought to give the impression that an alliance between the Lydians and the Babylonians was possible because Nabonidus ruled the latter. Reflex influences may have emanated from the gathering of treaty-makers in 585 B. C. Nabonidus was doubtless sent as the Babylonian plenipotentiary because of mediatorial abilities which would commend him to both Lydians and Medes.[139] At the same time he had the privilege of learning the character of the Lydian nation. Its sturdy culture, its courageous spirit, and its potential strength must have appealed to him. These influences may have inclined him to enter into an agreement with the

[137] Hall, *op. cit.*, p. 557f; *CAH* III, p. 222f.

[138] Herodotus I, 77.

[139] Cf. *CAH* III, p. 512f for evidence that Labynetus I, *i.e.* Nabonidus, represented the Lydians in the peace settlement in 585 B. C.

former enemies of the Medes. Whether there is justification for this somewhat theoretical reconstruction of events may be disputed by some, but all will agree that the language of Herodotus, without violent distortion, seems to lend itself to this interpretation.[140] Leaving this question for future discoveries to decide more definitely, emphasis may be placed upon that which is more certain. Nabonidus can no longer be looked upon as a puny historical figure. He cannot be regarded as a Babylonian with no claim to noble origin and with no early experience in carrying out governmental policies. He was in fact of princely ancestry and according to a reasonable interpretation of cuneiform sources had risen to a position of some responsibility as early as the eighth year of Nebuchadrezzar's reign. However, the clearest indication of his prominence is provided by Herodotus. In the twentieth year of Nebuchadrezzar's reign Nabonidus rendered a most important diplomatic service, being ranked worthy of representing the entire Babylonian nation and of collaborating with the Syennesis of Cilicia in adjusting the dispute between the Lydians and the Medes. This adds very much to the likelihood that Nabonidus, twelve years before, occupied a high post in a Babylonian city.

Herodotus' most remarkable reference to Nabonidus remains to be investigated. Since the Greek historian's words have proved misleading to some, an effort will be made to interpret them in the light of the discussion which has preceded. After explaining the achievements of Nitocris, Herodotus introduces his description of the campaign of Cyrus against Babylon as follows: ὁ δὲ δὴ Κῦρος ἐπὶ ταύτης τῆς γυναικὸς τὸν παῖδα ἐστρατεύετο, ἔχοντά τε τοῦ πατρὸς τοῦ ἑωυτοῦ τοὔνομα Λαβυνήτου καὶ τὴν Ἀσσυρίων ἀρχήν.[141] This sentence affirms (*a*) that Cyrus undertook an expedition against the son of Nitocris, (*b*) that the husband of Nitocris was Labynetus, *i.e.* Nabonidus, and (*c*) that the son of 'that woman' possessed the name of his father as well as the sovereign power of Babylonia.[142] Two different attitudes may be exhibited towards these assertions. They may be swept aside as containing nothing but historical chaff, or they may be

140 Of course the possible motive of opposition to Cyrus cannot be disregarded.

141 Herodotus I, 188.

142 That the Greek historian used Ἀσσυρίη and Βαβυλωνίη interchangeably and synonymously is shown in Herodotus I, 192.

sifted with the thought of conserving possible grains of truth.[143] The latter attitude will be maintained in the following evaluation of the data presented by Herodotus.

The generally accepted view concerning the passage which has just been quoted is that Herodotus was hopelessly confused in his knowledge of the events which he professed to record. On the assumption that he had Nebuchadrezzar in mind it is inferred that he regarded Nitocris as the wife of Nebuchadrezzar, and Nabonidus as the son of Nebuchadrezzar and Nitocris. Because this reasoning results in a conclusion entirely contrary to fact the veracity of Herodotus is questioned. Another procedure may be taken with equal propriety. The original premise, viz., that the Labynetus of Herodotus represents Nebuchadrezzar, may be probed as to its reliability. After all, this premise is purely suppositional and as such cannot be regarded as sacrosanct. In reality it has already been found wanting so far as Herodotus' first and second references to Labynetus are concerned. Let us now test its applicability to the third reference.

It should be stated, in the first place, that additional reason is at hand for impugning the view that Nabonidus was the son of Nebuchadrezzar and Nitocris. It is now known not only that Nabonidus' father was Nabû-balâṭsu-iqbi but that his mother in all probability was Shumûa-damqa.[144] Hence the usual elucidation of Herodotus' language leads to a double error. Of course the hypothesis that Herodotus had Nebuchadrezzar in mind instead of Nabonidus has been advanced, in the absence of explanatory data, with the idea of furnishing plausible interpretations for passages otherwise not understood. Perhaps no other historical method could have been pursued under the circumstances. However, since an entirely different background has been given to the problem by the decipherment of numerous cuneiform documents, a revision of theory has become possible. In this connection it is not enough to state that the old view convicts Herodotus of unbelievable inexactness; a new view must be presented

143 The question of Herodotus' veracity has been much discussed. See Sayce, *The Ancient Empires of the East, Herodotus I–III*, pp. xiii to xxxiii. Cf. Delitzsch, *Zu Herodots babylonischen Nachrichten*, in *Festschrift Eduard Sachau*, pp. 87–102; How and Wells, *A Commentary on Herodotus*, I, pp. 1–50. Note especially *Hérodote et ses critiques anciens et modernes* in Hauvette, *Hérodote*, pp. 63–180.

144 See pp. 18–27.

which appears more reasonable. The one which is here proposed is that Herodotus meant to inform posterity that Nitocris was the wife of Nabonidus and that Belshazzar, their son, exercised an authority comparable with that of his father.

In attempting to prove the acceptability of this interpretation primary consideration should be given to the fact that there is no basis for the opinion that the Labynetus of Herodotus represents any other person than Nabonidus in the passage dealing with the establishment of peace between the Lydians and the Medes and in that which refers to the alliance which Croesus concluded with the Babylonians. A much more emphatic statement may be made. Linguistic requirements, historical circumstances, and chronological facts present insuperable difficulties to the view that Herodotus mistook Nabonidus for Nebuchadrezzar in connection with the two events just mentioned. This being the case, one is driven to the conclusion that the import of the passage dealing with Nitocris and Nabonidus cannot hinge upon a similar confusion of characters. A writer who indulged himself in a contradictory use of terms would exhibit a most illogical attitude of mind. It is difficult to believe that Herodotus was guilty of such inconsistency. The three assertions which Herodotus makes concerning Labynetus cannot be considered apart from one another. If it is evident that two of them refer to Nabonidus, the third refers to him also.

The name Labynetus is applied to two persons in the passage which mentions Nitocris. The elder Labynetus is described as the husband of Nitocris; their son is regarded as possessing the name of his father and the rulership of Babylonia. Scholars have predominantly favored the view that the elder Labynetus was Nebuchadrezzar in Herodotus' conception of the historical situation and that the younger Labynetus was Nabonidus. This interpretation has been linked with the opinion that Herodotus in all his references to Labynetus was preserving the memory of Nebuchadrezzar rather than that of Nabonidus. The beclouding dilemmas which arise from this theory and the clarifying results which accrue from taking Herodotus at his word have already been indicated. How can the statement concerning Nitocris, Labynetus, and their son be explained so as to avoid predicament and secure elucidation? The answer to this question springs from a careful study of all pertinent data.

An initial readjustment of view may be suggested with regard to the meaning of the Greek text. Most interpreters of the passage have taken it for granted that the words convey the impression that Labynetus, the husband of Nitocris, was no longer living at the time Cyrus entered upon his campaign against the Babylonian king's son. The phraseology allows this inference but does not require it. One translator goes so far as to derive the unwarranted idea of 'inheriting' from ἔχοντα, as if the text implies that the son had no sovereign rights until his father's death.[145] It is natural to think that such was the case, but there is no basis for this supposition in the language used by Herodotus. The form of his statement permits the deduction that both Nitocris and Labynetus were alive when their son was attacked by the Persian king. This characteristic of the text is not presented as positive proof, for, in the absence of definite affirmation one way or the other, it must be regarded as an admissible rather than a necessary interpretation. Certainly a much more explicit manner of expression could have been used by Herodotus had he wished to assert indubitably that Labynetus and Nitocris as well as their son witnessed the Persian invasion of Babylonia. No attempt is being made to compress more meaning into Herodotus' words than they will bear. At the same time, cognizance must be taken of all possible aspects of the fragment of ancient writing which is under discussion. This method is pursued in the decipherment and interpretation of cuneiform inscriptions, and there is no reason why it should not be helpful in the appraisal of a classical document. In other words, no potential angle of approach to the real sense of an early record should be overlooked.

It is not a mere assumption that the three references of Herodotus to Labynetus represent connected rather than disjointed data. There is a unified progression as to time and circumstance in what is recorded concerning this historical character, who is depicted as having helped to settle the differences between the Lydians and the Medes in the reign of Nebuchadrezzar, who is described as having negotiated an alliance with the Lydians in his own reign, and who is mentioned as the husband of Nitocris and the father of the one against whom Persian military operations were mainly directed at the close of his

[145] See Godley's translation of Herodotus in *The Loeb Classical Library* I, p. 235.

reign. In reality Herodotus presents views of Nabonidus at three stages of his career. The first view is that of a citizen acting as a peace envoy; the second is that of a king shaping his foreign policy; the third is that of a ruler sharing his prestige and power with his son. The final view is all the more striking because it may be interpreted as giving a glimpse of the three most important characters of the last Neo-Babylonian reign, viz., king Nabonidus, queen Nitocris, and the energetic heir to the throne. This statement is made with the realization that exception will be taken to it by those who are inclined to minimize the accuracy of Herodotus' allusions to Babylonian affairs. The obvious answer to this objection is that much of the unfavorable attitude towards what the Greek historian has to say with reference to the period under consideration has been based upon limited information from cuneiform sources. This means that a real estimate of the veracity of some of the details presented by him has been practically impossible. Data from Neo-Babylonian tablets of wider range and of more specific contents may now be brought to bear upon this question. The judgment of the reader can be exercised independently in evaluating this vast amount of new material. It would be very surprising, however, if the study of this extensive array of documents should be found incapable of giving a fresh perspective to the corresponding data furnished by Herodotus. With this in mind, one may well examine every phase of the evidence in hand so as to throw all possible light upon the historical situation.

B. The Rôle of Nitocris

The queenly rôle of Nitocris gains much in significance from such a discriminating investigation. Herodotus emphasizes not only her prudence and foresight but also her ability to turn her wisdom to practical advantage. Manifestations of this were her efforts to ward off foreign attack and her endeavor to benefit her people.[146] The changing of the course of the Euphrates above Babylon so that it became more tortuous was directed against a potential Median invasion, and the building of a bridge across the Euphrates at Babylon aimed to confer a boon upon the inhabitants of both parts of the city.

[146] Herodotus I, 185, 186.

Thus Nitocris evinced an interest in a paramount military problem as well as in a pronounced domestic need. Heretofore critical students of Herodotus' account have favored the view that he really looked upon Nitocris as the wife of Nebuchadrezzar and the mother of Nabonidus. There is very little that can be used in defense of this interpretation. Enough evidence has been presented to make it apparent (*a*) that the Labynetus of Herodotus was Nabonidus, (*b*) that Nitocris was the wife of Nabonidus, and (*c*) that their son was a man of authority in the kingdom. Considerations of strong corroborative value may be presented. It is not conceivable that a queen would engage in national undertakings of strategic importance except in the extended absence of the king. The feats executed under the supervision of Nitocris were not accomplished in a short time. Now, it will be shown that Nabonidus did spend a large part of his reign at Têmâ in the northwest of Arabia, leaving the control of affairs in Babylonia to his eldest son, and it is altogether likely that the mother of the empowered crown prince remained at the national capital. One cannot imagine a more favorable opportunity for the achievement of the enterprises ascribed to Nitocris.[147] As the wife of the monarch who was reigning *in absentia* and the mother of the one who was functioning as sovereign in the homeland she would possess a prestige which would enable her to exercise leadership and direction in important matters.[148] Further-

[147] Berossus states that it was during the reign of Nabonidus that the river walls of the city of Babylon were constructed of burnt brick and asphalt. See Josephus, *Contra Apionem* I, 20. Comparison should be made with the passage in Herodotus I, 186, which asserts that Nitocris bricked the borders of the river flowing through Babylon. It is not surprising that Nebuchadrezzar during his long reign rebuilt the walls of Babylon. This work should not be confused with that of Nitocris. See Josephus, *Contra Apionem* I, 19; Cory, *Ancient Fragments*, etc., pp. 39f, 45f. There is no evidence that Nebuchadrezzar spent many years continuously in the Westland. Furthermore, he made no provision for political exigencies during his absence by appointing Amêl-Marduk as co-regent. At any rate no cuneiform intimation of such a step on his part has come to light. One must conclude, therefore, that Nebuchadrezzar ruled at his capital more directly than Nabonidus did. It was during the latter's reign that conditions were ripe for energetic deeds on the part of an absent king's consort.

[148] A striking parallel may be noted. Queen Naqi'a, the consort of Sennacherib and the mother of Esarhaddon, seems to have guided her son when he was king of Babylon during the latter part of Sennacherib's reign. It is thought that she may even have acted as Esarhaddon's representative when he was not in Babylon. See *CAH* III, p. 69. Cf. Meissner, *Babylonien und Assyrien*, I, p. 74f; II, p. 323.

more, there was no occasion, so far as records indicate, for defensive measures against the Medes in the time of Nebuchadrezzar, as they were then allies rather than enemies of the Babylonians. All this was changed in the time of Nabonidus,[149] due to the successful ambitions of Cyrus. The Persians and the Medes, who were so closely related racially that their united forces could be referred to as Median,[150] had become a distinct threat to the dynasty of Nabopolassar. It was this dire possibility of aggression from the east which inspired the protective efforts of Nitocris during the last reign of the Neo-Babylonian empire.

The origin of the name Nitocris has a bearing upon the question which is being discussed. Its Greek form Νίτωκρις cannot be connected with any known Babylonian personal name. That it is to be derived from an Egyptian source has long been recognized. A papyrus record indicates the possibility that there was a queen *Nt-'iqr-t* at the end of the Sixth Dynasty or the beginning of the Seventh Dynasty. Manetho mentions a Νίτωκρις for this period.[151] However, our main interest lies in the fact that there was a *Nt-'iqr-t* of great prominence in the Twenty-sixth Dynasty.[152] It will not be amiss to review the career of this Egyptian princess. She was the daughter of Psametik I, the sister of Necho, and the aunt of Psametik II. Her father, one of the greatest of the Pharaohs, caused her to be adopted by Shepnupet, Tirhakah's sister, who was the high priestess of Amon at Thebes. This adoption initiated Nitocris as a dedicated votress and she became the high priestess of Amon when Shepnupet died. Nitocris performed her sacerdotal functions until the reign of Psametik II, who caused his daughter Enekhnesneferibre to be adopted by the aged devotee of Amon. It is of no little significance that this exalted female priesthood of the Amon cult received royal sanction during the first half of the Twenty-sixth Dynasty.[153] The possible

[149] During the first part of Nabonidus' reign the Medes under the leadership of Cyrus were friendly to Babylonia. Later the trend of affairs was entirely different. In the ninth year of Nabonidus' reign Babylonians, Egyptians, and Lydians united to form an alliance against Cyrus. This indicates how real the menace from the east had become.

[150] Cf. Hall, *The Ancient History of the Near East*, p. 555.

[151] See Cory, *Ancient Fragments*, etc., p. 106; Breasted, *A History of Egypt*, p. 143.

[152] Breasted, *op. cit.*, pp. 567f, 585f.

[153] See Breasted, *Ancient Records of Egypt*, IV, p. 480, for table showing the place of Nitocris in the Twenty-sixth Dynasty of Egypt.

implications of this fact are widened when it is remembered that the Neo-Babylonian Empire was contemporaneous with the Twenty-sixth Dynasty. The following table indicates this synchronism:

Twenty-sixth Dynasty[154]			*Neo-Babylonian Kings*[155]		
Psametik I..........	663–609	B. C.	Nabopolassar....	626/625–605	B. C.
Necho....	609–593	"	Nebuchadrezzar.....	605–562	"
Psametik II.........	593–588	"	Amêl-Marduk.......	562–560	"
Apries (Hophra).....	588–569	"	Neriglissar..........	560–556	"
Ahmose II (Amasis)..	569–525	"	Lâbâshi-Marduk.....	556	"
Psametik III........	525	"	Nabonidus..........	556–539	"

The above eras of rule parallel one another in remarkable fashion. In the first place, there is essential concurrence chronologically. Both periods began in the seventh century B. C., the Egyptian several decades earlier so far as dynastic independence is concerned. It must be remembered, however, that Psametik I did not drive out all evidence of Assyrian control until about 651 B. C.[156] and that the Neo-Babylonian régime was preceded by strong insurgence against Assyrian domination.[157] Each governmental epoch survived beyond the middle of the sixth century B. C., the Neo-Babylonian hardly more than a decade, the Egyptian two and a half decades. In the second place, the two kingdoms were similar in origin and purpose. Each represented a revolution against authority which had its rise in the corresponding portion of its particular irrigation basin. The Egyptians threw off the yoke of Ethiopian kings who had extended their sway over the lower reaches of the Nile valley;[158] the Babylonians helped to deliver a fatal blow to Assyrian despotism which had tried to rule the lower part of the Tigris-Euphrates plain.[159] In each case the restoration of an older order of national life and the unfolding of a newer trend in political existence were made possible by the destruction of a competing power which sprang from colonial develop-

[154] Breasted, *A History of Egypt*, p. 601.
[155] See p. 7.
[156] Hall, *op. cit.*, p. 509.
[157] King, *A History of Babylon*, pp. 268–274.
[158] Breasted, *op. cit.*, p. 539–549.
[159] King, *op. cit.*, p. 268f.

ment, Egyptian culture having spread to the south[160] and Babylonian civilization having expanded to the north.[161] Furthermore, the rich delta of the Nile and the fertile alluvium of Babylonia had been invaded and devastated by the same Assyrian king.[162] Memphis and Thebes and Babylon had been sources of plunder to Nineveh. However, the two nations pursued their ambitions independently. Influenced by an incentive to attain freedom from outside rule and impelled by a desire for self-expression in cultural progress, the last truly native kingdoms of Egypt and Babylonia came into being. A certain degree of racial achievement was reached and then the rising might of Persia intervened. Babylon was captured by Cyrus in 539 B. C. and Egypt was conquered by Cambyses in 525 B. C. Thus the resuscitated empires of Egypt and Babylonia suffered eclipse at the hands of the same enemy. To the very end an unusual similarity in history was maintained.

This outward conformity in the evolution of events was not sufficient to eradicate a traditional rivalry for the control of Syria and Palestine. From early times the kings of the Tigris-Euphrates valley sought contact with the Westland, but the Egyptians always regarded the territory along the Mediterranean to their northeast as a preempted arena for the expansion of political influence. Therefore, when the sway of Assyria was threatened at the close of the seventh century B. C., the Dynasty of the Nile Delta made an effort to hold what it regarded as its legitimate share of the impending spoils. Necho entered upon a campaign which brought him victories at Megiddo and Kadesh.[163] His aim was to aid the Assyrians, who might continue as a bulwark against the Scythians,[164] but the conquest of Palestine and

[160] Breasted, *op. cit.*, p. 537.

[161] It has been the consensus of opinion that Assyria developed from Babylonian colonists. See Rogers, *History of Babylonia and Assyria*, II, p. 140; Jastrow, *The Civilization of Babylonia and Assyria*, p. 158; Goodspeed, *A History of the Babylonians and the Assyrians*, p. 127; Meissner, *Könige Babyloniens und Assyriens*, p. 92. The view that the Assyrians had an independent origin from Western Semites has been advanced by Sidney Smith. See his *Early History of Assyria*, ch. VIII, pp. 102–128. Smith submits cogent reasons for his conclusions and hence presents new possibilities with regard to the question of Assyrian origins.

[162] King, *op. cit.*, p. 272f. Ashurbanipal was compelled to deal with both Egypt and Babylonia.

[163] *CAH* III, p. 297f.

[164] See Gadd, *The Fall of Nineveh*, p. 15f.

Syria was the only real objective which he attained. However, Nabopolassar and Nebuchadrezzar were not disposed to abandon the Babylonian title to the Westland without a real contest. The issue was decided at the battle of Carchemish in 605 B. C., seven years after the fall of Nineveh. Nebuchadrezzar drove the Egyptians to the borders of their land and then hastened eastward across the desert to claim the throne which had been made vacant by his father's death.

An interesting query is suggested by this propinquity of Babylonians and Egyptians during the reign of Necho, whose sister Nitocris was high priestess of the god Amon at Thebes. The pedigree of the Nitocris, whom Herodotus designates as the wife of Nabonidus, requires explanation. Is it probable that a princess of the Twenty-sixth Dynasty became the consort of a Neo-Babylonian king? A paucity of documents dealing with facts which might throw light upon this problem prevents a final answer to the question which has been raised. However, data of no little significance may be presented for the purpose of showing whether such a marital alliance was possible.

C. Contact between Babylonia and Egypt

There has been considerable uncertainty as to how intimately the people of the Neo-Babylonian Empire were in touch with the dwellers of the Nile valley. Were these two civilizations connected with one another by social intercourse, trade relations and the ties of past political coöperation? Evidence is at hand which enables an affirmative answer. The famous Têmâ stone of the sixth century B. C., found in Northwest Arabia, bears mute witness of a positive character.[165] Inscribed in the Aramaic language and decorated with interesting reliefs it is a most valuable Arabian antiquity. The contents of the inscription need not be given in detail. Suffice it to say that there is clear proof that Babylonian culture mingled with Egyptian influence at Têmâ.[166] In lists of Neo-Babylonian names it

[165] Cf. Cooke, *North Semitic Inscriptions, pp. 195–199; RA* I, pp. 41–45.

[166] Assyro-Babylonian influence is indicated by the art displayed in the figures depicted upon the stone. Cooke, *ibid.*, p. 196, comments as follows: "On one side of the stone the god Ṣalm of Hajam is represented in Assyrian fashion, and below him a priest stands before an altar." Beneath the figure of the priest are the words 'Ṣalm-shezeb, the priest.' Ṣalm-shezeb is described as the son of Peṭ-osiri in the main in-

is possible to find instances of *Mi-ṣir-a-a*, 'Egyptian,'[167] mentioned as the name of the father or the grandfather of a man bearing a Babylonian name. Such occurrences of *Mi-ṣir-a-a* are frequent enough to warrant the conclusion that intermarriage between Babylonians and Egyptians was not uncommon from Nebuchadrezzar's reign to that of Nabonidus.[168] In the time of Nebuchadrezzar there were inhabitants of Egyptian ancestry in Babylonia, the father in some cases bearing a Babylonian name and the grandfather being designated as *Mi-ṣir-a-a*, 'Egyptian.'[169] Apparently, then, this condition of social contact between the Babylonians and the Egyptians existed in Nabopolassar's reign also. Taken as a whole, therefore, the Neo-Babylonian Empire cannot be regarded as having been in a state of isolation with respect to Egypt.[170]

The route by which Egypt and Babylonia interacted upon one another deserves consideration. The old view was that the only feasible road went through Palestine and Syria. The Têmâ Stone and Neo-Babylonian inscriptions referring to Têmâ[171] indicate that a southern line of march across the Arabian desert was used by travelers in the sixth century B. C. It cannot be asserted that this wilderness

---

scription. Smith *BHT* p. 79f, discusses the import of both names as follows: "It has frequently been pointed out that Peṭosiri is an Egyptian name; the historical evidence now points to Ṣalamshuzub being a Babylonian one, and a Babylonian name particularly of the period of Nabonidus. The deity called Ṣalam, 'the image,' sometimes distinguished as belonging to various localities in the main inscription, seems to be peculiar to Taimā, and is possibly 'the image' of Sin, already shown to have been important in Nabonidus' times. Yâqût speaks of a place near Ḫarrân called Ṣalamsin, which he rightly translates 'the image of the moon-god'; and the name Ṣalamshuzub has a true Babylonian form." On the basis of the reading Ṣalmshuzub, which is the Babylonian equivalent of the characters upon the stone, one may conclude that the Têmâ monument deals with a man of Babylonian affiliations who had an Egyptian father. For other evidences of Babylonian influence see *JAOS* XLII, p. 309, and *BHT* p. 80.

167 Consult the names listed under *Mi-ṣir-a-a* in Tallqvist, *Neubabylonisches Namenbuch*, p. 111.

168 The same situation prevailed in the Persian period, as may be concluded from the textual origin of some of the names listed under *Mi-ṣir-a-a* in Tallqvist, *ibid.*, p. 111.

169 *E.g.* Bêl-uballiṭ, the son of Bêl-shum-ishkun, son of Miṣirâ; *StrNbk* 164: 40. Cp. *StrNbk* 328: 14.

170 The possibility that some of the Egyptian ancestors of persons with Babylonian names were captives taken in war must be kept in mind.

171 See pp. 114–117. Consult map on plate II, opposite page 140.

track, the monotony of which was broken by convenient oases, formed the sole means of communication between the two centers of ancient empire. However, the caravan course by way of Têmâ may have had its peculiar advantages.[172] Be this as it may, the fact that there were two main land routes, in addition to the sea passage around the peninsula of Arabia,[173] makes contact between the Twenty-sixth Egyptian Dynasty and the Neo-Babylonian Empire much more intelligible. Furthermore, that the peoples of Babylonia and Arabia intermingled in the sixth century B. C. is indicated by the following personal names borne by Babylonians: *A-ra-bi, Ar-a-bi, Ar-ra-bi, Ar-rab-bi, Ar-bi, Ar-rab, Ar-rab-tum, Ar-rab-tu, Ar-rab-ti, Ar-ra-ab-tum, A-ra-ab-tum.*[174] The data presented cannot be used to support the view that Arabia was an effective barrier between the Babylonians and the Egyptians. Its arid terrain was not an impassable bridge between the two extensive areas of early irrigation culture. Its people, in the period under discussion, were not committed to the policy of complete isolation. In a word, Arabia was a real part of the ancient Oriental world and did not exist as an impenetrable waste between Babylonia and Egypt.

If the inhabitants of Babylonia and Egypt had intimate social relations with one another in the sixth century B. C., one would expect to find some evidence of trade between the two peoples. Proof of such commercial activity exists, for Neo-Babylonian tablets refer repeatedly to the *gabû* (*gabbû*) stone which was obtained from Egypt.[175] The unique quality of this stone or gem is indicated by the fact that it was used in decorating vestments which were employed in the worship of Babylonian deities.[176] There was no need for the interchange

172 See Moritz, *Arabien—Studien zur physikalischen und historischen Geographie des Landes*, p. 31, note, for instances of crossing North Arabia in antiquity.

173 It seems that it was possible for Babylonians even in very early times to make the sea journey from the Persian Gulf to Egypt via the Indian Ocean and the Red Sea. Cf. *CAH* I, p. 582f. See *ibid.*, p. 224, for map of ancient trade routes. That these routes were known and used in Neo-Babylonian times seems certain.

174 See Tallqvist, *op. cit.*, p. 15f. *StrNbn* 297: 5, 6, refers to a man in charge of Arabs in the eighth year of Nabonidus' reign.

175 Cf. *CD* p. 209. See *AENN* 327: 1–3; *REN* 168: 11, 12; *ContCN* 84: 5, 6.

176 Note the following from *StrNbn* 938: 1, 2: *8 ma-na* ^{aban}*gab-bu-ú a-na dul-lum ša ku-si-tum*, 'Eight minas of the *gabbû* stone for the making of a vestment.' *AENN* 175: 1–5 is apropos because it associates the *gabû* stone with a cloth or garment from Arabia.

of ordinary commodities between Babylonia and Egypt as each country was practically self-sufficient as to articles of food and clothing. Timber was in a class by itself, for both countries looked to the cedar forests of Lebanon for hard wood. The situation was different with respect to precious stones. Egypt controlled dependable mines which supplied her with various kinds of valuable stones,[177] whereas the alluvial plains of Babylonia lacked such deposits. Mountains to the east and north could furnish Babylonian artisans with certain rock materials, but it is evident that Egypt was the source of the much-prized *gabû* stone.[178] Its importation into Babylonian cities is sufficient indication that Egypt was not beyond the reach of Babylonian commercial operations.[179]

A background of political coöperation between the Babylonians, the Egyptians, and Arab tribes against Assyrian encroachment should not be overlooked. Merodach-baladan's plot against Sennacherib at the close of the eighth century B. C. was able to win support from the disaffected elements of Arabia.[180] Arabs fought for Hezekiah at the siege of Jerusalem.[181] Furthermore, it is not improbable, as Sidney Smith has noted, that Egypt had a share in the conspiracy instigated by Merodach-baladan.[182] About the middle of the seventh century B. C., *i.e.* shortly after the beginning of the Twenty-sixth Egyptian Dynasty, Shamash-shum-ukîn, whom Esarhaddon had made king of Babylon, revolted against Ashurbanipal, his brother, the king of As-

---

The text reads as follows: *1 šiqlu šal-šu 1 šiqil kaspi šîm 12 qa* ^{aban} *gab-ú ina kaspi šîm* $^{\text{kitû (or ṣubât)}}$ *A-ra-bu ša* ^{md}*Nabû-iq-bi ša ina makkûri* ^{md}*Nabû-iq-bi iššî*, 'One shekel(and) one-third of one shekel of silver, the price of twelve *qa* of *gabû* stones, (part) of the silver (which is) the price of the Arabian cloth (or garment) of Nabû-iqbi, which Nabû-iqbi to(?) the treasury brought.' This text is dated in the forty-second year of the reign of Nebuchadrezzar.

[177] See Schoff, *The Ship "Tyre,"* p. 118.

[178] In this connection it is necessary to keep in mind that there was an Arabian *Muṣur* as well as an Egyptian *Muṣur*. See Hommel, *Ethnologie und Geographie des Alten Orients*, pp. 600–603.

[179] Arabia was also famed for its precious stones. Diodorus says: "And therefore neither the Marble of *Paros*, nor any other Stone (tho' never so admirable) are (sic) comparable to the Stones in *Arabia*, which exceed all others for Lustre, Weight, and Delicacy." See Booth, *The Historical Library of Diodorus the Sicilian*, p. 80.

[180] *CAH* III, p. 62f.

[181] See Luckenbill, *Ancient Records, Assyria and Babylonia*, II, p. 120f.

[182] *CAH* III, p. 71f.

syria. The Babylonian king made an alliance which included the Elamites, the Aramaeans, the Arabs, and the Egyptians.[183] Half a century later, when the Babylonians, the Medes, and the Scythians were leagued against Nineveh, the Egyptians allied themselves with the Assyrians. It is likely that this was due only partially to a desire to control Palestine and Syria. A stronger motive was fear of the Scythian menace.[184] An inherent antagonism towards Babylonia could not have been the Egyptian justification for taking a pro-Assyrian part in the struggle.[185] Necho believed that he was fighting for the preservation of his dynasty against a horde of barbarian invaders. This ranged his forces against Nebuchadrezzar with resultant defeat at Carchemish.[186]

D. The Consort of Nabonidus

The foregoing presentation of facts has prepared the way for a discussion of the question as to whether Nabonidus could have had a wife of Egyptian or half-Egyptian origin. The simplest explanation of the name Nitocris, borne by his consort according to Greek history, is that it denotes connection in some way with the contemporary Egyptian dynasty which had furnished a princess called Nitocris for the exalted worship of Amon at Thebes.[187] It will be best to consider every phase of the situation. Three main theories are possible. Nabonidus may have married (*a*) an Egyptian woman who was not of royal rank, or (*b*) an Egyptian princess direct from the court of Pharaoh, or (*c*) a descendant of an Egyptian princess who had become the wife of a Neo-Babylonian king. In attempting to determine which one of these theories is the most probable it is necessary to keep in mind pertinent data supplied by careful research. Nabonidus was of noble but not of royal descent;[188] more than forty years before he became king he was old enough, according to cuneiform intimation,

[183] *CAH* III, pp. 121, 393.

[184] See note 164.

[185] The Egyptians were ready to enter into an alliance with Nabonidus according to Herodotus I, 77.

[186] It is not impossible that Necho was also fearing the rising power of Media

[187] See p. 44f.

[188] See p. 18.

to direct the affairs of a Babylonian city;[189] a generation before he was crowned he helped to make peace between the Lydians and the Medes;[190] he married long enough before he ascended the throne to have a son sufficiently mature to act as his co-regent as early as the third year of his reign.[191] A proper weighing of all these factors in the career of Nabonidus ought to throw some light upon the identity of his consort.

(*a*) That Nabonidus was wedded to an Egyptian woman of no rank whatsoever seems out of the question. Of patrician ancestry himself, it is improbable that he would have been content with a foreign wife from the lower level of society. We may think of him as a nobleman striving to attain certain ambitions during the first and second decades of Nebuchadrezzar's reign. According to available chronological data this was the period during which he married. While there appears to have been an appreciable amount of intermarriage between Babylonians and Egyptians in the Neo-Babylonian era, there is nothing to indicate that marital union between a Babylonian of princely extraction and an Egyptian woman of low pedigree was likely to take place. We may consider, in the next place, the possibility that Nabonidus married an Egyptian woman of some degree of nobility, but not of the family of Pharaoh, *i.e.* that he took a wife from the Egyptian social class which corresponded to his own in Babylonia. While this may be regarded as reasonable, an element of improbability should be noted. If, as the records intimate, Nabonidus was interested in political self-advancement, elevation in the ranks of gentility would be of the greatest assistance to him. This he could not achieve if he married an entirely alien woman of no higher station in life than himself. A Babylonian wife who equalled him in aristocratic status would have furthered his plans more surely.

(*b*) Our thought proceeds to the possibility that Nabonidus married a daughter of one of the Pharaohs of the Twenty-sixth Dynasty. The period during which he in all probability chose his wife synchronizes with the last part of the reign of Necho and the first part of the reign of Psametik II.[192] At this stage of his life Nabonidus was an active

[189] See p. 31.
[190] See p. 36.
[191] See p. 106f.
[192] See table on page 45.

official with his career beginning to unfold but with no promise that he would ever be king of Babylon. It is hard to believe that a Babylonian of no royal affiliations would have found it possible to court and win an Egyptian princess of Pharaoh's household. A sovereign's daughter was more likely to be espoused to a king or a crown prince in the negotiation of a foreign marriage.[193]

(*c*) This introduces us to the remaining possibility, viz., that Nabonidus married the daughter of an Egyptian princess who had become the consort of a Neo-Babylonian king. Since there is cuneiform evidence that Belshazzar, Nabonidus' firstborn son, was old enough in 560 B. C., Neriglissar's accession year, to occupy an important governmental position,[194] Nabonidus must have married, one may surmise, at least twenty-five and possibly thirty years before that date. This is sufficient basis for the inference that Nabonidus could with little probability have married a daughter of Amêl-Marduk, the son and successor of Nebuchadrezzar.[195] For the same reason Neriglissar, Nebuchadrezzar's son-in-law, could hardly have been the father-in-law of Nabonidus.[196] The youthful Lâbâshi-Marduk need not be considered in this connection, as he reigned less than a year immediately prior to the accession of Nabonidus. This narrows the investigation to Nabopolassar and Nebuchadrezzar. Not much is known concerning the early career of Nabopolassar. There are indications, however, that his father was of non-royal origin.[197] As Nabopolassar appears to have died of old age after a reign of thirty years, it will be seen that he passed the major portion of his life as a Baby-

[193] Examples of this are the marriage of the daughter of Alyattes to Astyages, the son of Cyaxares (Herodotus I, 74), and the marriage of Nebuchadrezzar prior to his reign to Amuhean, the daughter of Ashdahak, leader of the Medes (*CB* p. 27; Gadd, *The Fall of Nineveh*, pp. 10f, 30). It should be noted that both these instances represent international alliances. Nabonidus, who was not the son of a king, could hardly have figured in such a marriage.

[194] See p. 67f.

[195] Amêl-Marduk became king in 562 B. C. If, as seems highly probable, Nabonidus was already married in 585 B. C., it is conceivable that the one who became his wife was born at least twenty years before that date, *i.e.* in 605 B. C. This takes us back to the beginning of Nebuchadrezzar's reign. Nebuchadrezzar married the Median princess Amuhean nine years before he became king.

[196] There is not the slightest foundation for the belief that Nabonidus married the widow of Neriglissar.

[197] *CAH* III, p. 207f.

lonian citizen. How soon he entered upon the course of events which brought him the kingship has not been revealed. As sovereign he was able to maintain himself against the weak kings which followed Ashurbanipal and ultimately with the help of allies to overthrow the Assyrian power. Extant cuneiform and classical sources give no information concerning the wife of Nabopolassar. Thus the question as to whether he married an Egyptian princess is thrown into the realm of conjecture.[198] The problem may be attacked with definiteness, however, by dividing Nabopolassar's career into three parts and estimating probabilities. Nabopolassar spent the pre-regnal part of his life in activities of which no record has been found. That he inherited no title of any kind is indicated by the fact that his royal inscriptions make no reference to his lineage.[199] One may infer from this that he did not marry an Egyptian princess before he became king. The improbability that an ordinary Babylonian could achieve such a marriage is very great. The first portion of his reign constitutes the second part of his life. During this period (626–616 B. C.) he was fortifying his hold in Babylonia and gathering strength for his complete break with Sin-shar-ishkun, the king of Assyria.[200] The last part of his life represents his aggressive campaign against Assyria and Egypt (616–605 B. C.).[201] The Egyptians were already fighting with the Assyrians in 616 B. C.[202] It may be taken for granted that Nabopolassar did not secure a wife from the house of Pharaoh during this portion of his career. Aggressive opposition on the part of the Egyptians warrants this conclusion and suggests that no Egypto-Babylonian alliance could have been made during the preceding period. If Nabopolassar had wedded an Egyptian princess during the first part of his reign, this would have symbolized a strong international treaty. Succeeding incidents do not prove that such a treaty was negotiated. All known events seem to rule out the possibility that a daughter of Pharaoh became the consort of Nabopolas-

[198] The probability that Nabopolassar before he became king married an Egyptian woman of ordinary status is not great.

[199] See *NKI* pp. 60–71. Cf., however, *OLZ* XXVIII, 346f.

[200] *CAH* III, p. 296.

[201] See Gadd, *The Fall of Nineveh*, pp. 3–5, for data indicating that the real revolt of Nabopolassar began in the period 620–617 B. C.

[202] Cf. Gadd, *ibid.*, pp. 6f, 24, 31, 37.

sar either before or after he became king. Nebuchadrezzar cannot be disposed of so easily. The record of his marriage to a Median princess while he was still crown prince must not be overlooked.[203] At the same time, of all Neo-Babylonian kings he is the only one whose career was intertwined with Egypt closely enough to make marriage with an Egyptian princess possible. These two factors in his life, viz., his early marriage to the daughter of a Median king and his dramatic approach to Egypt at a critical time in the relations between that land and his own, require careful consideration. In 614 B. C., two years before the capture of Nineveh, Nabopolassar made an alliance with the Medes at Ashur. Both Alexander Polyhistor and Abydenus, using Berossus as their source, record the fact that Nabopolassar in treating with the Medes acquiesced in an agreement whereby Amuhean, the daughter of Ashdahak, became the wife of Nebuchadrezzar.[204] It is important to notice that this event took place nine years before Nebuchadrezzar became king. There is no reference to this Median consort of Nebuchadrezzar in extant cuneiform inscriptions, but this cannot be used as evidence against the historicity of the marriage. Berossus, according to Josephus, explained that Nebuchadrezzar, after he became king, built a suspended park (κρεμαστὸν παράδεισον) in order to please his queen, 'because she had been brought up in Media, and was fond of a mountainous situation.'[205] Hence no opportunity is presented for surmising that the Median wife of Nebuchadrezzar died before he became king. Now comes the question as to what diplomacy achieved in 605 B. C. after Nebuchadrezzar had defeated the Egyptians at Carchemish and caused their retreat to the borders of their country.[206] On account of this debacle the Babylonian army was on the verge of invading Egypt. Such a sequel did not materialize, however, and it is natural to suppose that a treaty was negotiated. The record of Berossus warrants the conclusion that the contending leaders engaged in a parley.[207] Nebuchadrezzar's

[203] See note 193.

[204] Both Alexander Polyhistor and Abydenus, as quoted by Eusebius, chronicle this event. *CB* pp. 22, 27.

[205] Josephus, *Contra Apionem* I, 19.

[206] Jeremiah 46: 2.

[207] Berossus states that Nebuchadrezzar set in order the affairs of Egypt and the other countries. See Josephus, *Contra Apionem* I, 19.

victory was not so complete that he could demand entire submission on the part of the Egyptian nation. Hence it is very unlikely that he left for Babylonia without initiating, if not consummating, some agreement with the Egyptian king who desired to save his dynasty from further humiliation, while he himself wished to hasten home to assume the throne, although there is no foundation for the belief that he had a rival. Could anything be more natural than that Necho should have come to terms with Nebuchadrezzar and that their treaty should have been sealed by the giving of Necho's daughter to Nebuchadrezzar as a secondary wife?[208] So far as is known, further hostilities did not take place. However, the terms of the amicable settlement,[209] which one may predicate as having been made, are not available. Only by studying the relations which existed between the two nations during the reign of Nebuchadrezzar can any inkling be obtained as to whether a general policy of approximate peace or one of aggressive warfare prevailed. Events in Palestine and Syria were the most liable to cause contention between Egypt and Babylonia. Therefore an investigation of the international effect of occurrences in Judah and Phoenicia in the time of Nebuchadrezzar should prove very revealing.

Unfortunately only the barest details of the history of this period are known. Translated Babylonian inscriptions of the reign of Nebuchadrezzar and deciphered Egyptian documents of the corresponding years of the Twenty-sixth Dynasty are destitute of data which can be used in settling the question under discussion. The one exception is a possible cuneiform reference to Nebuchadrezzar's conflict with Egypt in his thirty-seventh year.[210] This lack of information from Neo-Babylonian and Egyptian sources should not be given too much weight. After all it is probable that many of the historical records of the time have not been recovered. Future discoveries may

[208] Sennacherib seems to have had two official consorts, Tashmêtum-sharrat and Naqi'a. See Olmstead, *History of Assyria*, p. 337; Luckenbill, *Ancient Records, Assyria and Babylonia*, II, p. 194; Meissner, *Babylonien und Assyrien*, I, p. 74f. Tiele, *Babylonisch-assyrische Geschichte* I, p. 423, advances tentatively the view that Nebuchadrezzar could have had more than one consort.

[209] Breasted takes it for granted that a 'compact' was arranged between Necho and Nebuchadrezzar. See Breasted, *A History of Egypt*, p. 584f.

[210] *StrNbk* 329.

throw more light upon the situation. Furthermore, there are indications that important domestic enterprises claimed the attention of the sovereigns of both countries. Hence the military expeditions of Nebuchadrezzar and the unsuccessful countermoves of Egypt may not have been regarded as worthy of annalistic notice. Be this as it may, we are dependent at present upon evidence which must be judged without the aid of corroborative material from Babylonia and Egypt.

No helpful end would be served by enumerating events in detail. It will be best to summarize conclusions for each Egyptian reign which synchronized with the period during which Nebuchadrezzar ruled in Babylonia. There is no evidence of anti-Babylonian action on the part of Necho after his defeat in 605 B. C. No records indicate that Egypt exercised an instigating influence upon Judah at the time of Jehoiakim's revolt, and there is not the slightest intimation that Necho attempted to intervene in favor of his appointee upon the throne in Jerusalem. Nebuchadrezzar, on his part, had not endeavored to oust Jehoiakim after the battle of Carchemish, in spite of the latter's belated, sullen submission.[211] The chastisement of Judah in 597 B. C. was not caused by any overt act of Necho; it was due to the Southern Kingdom's confidence that it could withstand the arms of Babylonia. What other inference can be drawn than that Necho remained true to the pact which he had made with Nebuchadrezzar? Necho's son, Psametik II, reigned in peace with the king of Babylon. Evidence of this is the non-hostile visit which Psametik II paid to Phoenicia in 591 B. C.[212] The alliance with Nebuchadrezzar continued unbroken. The youthful, headstrong Apries (Hophra) was the next Pharaoh. In a succession of reigns it was difficult to maintain a permanent foreign policy. Old aims kept clamoring for attention despite treaties between kings. It is little to be wondered at that an irresponsible sovereign like Apries should project rash expeditions into Phoenicia and Palestine.[213] What is cause for real astonishment is that no major conflict between the Egyptians and the Babylonians was precipitated. If Egypt ever was undependable it was during Apries' reign, for he seems not to have risked a single battle with the

[211] II Kings 24: 1.
[212] *CAH* III, p. 300.
[213] Breasted, *op. cit.*, p. 586f.

Babylonians as a help to beleaguered Jerusalem or besieged Tyre.[214] His reign came to an ignominious end at the hands of Amasis, who for a time had acted as co-regent.[215]

For almost four decades Babylonians had not clashed with Egyptians in open struggle. Jeremiah's words, 'they departed from Jerusalem,'[216] with which he describes the action of the Babylonian encompassers of Jerusalem when they heard of Apries' sally from Egypt, are more suggestive of retirement northwards to seek safety than of advancement southwards to meet the Egyptian army.[217] It seems, then, that during all these years actual warfare did not break out between the two nations. No acts of Necho and Psametik II were capable of inciting it, and the aggressions of Apries seem to have been overlooked. Howbeit, whatever restraining influence may have existed was brushed aside in Nebuchadrezzar's thirty-seventh regnal year, when, according to a fragmentary text published by Strassmaier, the Babylonian king fought with Amasis.[218] It should be noted that this event took place almost two decades after Nebuchadrezzar's capture and destruction of Jerusalem in 586 B. C. and at least five years after the close of the Babylonian investment of Tyre.[219] This makes it difficult to consider Nebuchadrezzar's anti-Egyptian campaign as a punitive expedition on account of the aggressions of Apries. That the Babylonian king should have waited so long to wreak vengeance is hard to believe. It is all the more difficult to ascribe this retributive motive to Nebuchadrezzar, because Apries was not in full power at the time.[220] The cuneiform document dealing with the campaign is definite in the impression which it conveys. Nebuchadrezzar fought not with Apries but with Amasis and

[214] Hall, *The Ancient History of the Near East*, p. 545f.

[215] Breasted, *op. cit.*, p. 589.

[216] Jeremiah 37: 5.

[217] *CAH* III, p. 213.

[218] See note 210.

[219] 586–573 B. C.

[220] Apries died about 567–566 B. C., Amasis having been made co-regent in 569 B. C. *CAH* III, p. 302f. Nebuchadrezzar's expedition against Amasis took place in 568 B. C. During the co-regency it seems that Amasis exercised superior authority. See Breasted, *op. cit.*, p. 589.

his mercenaries and achieved a decisive victory.[221] In this connection considerable significance should be attached to the fact that Apries was of the house of Necho, whereas Amasis was not. Furthermore, if one remembers that Amasis' subversive movement accomplished the overthrow of Apries, the possibility of another aim on the part of Nebuchadrezzar emerges, granting that the treaty which he made with Necho in 605 B. C. was sealed with the marriage of the latter's daughter to the Babylonian king. During an unusually long reign the son of Nabopolassar may have guided his foreign policy in harmony with a strong compact with Necho and his regular successors. Having as one of his consorts a daughter of Necho and a niece of Nitocris, the high priestess of Amon at Thebes, it is not impossible that he may have felt himself closely linked with the interests and fortunes of the lawful kings of the Twenty-sixth Dynasty. An Egyptian princess, even as a secondary queen, could have wielded considerable influence upon him. It has been shown that the relations between Babylonia and Egypt during the reign of Nebuchadrezzar, following the battle of Carchemish in 605 B. C., are not against such an interpretation of the historical situation. Moreover, if Nebuchadrezzar after he became king was induced by an Egyptian wife to adopt a pro-Egyptian policy during the reigns of Necho, Psametik II, and Apries, an opposite attitude towards Amasis would be the natural consequence.

All the facts which have been presented—and there has been an endeavor to omit no important fact—indicate the probability as well as the possibility that Nebuchadrezzar wedded an Egyptian princess.

[221] *NKI* p. 206f, no. 48, lines 13–26. In line 15 occurs . . . . *a-su šar Mi-ṣir*, which should evidently be restored to [*A-ma*]-*a-su šar Mi-ṣir*, 'Amasis, the king of Egypt.' The inscription reveals that Amasis mustered his numerous troops and that they were overwhelmingly defeated, presumably by Nebuchadrezzar, although his name is not mentioned in the last fragmentary lines of the text. There is general agreement, however, that the record deals with Nebuchadrezzar's military triumph over Amasis in the 37th year of the former's reign. See *TSBA* VII, pp. 210–225, *KB* III, 2, p. 140f, *Der Alte Orient*, VII, 2, p. 30f. It may be possible that Amasis made an aggressive campaign against Babylonian power and that Nebuchadrezzar's military operations were defensive in character. Such a reconstruction of the history of the time would not weaken the argument in favor of an alliance between Nebuchadrezzar and the loyal kings of the Twenty-sixth Dynasty, as an international agreement could well have been repudiated by Amasis who usurped the throne in a spirit of rebellion against Apries.

There is little likelihood that Necho had a sister young enough to become the bride of Nebuchadrezzar. It is much more credible that a daughter of Necho was given in marriage to the Babylonian king who was just ascending the throne. That a daughter of Nebuchadrezzar by his Egyptian consort should have been named Nitocris[222] is entirely believable, and that this daughter should have become the spouse of Nabonidus may be looked upon as a normal incident in the course of events.

The view that Nabonidus was connected with the family of Nebuchadrezzar by marriage is supported by a reasonable interpretation of data derived from ancient documents, as the following summary reveals:

(*a*) It is an established fact that Nabonidus married long enough before he became king to have a son old enough to be entrusted with the kingship in the third year (553 B. C.) of his reign.[223] In addition to this, there is evidence that Belshazzar was mature enough in the accession year (560 B. C.) of Neriglissar to perform the functions of a chief officer of the king.[224] Therefore it is very probable that Nabonidus was no longer unmarried in 585 B. C., when he acted as a mediator between the Lydians and the Medes. If Nitocris, his wife, was a daughter of Nebuchadrezzar, his appointment as a peace envoy to act with the Syennesis of Cilicia finds a ready explanation. A most suggestive parallel exists in the part played by Neriglissar, a son-in-law of Nebuchadrezzar, at Jerusalem in 586 B. C.[225]

[222] The name *Nt-'iqr-t* (= Νίτωκρις) means 'The goddess Neit is excellent.' See Erman and Grapow, *Aegyptisches Handwörterbuch*, p. 19. Cf. *AJSL* XLV, p. 187f.

[223] *BHT* pp. 84, 88, col. II, line 20.

[224] See pp. 67f.

[225] Jeremiah 39: 3. See *AJSL* XLII, 2, p. 130, for the discussion of a text published by Unger in *Theologische Literaturzeitung 50*, XXI, (Oct. 17, 1925) referring to *Nergal-šar-uṣur* as one of the *rabûti ša* [mât]*Akkadîm*, 'princes of the land of Akkad.' This accords with the title *Rab-mag* given to Nergal-sharezer. Contract tablets dated in the reigns of Nebuchadrezzar and Amêl-Marduk indicate that Neriglissar was prominent in affairs before he became king. The slaves of Neriglissar are referred to in *StrNbk* 83: 3; 266: 2, 5; 322: 4, 5; 419: 2. His [amêl]*rab bîti*, 'major-domo,' is mentioned in *StrNbk* 411: 3, 4. His [amêl]*si-pi-ri*, 'scribe,' is alluded to in *StrNbk* 413: 3–5. Tablets dated in the reign of Amêl-Marduk prove that certain things were done at the command of Neriglissar; see *EMNL* 9: 8; 14: 10; 19: 9; 22: 14. These facts are in harmony with the view that Neriglissar occupied an influential position during the reign of Nebuchadrezzar, his father-in-law, and during that of Amêl-Marduk, his brother-in-law.

(*b*) If the wife of Nabonidus was a daughter of Nebuchadrezzar, one would expect the firstborn son of this union to be given responsibility in a position of prominence as soon as he was old enough to assume it. A grandson of Nebuchadrezzar would rise quickly to a post of authority. The reference to a Belshazzar who served as a chief officer of the king before Nabonidus ascended the throne supplies this link in the chain of evidence.[226]

(*c*) The necessity arising for Babylonians to choose a king because a vacancy existed, one can understand that they would select a man who had shown marked ability in governmental affairs, especially if he was a son-in-law of the most notable sovereign of the dynasty. Nabonidus was made king by common consent after the death of Lâbâshi-Marduk.[227] A precedent was the accession of Neriglissar to the throne after the assassination of Amêl-Marduk,[228] although different factors were involved in the elevation of Nabonidus to the kingship.

(*d*) Had Nabonidus been an ordinary usurper, enjoying no relationship by marriage with the ruling dynasty, it is difficult to understand how he could have felt himself in harmony with the reigns of

---

In a number of the texts which have been quoted Neriglissar is referred to as the son of Bêl-shum-ishkun. The royal inscriptions of Neriglissar corroborate this, with lofty titles ascribed to Bêl-shum-ishkun, viz., *šar Bâbili*[ki], 'king of Babylon,' *NKI* p. 210, no. 1, col. I, line 14; *rubû e-im-ga*, 'wise prince,' *NKI* p. 214, no. 2, col. I, line 11; *id-lum gi-it-ma-lum*, 'perfect hero,' *ibid.*, line 12; *na-ṣi-ir ma-aṣ-ṣa-ar-tim Ê-sag-ila u Bâbili*[ki], 'keeper of the fortresses of Êsagila and Babylon,' *ibid.*, lines 12, 13. With the data now at our disposal identification of Bêl-shum-ishkun with any known sovereign is difficult. Pinches in *The Old Testament in the Light of the Historical Records of Assyria and Babylonia*, p. 409, intimates that the record is in error which states that the father of Neriglissar was king of Babylon. Tiele in *Babylonisch-assyrische Geschichte*, p. 465f, expresses the view that Bêl-shum-ishkun may have been the Assyrian king whose name ended in -ishkun; see I *R*, p. 8, no. 6. This is now known to be impossible, because the king's name in reality was Sin-shar-ishkun. A discussion of importance with reference to this question is that of Schnabel in *OLZ* XXVIII, 345–349, as it gives a reconstruction of the chronology of the end of the Assyrian empire. However, the evidence of Neriglissar's noble ancestry cannot be disregarded, as it furnishes a basis for his importance as a man of affairs before he became king and explains his ability to make a marital alliance with the house of Nebuchadrezzar. The similarity of Nabonidus' rôle is striking.

[226] See pp. 67f.

[227] See p. 78.

[228] *CB* pp. 30, 35.

any of his predecessors. On the other hand, he would certainly regard himself as a legatee of the former kings, if he had wedded a princess of the royal line. There are definite indications that the second supposition points to the true situation.[229]

(*e*) Belshazzar was made co-regent in the third year of Nabonidus' reign.[230] His early exaltation to kingly rank may be best explained on the assumption that he was Nebuchadrezzar's grandson through Nitocris, his mother. With the blood of the kings of the Neo-Babylonian dynasty in his veins, he could inspire an allegiance equal to that which was shown his father, who as actual king was not debarred from his supreme position until Cyrus captured Babylon in 539 B. C.[231]

(*f*) The extensive projects which Nitocris,[232] it may be assumed, brought to completion during the absence of Nabonidus in Arabia cannot be ascribed to one who was not moved with an intense impulse to protect the kingdom. The strength of such an inclination would receive its main stimulus from connection with one who had helped to place the empire upon a firm foundation. Nitocris as the daughter of Nebuchadrezzar could not have looked upon impending national danger without striving to avert it. As the wife of the ruling sovereign and as the mother of the heir apparent, who was acting as co-regent, she had good cause to interest herself in measures of defense, it is true, but a special incentive would exist if she had been saturated with the *esprit de corps* of the court of Nebuchadrezzar.

(*g*) The dedication of Bêl-shalṭi-Nannar, the daughter of Nabonidus, as an *entu*, or high priestess, of the moon god at Ur[233] may have been due partly to the fact that she had a grandmother who was the daughter of Necho and the niece of the Nitocris who was high priestess of Amon at Thebes. The mother of Nabonidus was high priestess of the moon god at Ḫarrân,[234] but she could not have taken vows as a fully-dedicated votress, and she was not established in her office by the decree of a king who was her father. Hence, while Shumûa-damqa, the paternal grandmother of Bêl-shalṭi-Nannar, exerted a good

[229] *NKI* p. 276f, col. V, lines 14–24.
[230] See pp. 106ff.
[231] See pp. 170ff.
[232] Herodotus I, 185, 186.
[233] *MI* 45; see *ibid.*, pp. 66–75.
[234] See pp. 18ff.

example by her long life of religious devotion at Ḫarrân, the real precedent for the act of Nabonidus in consecrating his daughter to the moon god's service at Ur must be looked for elsewhere. Apparently a practice existed whereby a Babylonian king might dedicate his eldest daughter as a high priestess at Ur,[235] but Nabonidus may also have been moved by other considerations.

(*h*) In the time of Darius the Great two persons, viz., Nidintu-Bêl, the Babylonian, and Araḫu, the Armenian, pretended to be Nebuchadrezzar, the son of Nabonidus, for the purpose of stirring up revolt against the Persian king.[236] This indicates that Nabonidus must have had a son who was called Nebuchadrezzar, or else such claims could not have been made. What is more natural than that a son of Nabonidus should have been called Nebuchadrezzar if Nitocris, the mother, was a daughter of Nebuchadrezzar, the famous Neo-Babylonian king?

Some of the eight points which have just been enumerated have already been dealt with in detail. The real significance of others will appear as the discussion proceeds. An inquiry of the type which has been undertaken is so intricate that a summary of the argument is always in order, even if this anticipates full treatment of certain questions.

E. The Son of Nitocris and Nabonidus

It is necessary to revert at this point to Herodotus' assertion concerning the son of Nitocris and Labynetus. The Greek historian's statement will bear repetition and careful examination. It is as follows: ὁ δὲ δὴ Κῦρος ἐπὶ ταύτης τῆς γυναικὸς τὸν παῖδα ἐστρατεύετο, ἔχοντά τε τοῦ πατρὸς τοῦ ἑωυτοῦ τοὔνομα Λαβυνήτου καὶ τὴν Ἀσσυρίων ἀρχήν.[237] The foregoing discussion has drawn two highly-probable deductions from this passage, viz., (*a*) that Nitocris was the wife of Labynetus (Nabonidus), and (*b*) that Nitocris was the daughter of Nebuchadrezzar by an Egyptian wife. We are prepared, therefore, to investigate the credibility of a resulting inference, *i.e.* that what

[235] See Woolley, *The Sumerians*, p. 76f.

[236] See the British Museum publication, *The Sculptures and Inscription of Darius the Great*, pp. 170ff, 194ff, 198f. Cf. also *KA* pp. 22–27, §§16–20; pp. 54–57, §§49, 50; 56–61, §52.

[237] Herodotus I, 188.

Herodotus affirms concerning the son of Nitocris and Labynetus, to the effect that he possessed the name of his father and the rulership of the Assyrians (Babylonians), may be interpreted as descriptive of the position occupied by Belshazzar during his father's reign. The full appraisal of Herodotus' words requires brief allusion to data which will be reviewed more exhaustively in other parts of this monograph. Cross references are given as aids in weighing the argument.

In reality three circumstances in the career of the son of Nitocris and Labynetus are recorded by Herodotus. They may be summarized as follows: (*a*) The campaign of Cyrus for the conquest of Babylon was directed against the son of Nitocris and Labynetus; (*b*) The son of Nitocris and Labynetus was regarded as possessing the name of his father; (*c*) The son of Nitocris and Labynetus possessed royal power in the kingdom. The probable applicability of these statements to the rôle played by Belshazzar may be indicated in a few brief paragraphs.

(*a*) In order to prove that it is possible to deem the Persian attack in 539 B. C. a premeditated blow against Belshazzar it is necessary to show that he was in a position of unique authority as a Babylonian crown prince. An indubitable demonstration of this fact is not wanting. The extended absence of Nabonidus in Arabia is now an established historical episode.[238] Indeed, so far as available evidence is concerned, Nabonidus seems to have spent nearly all his reign at a great distance from the throne which he ascended, while Belshazzar directed administrative and military affairs in Babylonia.[239] A cuneiform record states that Nabonidus entrusted the kingship to his eldest son,[240] *i.e.* to Belshazzar, and there is intimation that the latter dominated the aristocratic and belligerent party in Babylon during fourteen of the seventeen years of his father's reign. That this resulted in the establishment and recognition of Belshazzar as the *de facto* leader of the dynasty in Babylonia, while Nabonidus pursued other ambitions in Arabia, need not cause surprise. It is altogether likely that Cyrus after having conquered all of the rest of Asia, including, one must surmise, the Arabian domain of Nabonidus,

[238] See pp. 106–137.

[239] See pp. 111–137.

[240] See note 223. Cf. p. 106f.

turned his attention last of all to the sphere in which Belshazzar had been the chief moving spirit.[241] There is little difficulty in harmonizing Xenophon's account[242] with this view, and the fifth chapter of Daniel accords with it in remarkable fashion.[243] Hence the first of Herodotus' statements concerning the son of Nitocris and Labynetus may be regarded as describing the advance of Cyrus' hosts against the concentration of Babylonian defense which, so far as we know, may have been headed by Belshazzar.[244]

(*b*) Herodotus' statement that the son of Nitocris possessed the name of Labynetus, his father, produces no difficulty in the interpretation which is proposed. When Nabonidus cast his lot with the Westland, Belshazzar stepped into his place in Babylonia. The fact that Nabonidus 'entrusted the kingship' to him is supported by an abundance of documentary evidence.[245] Belshazzar functioned as ruler in Babylon so far as the practical administration of affairs was concerned. However, all fully-dated cuneiform inscriptions mention Nabonidus as king. This means that Belshazzar performed royal functions in the name of the absent monarch, his father. If, as seems

[241] There is no indication that Nabonidus returned to Babylon from his court at Têmâ in Arabia before the final months of his reign. Certain records suggest that Cyrus conquered Arabia before he advanced upon Babylon. See pp. 161–166. Nabonidus may have maintained his residence in Arabia until a Persian expedition compelled him to retreat to the homeland.

[242] *Cyropaedia* VII, 5, 1–32.

[243] See pp. 191–200.

[244] The *Nabonidus Chronicle* states that Belshazzar was with the princes and the troops in Akkad, *i.e.* Babylonia, in the seventh, ninth, tenth, and eleventh years of Nabonidus' reign. See pages 111f. During these years Nabonidus was at Têmâ. The *Nabonidus Chronicle* indicates that Nabonidus was in Babylonia in 539 B. C. when Babylon was captured by Cyrus. See pp. 170f; 195f. There is no available cuneiform information as to where Nabonidus was from the twelfth to the seventeenth year of his reign. No deciphered Babylonian document mentions Belshazzar by name after the twelfth year of Nabonidus' reign and no clay record refers to him by title after the fourteenth year of Nabonidus' reign. The *Nabonidus Chronicle* in its mutilated state does not allude to him in connection with the fall of Babylon. No definite conclusion, one way or the other, can be drawn from this silence. It is possible that future discoveries will throw more light upon the situation. Hence an unequivocal statement with reference to Belshazzar's position in 539 B. C. cannot be made, but it is highly probable that his authority as co-ruler continued until the downfall of the kingdom. See p. 191f.

[245] See pp. 106–137.

to be indicated, Nabonidus was continuously absent from Babylon over a long period of years, Belshazzar's rôle as a temporary substitute on the throne vanishes and he assumes prominence as the only male representative of the dynasty at the capital of the empire.[246] That a post-Babylonian view of this situation should have been expressed in words such as Herodotus used is entirely natural. The following testimony of Josephus is apropos: Μετ' αὐτὸν δὲ εἰς τὸν υἱὸν αὐτοῦ Λαβοσόρδαχον ἀφικνεῖται τῆς βασιλείας ἡ διαδοχὴ, καὶ μῆνας ποιήσασα παρ' αὐτῷ τοὺς πάντας ἐννέα, τελευτήσαντος αὐτοῦ μεταβαίνει πρὸς Βαλτάσαρον τὸν καλούμενον Ναβοάνδηλον παρὰ τοῖς Βαβυλωνίοις.[247] This passage records that Labosordachus (Lâbâshi-Marduk) reigned about nine months, after which sovereignty passed to Baltasar (Belshazzar), who was called Naboandelus (Nabonidus) by the Babylonians. If Josephus was not influenced by Herodotus in making this statement, we possess two strikingly similar interpretations of the political situation which existed during the last reign of the Neo-Babylonian empire. If the view expressed by Josephus was due to a knowledge of Herodotus' words, the Jewish historian's assertion furnishes a precedent in favor of the identification of the son of Nitocris and Labynetus with Belshazzar.[248]

(c) The facts which have been presented indicate that Herodotus' third statement concerning the son of Nitocris and Labynetus, i.e. that he possessed τὴν Ἀσσυρίων ἀρχήν, 'the rulership of the Assyrians,' may be regarded as harmonizing with the view that the exalted position of the crown prince during Nabonidus' reign is chronicled by the Greek historian. Herodotus uses the terms 'Assyria' and 'Assyrians' as synonymous with 'Babylonia' and 'Babylonians.'[249] That Belshazzar was in reality the acting sovereign of Babylonia, while Nabo-

---

[246] It seems probable that Queen Nitocris, the mother of Belshazzar, was in Babylonia during Nabonidus' absence in Arabia. There can be no doubt that she exercised considerable influence in governmental matters.

[247] See Dindorfius, *Flavii Josephi Opera*, Paris, MDCCCLXV, *Antiq. Jud.*, X, 11, 2, p. 392. The Latin translation of the passage is, *At post illum ad filium ejus Labosordachum successionis jure regnum pervenit, quumque ei menses solummodo novem manisset, eo sublato transit ad Baltasarum, qui Naboandelus a Babyloniis vocatur.* Cf. Whiston's translation of *The Works of Flavius Josephus*, p. 317.

[248] It is possible that Josephus was endeavoring to harmonize Jewish and Greek traditions concerning the name of the Babylonian ruler who was conquered by Cyrus.

[249] See note 142.

nidus exercised a reduced influence upon home affairs during his extended absence in Arabia, is the only conclusion which can be drawn from the vast amount of cuneiform data, now available, dealing with the era under discussion.[250] Hence, in every assertion made, the words of Herodotus which have been quoted can be shown to fit, in a general way, the situation which obtained during the last reign of the Neo-Babylonian empire.

An attempt has been made to discuss everything having a bearing upon the prominence of Nabonidus before he ascended the throne. Both direct demonstration and indirect evidence have been incorporated in the argument. An element of certainty arises from data based upon definite proof. At the same time, conjecture is not without its place in the reconstruction of past events. However, all suppositions have been propounded under a strict guiding principle. The greatest weight has been given to known facts and every theoretical proposition has been formed accordingly. A meticulous investigation of all available records has resulted in a conclusion which is contrary to previous opinion as to Nabonidus' early career. From now on it would seem that he must be regarded as one who, under the advantage of noble birth and natural ability, rose high in the counsels of state long before he was chosen king.

2. Belshazzar's Prominence before Nabonidus Became King

A tablet in the Yale Babylonian Collection,[251] dated at Babylon in the accession year of Neriglissar, contains an interesting reference to a chief officer of the king by the name of *Bêl-šar-uṣur, i.e.* Belshazzar. The main part of the inscription is as follows:

[1]*1 ma-na 17 šiqil kaspi ša ina 1 šiqil pit-qa* [2]*ša* ^{md}*Bêl-šar-uṣur* ^{amêl}*šaqû šarri ina muḫ-ḫi ša*[252] [3] ^{m}*Ri-mut apil-šu ša* ^{md}*En-lil-ki-din-nu* [4]*kaspu ša ina qât* ^{md}*Nergal-da-a-nu apil-šu ša* [5] ^{m}*Mukîn-zêr a-na ḫarrâni mimma ma-la* [6]*ina muḫ-ḫi ip-pu-uš a-ḫi ina ú-tur* [7]*it-ti* ^{md}*Nergal-da-a-nu ik-kal.*

[1](As to) one mina (and) seventeen shekels of silver, which are in one shekel pieces, [2]belonging to Belshazzar, the chief officer of the king, (charged)

[250] See pp. 106–137.

[251] *YBC* No. 3765. See pl. I, 1, opposite p. 68.

[252] The *ša* seems to be a mistake of the scribe, as the usual idiom would be *ina muḫ-ḫi* ^{m}*Ri-mut.*

against [3]Rîmût, the son of Enlil-kidinnu, [4]the silver which is from Nergal-dânu, the son [5]of Mukîn-zêr, for the road,[253] whatsoever [6]he shall gain upon it, half of the profit[254] [7]he shall share with Nergal-dânu.

The above document records a transaction relative to money belonging to Belshazzar, the chief officer of the king. The money was at the disposal of Nergal-dânu, who lent it to Rîmût in order that the latter might engage in some profitable enterprise, with the stipulation that half of the gain should be paid to the former. The reference to Belshazzar is most interesting. It is not surprising that the name of his father is not indicated. In writing Neo-Babylonian contracts it was the usual custom of scribes to make no mention of the parentage of a chief officer of the king.[255] Such an official was distinguished sufficiently from other people of the same name without reference to his lineage. There is, therefore, no registered proof, from the documents now at our disposal, that the Belshazzar who was a chief officer of the king in the time of Neriglissar was the son of Nabonidus and hence the Biblical Belshazzar. However, the facts are strongly in favor of such an identification. If Nabonidus was old enough to hold an official position in the eighth year (597 B. C.) of Nebuchadrezzar's reign[256] and was sent as a treaty-maker in the twentieth year (585 B. C.) of Nebuchadrezzar's reign,[257] Belshazzar, the firstborn son of Nabonidus, could easily have been mature enough to be a chief officer of the king in the accession year (560 B. C.) of Neriglissar's reign. It

[253] The word *ḫarrânu*, 'road,' 'way,' in this context denotes a journey for business purposes. See Bezold, *Babylonisch-assyrisches Glossar*, p. 127, for the meanings 'Handelsreise,' 'Handelsunternehmung.'

[254] The term *ú-tur* occurs in the same context in *StrCyr* 148: 7. In *StrNbk* 261: 6 the form *ú-tir* occurs in the same syntactical construction. In *StrNbk* 51: 4 the form *ú-tur-šu-nu* is used. In all cases the expression is employed with the verb *ik-kal*. Cf. *ContCN* 40: 6. Tallqvist, *Die Sprache der Contracte Nabû-nâ'ids*, p. 69, lists the forms under *atru*, 'excess.' See Moldenke, *Cuneiform Texts in the Metropolitan Museum of Art*, 13: 6; 15: 5; pp. 8, 15. Moldenke, *ibid.*, p. 9, connects *ú-tur* with *atru*, 'more,' 'exceeding,' and with Hebrew יוֹתֵר, 'that which remains over,' then 'profit.' See Gesenius-Buhl[17], p. 296. Hence the expression *a-ḫi ina ú-tur* seems to mean 'half of the profit.' This comports with the general sense of the context. Cf. Koschaker, *Babylonisch-assyrisches Bürgschaftsrecht*, p. 149, n. 2.

[255] See p. 30.

[256] See p. 29f.

[257] See p. 34f.

PLATE I

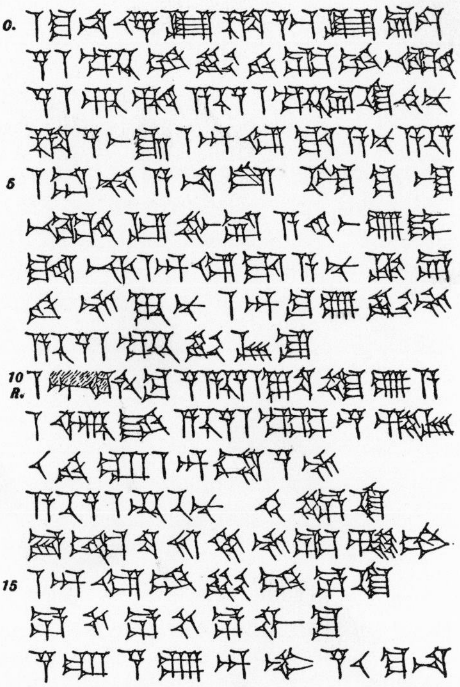

1. *Text of Tablet No. 3765, Yale Babylonian Collection*

See page 67

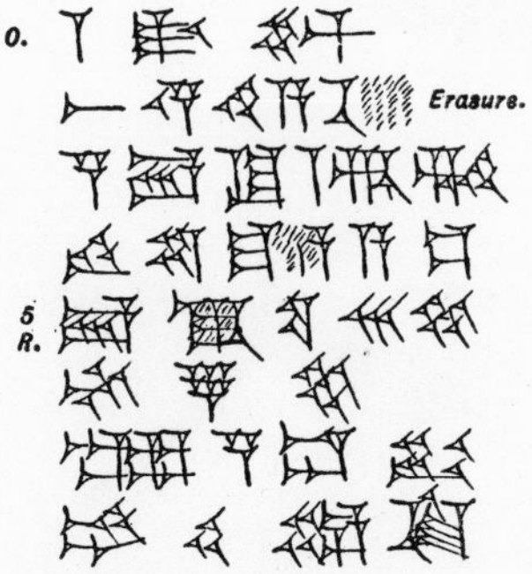

2. *Text of Tablet No. 117520, British Museum*

See page 117

has been shown that Nabonidus was not a Babylonian of ordinary origin and that he performed honorable and distinguished service in the time of Nebuchadrezzar. If, in addition, he was a son-in-law of Nebuchadrezzar, it is extremely probable that his firstborn son, Belshazzar, rose to a position of importance during the reign of Neriglissar.

3. *Survey of Evidence*

Different sources have been employed in the preceding attempt to determine the degree of prominence enjoyed by Nabonidus and Belshazzar before the former ascended the throne. A critical evaluation of the evidence is now in order. It should be kept in mind, first of all, that the data presented cannot be regarded as isolated or detached. Related information must not be overlooked in passing judgment upon the meaning of statements quoted from ancient writings. Too much weight cannot be attached to what is now known concerning the exalted ancestry of the last Neo-Babylonian king. The social rank of his father and the religious prestige of his mother prepared the way for Nabonidus' early eminence. Hence a suitable background exists for the interpretations drawn from the records discussed in this chapter.

That Nabonidus was capable of governing a Babylonian city as early as the eighth year of Nebuchadrezzar's reign is entirely credible. The cuneiform text which refers to a Nabû-nâ'id who filled such a position does not intimate in direct language that it was the Nabû-nâ'id who became king. However, such a suggestion cannot be expected from the Babylonian scribe, as it is doubtful if even Nabonidus himself anticipated at that stage of his life that he would ever be chosen as sovereign. What the record does prove is that there was a municipal ruler by the name of Nabû-nâ'id in the year specified whose titles may be regarded as indicating a rank similar to that which Nabonidus possessed as a young man. Although the existence of identity in personality is conjectural, no known circumstance suggests its improbability. In reality the weight of presumption is in favor of the view that the Nabû-nâ'id who conducted the affairs of a Babylonian city in the eighth year of Nebuchadrezzar's reign was the man by that name who afterwards served as the nation's monarch.

The statements of Herodotus require little further elucidation. Arguments for their trustworthiness have been presented. Nabonidus' career is summarized in three brief assertions of convincing veracity if Labynetus I is identified with Nabonidus, and Labynetus II with Belshazzar. Herodotus' third statement is the most involved, but its apparent haziness does not belie the facts which are recorded. It may be granted that the Greek historian preserved a tradition, the full meaning of which was not clear in his mind. However, the essential authenticity of a tradition need not be impaired by a lack of comprehension on the part of the one who transmits it. Information concerning the fact that Belshazzar was the co-regent of Nabonidus may have come to Herodotus in a slightly garbled form. Evidently Josephus experienced the same handicap. The modern interpreter must take such possibilities into account. It seems that Nitocris fared well at the hands of Herodotus. The career which his chronicle ascribes to this queen as the wife of Nabonidus accords with the general situation which existed during the last Neo-Babylonian reign. Whether the consort of Nabonidus was actually the daughter of an Egyptian princess married to Nebuchadrezzar will be decided as the work of cuneiform decipherment proceeds. The theory submitted has resulted from the subjection of data now at hand to a consistent analysis. Future discoveries will verify or refute the hypothetical solution which has been presented.

The Babylonian record which refers to a Belshazzar who was a chief officer of the king in the accession year of Neriglissar's reign possesses a significance which cannot be ignored in an attempt to unravel the events which introduced the last reign of the Neo-Babylonian empire. This text supplements evidence, already adduced, that the stage for the rôles played by Nabonidus and Belshazzar was prepared with more elaborateness than has hitherto been supposed. Neither was inducted into a position of leadership in the kingdom entirely untrained and untried. With this general conclusion in mind, we may proceed to a detailed scrutiny of the manner in which Nabonidus was elevated to the throne.

VI

NABONIDUS' ACCESSION TO THE THRONE

There has been wide acceptance of the belief that Nabonidus was an ordinary usurper. It is possible to show, however, that available data dealing with his accession to the throne will bear another interpretation. All pertinent documentary evidence should be approached with the historical perspective provided by new cuneiform inscriptions. Such a procedure cannot help bringing about a different alignment of events and a consequent adjustment of views.

1. Cuneiform Data

One of the longest inscriptions found among Nabonidus texts is a religious chronicle interspersed with historical statements.[258] Ranging as it does from the time of Sennacherib to Nabonidus' restoration of the temple Êḫulḫul in Ḫarrân, it contains much interesting material. Of special value are the passages which deal with the transition from the reign of Lâbâshi-Marduk to that of Nabonidus. The brevity of the record at this point is to be regretted. In spite of this handicap certain implications are reasonably sure.

The first passage which should be quoted is that which refers briefly to Lâbâshi-Marduk. It is the last part of column IV of the inscription:

[34]*Iš-tu ū-um* [35]*im-lu-ú iṣ-ba-tú* [36]*ú-ru-uḫ ši-im-ti* [37] *[m]La-a-ba-ši-[d]Marduk* [38]*mâri-šú ṣa-aḫ-ri* [39]*lâ a-ḫi-iz ri-id-di* [40]*kîma lâ libbi ili-ma* [41]*ina [iṣ]kussî šarru-ti* [42]*ú-ši-im-ma.*[259]

[34]From the time when (his) day [35]was filled (and) he took [36]the way of fate, [37]Lâbâshi-Marduk, [38]his young son, [39]who had no ability in governing, [40–42]sat on the throne of the kingdom contrary to divine wish.

Lines 34–36 allude to the death of Neriglissar, the father of Lâbâshi-Marduk. The remaining lines indicate that Lâbâshi-Marduk then took possession of the throne although he was ill-endowed for the position in three respects. That he was a mere youth is shown by the

[258] *NKI* pp. 270–289, no. 8, cols. I–XI.
[259] *NKI* p. 276f, col. IV, lines 34–42.

words *mâri-šu ṣa-aḫ-ri*, 'his young son;' that he had no inherent capacity for rulership is suggested by the statement *lâ a-ḫi-iz ri-id-di*, literally, 'who did not have understanding;' and that his suzerainty lacked the favor of the gods may be gathered from the phrase *kîma lâ libbi ili-ma*, literally, 'contrary to the heart of a god.' There may be an element of political bias in the record, it is true, but the essential probability of the rôle ascribed to Lâbâshi-Marduk must be recognized. The text contains no intimations as to the character of his reign or the manner of his death.

The inscription passes abruptly in column V to the ceremony which inducted Nabonidus into the kingship. This illuminating passage reads thus:

[1]*A-na qi-rib ê-kal*(?) [2]*ub-la-'-in-ni-ma* [3]*kul-lat-zu-nu a-na šêpi-iá* [4]*iš-šap-ku-nim-ma* [5]*ú-ša-aš-ši-qu še-pa-a-a* [6]*ik-ta-na-ar-ra-bu* [7]*šarru-ú-ti* [8]*i-na a-mat* ^{d}*Marduk bêli-iá* [9]*a-na be-lu-ti mâti* [10]*an-na-ši-ma* [11]*e-ma ú-za-am-ma-ru* [12]*a-bi mâti-ma* [13]*ša-ni-ni ul i-ši*.[260]

[1]Unto the midst of the palace(?) [2]they brought me and [3,4]all of them cast themselves at my feet and [5]kissed my feet (and) [6,7]paid homage to my royalty. [8]At the command of Marduk, my lord, [9,10]I was raised to the sovereignty of the land, [11]while they exclaimed, [12,13]"Father of the land! He does not have an equal!"

No clearer statement as to the way in which Nabonidus came to the throne need be desired. Self-aggrandizement such as would belong to deliberate usurpation of power cannot be ascribed to Nabonidus on the basis of the record which has been quoted. There is definite indication of spontaneous and unanimous action on the part of the people in investing him with supreme authority. Furthermore, the indubitable import of the record is not that Nabonidus raised himself to the kingship in impious fashion but that he was elevated in accordance with the will of Marduk. The words of acclaim at the close of the passage are very significant, since they imply that factors in Nabonidus' previous career contributed to his selection as king. There is definite intimation in the words "Father of the land! He does not have an equal!" that Nabonidus for a period of years had taken such an influential part in the affairs of the nation that he was

[260] *NKI* p. 276f, col. V, lines 1–13.

regarded as its most capable leader at a time of critical political need. This accords with what has been presented in the preceding chapter concerning his early prominence.

Nabonidus made no claim that he was establishing a new dynasty; he regarded himself as in entire accord with the great kings of the Neo-Babylonian empire. The passage describing his election as king is followed by these words:

[14]*Ša* ^{md}*Nabû-ku-dur-ri-uṣur* [15]*ù* ^{md}*Nergal-šar-uṣur* [16]*šarrâni*^{meš} *a-lik maḫ-ri-ia* [17]*na-aš-pa-ar-šú-nu* [18]*dan-nu a-na-ku* [19]*um-ma-na-ti-šú-nu* [20]*ga-tu-ú-a paq-da* [21]*a-na qi-bit-šú-nu* [22]*lâ e-ga-ku-ma* [23]*ka-bat-ta-šú-nu* [24]*šú-ṭu-ub-ba-ak.*[261]

[14]As for Nebuchadrezzar [15]and Neriglissar, [16]the kings who preceded me, [17,18]I am their mighty delegate. [19,20]Their troops have been entrusted into my hand. [21,22]Towards their command I am not dilatory; [23,24]I rejoice their heart.

The next ten lines contain a partially-preserved record concerning Amêl-Marduk and Lâbâshi-Marduk.[262] There is no evidence in any of the lines that Nabonidus considered himself guilty of usurpation. He felt himself at one with Nebuchadrezzar and Neriglissar. Apparently there is sufficient ground for the view that the last reign of the Neo-Babylonian empire was an integral part of the Neo-Babylonian dynasty.

The above passages comprise our sole cuneiform information concerning Nabonidus' accession to the throne. That they come from an inscription dated in the reign of Nabonidus indicates that they were written not long after the events recorded took place. This increases their value and causes one to believe that there is a measure of truth in their statements which cannot be ignored. Until further light is obtained from cuneiform sources these passages must remain in a position of unique authority, for they represent a contemporary view of the way in which Nabonidus became king. Even though the record is not entirely disinterested, it cannot be regarded as worthless on that account.

Chronological data secured from contract tablets belonging to the period of transition from Lâbâshi-Marduk's reign to that of Nabonidus

[261] *NKI* p. 276f, col. V, lines 14–24.
[262] *NKI* pp. 276–279, col. V, lines 25–34.

appear to suggest a state of uncertainty in the kingdom. Dated documents indicate an overlapping of reigns and hence a condition of political confusion. The known texts connected with Lâbâshi-Marduk's occupancy of the throne range from the twelfth day of the second month to the twelfth day of the third month of his reign. The earliest tablet of Nabonidus' reign is dated on the fifteenth day of the second month of his accession year, only three days after the earliest tablet of the reign of Lâbâshi-Marduk.[263] The accession year of Lâbâshi-Marduk was the latter part of the preceding calendar year. It is difficult to determine the exact length of the reign of Lâbâshi-Marduk because so few texts belonging to his time have been published.[264] If the records are to be taken as they stand, the official chronology of the period indicates a regnal overlapping of nearly a month. The real reason for such a situation can be conjectured with difficulty. Other tablets dated at the end of Lâbâshi-Marduk's reign and at the beginning of Nabonidus' reign will probably furnish information as to the true course of events.[265]

2. Greek Data

After a lapse of more than two centuries Megasthenes wrote a very abbreviated history of Neo-Babylonian kings. His account was quoted by Abydenus, the extant fragment of whose literary work has been preserved by Eusebius. The passage concerning the beginning of the last Neo-Babylonian reign follows the statement that Neriglissar had only one living son remaining, *i.e.* Λαβασσοάρασκον (Lâbâshi-Marduk). Megasthenes continues thus: τούτου δὲ ἀποθανόντος βιαίῳ μόρῳ Ναβαννίδοχον αποδείκνυσι βασιλέα, προσήκοντά οἱ οὐδέν.[266] Aucher's Latin translation of the Armenian version of this passage is: *Cui etiam contigit tristi fato occumbere vi illata. Nabonedochum in regni solium evehi jussit, ad quem nullo modo pertinebat.*[267] Schoene's interpretation of the same Armenian text varies as follows: *Huic etiam sors contigit* (*contingebat*) *volentiae morte* (*fato*) *mori. Nabone-*

[263] See *BE* VIII, 1, 39: 18–20, and discussion in *Klio*, XVIII, p. 57.
[264] See *EMNL*, *Lab.* 1–6.
[265] See note 557 for a discussion of a similar confusion at the end of Nabonidus' reign.
[266] *CB* p. 29f; *CLP* cols. 41, 42.
[267] *CB* p. 29f.

dokhum in regni solium evehi jussit (jubebat s. jubebatur), quod nullo modo ejus erat.[268]

The proper understanding of the above Greek passage from Megasthenes is dependent upon a recognition of the linguistic problems which it presents. One uncertainty arises from a difference of opinion concerning the number of its main verb which is in the historic present. Some read ἀποδείκνυσι, while others read ἀποδεικνῦσι. Aucher feels that the Armenian version decides in favor of the singular number.[269] This results in an unexpected conclusion, as one is driven to assume from the context that Neriglissar appointed Nabonidus as king, for Megasthenes states that Neriglissar put Amêl-Marduk to death and that Lâbâshi-Marduk died, but he makes no mention of the death of Neriglissar, unless one interprets λεῖπε παῖδα Λαβασσοάρασκον, 'he left a son Labassoarascus,' as intimating that Neriglissar died before Lâbâshi-Marduk assumed the reins of government.[270] This is what one would expect, for it would be hard to understand why a king would relinquish his throne after a reign of only four years and entrust it to an inexperienced boy. It must be recognized, however, that Megasthenes makes a pronounced exception in the case of Neriglissar. He brings the reigns of Nebuchadrezzar, Amêl-Marduk, and Lâbâshi-Marduk to an end by a record concerning the demise of each king.[271] The reign of Nabonidus closed with the capture of Babylon by Cyrus, but Nabonidus continued to live in Carmania. There is no direct statement that Neriglissar's period of rule ended because he died.[272] Does this mean that Megasthenes wished to convey the impression that Neriglissar abdicated as an old man in favor of his son? Such an interpretation of his record is suggested not only by his silence concerning the death of Neriglissar but also by the necessity for a singular subject for the verb ἀποδείκνυσι. It is significant that Berossus gives a similar impression, for he records the deaths of Nabopolassar, Nebuchadrezzar, Amêl-Marduk, and Lâbâshi-

[268] *CLP* cols. 41, 42.

[269] *CB* p. 30, note 2.

[270] *CB* p. 29.

[271] *CB* p. 29f; Cory, *Ancient Fragments*, etc., p. 45.

[272] Josephus states that Neriglissar reigned forty years and then died. See Dindorfius, *Flavii Josephi Opera, Antiq. Jud.* I, 11, 2; Whiston's translation of *The Works of Flavius Josephus*, p. 317.

Marduk as terminating their reigns, but gives no hint that Neriglissar died before Lâbâshi-Marduk became king.[273] Nabonidus was sent to Carmania and died there. For some compelling reason both Megasthenes and Berossus did not feel warranted in asserting that Neriglissar's death caused the end of his reign. The idea that Neriglissar continued to live after he ceased to reign is at variance with previous interpretations of the records, as the death of Neriglissar before Lâbâshi-Marduk became king has been taken for granted. A cuneiform passage (see p. 71) asserts that Lâbâshi-Marduk sat on the throne contrary to divine wish from the time when Neriglissar's period of life was completed and he had taken the way of fate. It should be noted that the record emphasizes the fact that Lâbâshi-Marduk's reign was contrary to divine ordering from its very beginning. There is the possibility, then, that Neriglissar, who as king was the main embodiment of the will of the gods, may not have designated his ill-prepared son as his successor, but may have sanctioned Nabonidus as the one who should ascend the throne. This view is rendered plausible by the prominence which Nabonidus had attained in national affairs and by the possibility that he like Neriglissar was a son-in-law of Nebuchadrezzar. The fact that a Belshazzar, in all probability the son of Nabonidus, was a chief officer of the king in Neriglissar's reign, should not be overlooked in this connection. Furthermore the way in which Nabonidus refers to himself as the mighty delegate or legatee of Nabuchadrezzar and Neriglissar (see p. 73) suggests that he may have regarded both as having favored his ultimate elevation to the kingship. Megasthenes, in not recording the death of Neriglissar and in ascribing the appointment of Nabonidus as king to Neriglissar, seems to have been influenced by some faint tradition of the actual course of events. Be this as it may, the chronicle of Megasthenes accords with cuneiform data in an important respect. Nabonidus did not gain the throne through aggressive usurpation on his part; other influences were at work to make him king.

The last part of Megasthenes' statement contains the words *προσήκοντά οἱ οὐδέν*. The general view is that this clause indicates that Nabonidus had no right to the kingdom, on the supposition that

[273] Josephus, *Contra Apionem* I, 20.

προσήκοντα agrees with Ναβαννίδοχον and that οἱ refers to the idea contained in βασιλέα. The Latin translations *ad quem nullo modo pertinebat*[274] and *quod nullo modo ejus erat*[275] exemplify this interpretation. A further instance is furnished by the comment *qui nulla ratione haereditatem regni habebat.*[276] The smallest word in the clause makes it difficult to derive such a meaning from the passage, for οἱ has a reflexive force[277] and hence refers to the singular subject of ἀποδείκνυσι. On the basis of this construction it is impossible to regard προσήκοντα as agreeing with βασιλέα. Therefore, no ground exists for the following translation: 'When this one (Lâbâshi-Marduk) had gone to his death by a violent fate, he (Neriglissar) made Nabonidus king, (since the kingship) was not suitable to himself in any way.' The word βασιλέα cannot be construed as having the meaning of βασιλείαν in the interpretation of the participial clause. It should not be asserted with historical finality that Neriglissar was the one who elevated Nabonidus to sovereignty, but this is an inference which may be derived from the language used by Megasthenes. However, the syntax of the passage does not sanction the view that Neriglissar felt it inappropriate that he himself should administer the government, nor is there any basis for the conclusion that Nabonidus could not fittingly occupy the throne. A logical treatment of the words of the record makes it necessary to regard προσήκοντα as agreeing with Ναβαννίδοχον and οἱ as referring to the subject of ἀποδείκνυσι. Therefore the final clause must be translated: 'who was not related to himself in any way.'[278] This would mean that Neriglissar appointed Nabonidus as king, although the latter was no kin of his. There certainly was no blood relationship between the two, but if Nabonidus as well as Neriglissar was a son-in-law of Nebuchadrezzar they were allied by marriage. Strong intimations that Nabonidus married a daughter of Nebuchadrezzar have been noted. Hence the implication of Megasthenes' words must be weighed with this possibility in mind. How-

[274] *CB* p. 30.
[275] *CLP* cols. 41, 42.
[276] *CB* p. 30, note 3.
[277] See Goodwin, *A Greek Grammar*, p. 213.
[278] Confirmed by Professor Sturtevant. The Latin translation, *nulla cum eo affinitate conjunctum*, is in line with this interpretation. See *CB* p. 30, note 3.

ever, there is one assured inference; Megasthenes does not state that Nabonidus had no right at all to the throne.

The record of Berossus remains to be considered. It is so significant in its implications that the sections having a bearing upon the question under discussion will be quoted in full. The text is as follows: *Μετὰ δὲ τὸ ἀναιρεθῆναι τοῦτον, διαδεξάμενος τὴν ἀρχὴν ὁ ἐπιβουλεύσας αὐτῷ Νηριγλισσόορος, ἐβασίλευσεν ἔτη τέσσαρα. Τούτου υἱὸς Λαβοροσοάρχοδος ἐκυρίευσε μὲν τῆς βασιλείας παῖς ὢν μῆνας ἐννέα, ἐπιβουλευθεὶς δὲ, διὰ τὸ πολλὰ ἐμφαίνειν κακοήθη, ὑπὸ τῶν φίλων ἀπετυμπανίσθη. 'Απολομένου δὲ τούτου, συνελθόντες οἱ ἐπιβουλεύσαντες αὐτῷ, κοινῇ τὴν βασιλείαν περιέθηκαν Ναβοννήδῳ τινὶ τῶν ἐκ Βαβυλῶνος, ὄντι ἐκ τῆς αὐτῆς ἐπισυστάσεως.*[279] The salient points of this account may be summarized in a few brief paragraphs.

(1) Amêl-Marduk was slain as the result of a conspiracy and was followed by Neriglissar[280] who had plotted against him. Neriglissar reigned four years.

(2) The next king was Lâbâshi-Marduk, the youthful son of Neriglissar. Nothing is stated as to the way in which Neriglissar's reign came to a close. Because Lâbâshi-Marduk exhibited evil tendencies he was conspired against and tortured to death by his friends after he had reigned only nine months.

(3) Upon the death of Lâbâshi-Marduk those who had planned his downfall assembled and by common consent bestowed the sovereignty upon Nabonidus, one of those from Babylon who was in the same insurrection.

The narrative of Berossus shows that there was a defection from Lâbâshi-Marduk, who was a mere boy (*παῖς*),[281] even on the part of his friends (*ὑπὸ τῶν φίλων*), but there is no indication that the insurrection occurred for the avowed purpose of making Nabonidus king. The general revolt was due to the weak and inefficient rule of Lâbâshi-Marduk. After the conspirators had succeeded in getting rid of him, they placed Nabonidus on the throne by general agreement (*omnium consensu*, var. *communiter*).[282] The record practically intimates that

[279] Josephus, *Contra Apionem* I, 20.

[280] Neriglissar had married the sister of Amêl-Marduk. See reference in preceding note.

[281] The corresponding cuneiform statement is *mâri-šú ṣa-aḫ-ri*, 'his young son.' See *NKI* p. 276f, col. IV, line 38. See p. 71.

[282] Compare with *kul-lat-zu-nu* 'all of them,' in *NKI* p. 276f, col. V, line 3. See p. 72.

the elevation of Nabonidus was an afterthought, the result of deliberative action subsequent to the death of Lâbâshi-Marduk. Nothing in the statement of Berossus proves that Nabonidus headed the insurrection against his predecessor as an inciter of the movement or as one who expected to profit by it. All that can be said is that he may have sympathized with it because he disapproved of prolonged sovereignty on the part of a puny successor of Nebuchadrezzar and Neriglissar. Such would be his attitude all the more if, as has been shown, he was a titled Babylonian and a man of prominence in the reign of Nebuchadrezzar. Although the way is open for speculation as to certain implications of Berossus' account, conclusiveness is possible on one point. Nabonidus did not become king as a dictator who forced his way upon the throne. Both sources of information, cuneiform and Greek, agree as to the non-audacious manner in which the last Neo-Babylonian king gained his position of authority.

A suitable summary of what has thus far been presented concerning Neo-Babylonian kings is the following dynastic table:

NABOPOLASSAR
(*Founder of Dynasty*)

NEBUCHADREZZAR
(*Son of Nabopolassar*)

AMÊL-MARDUK
(*Son of Nebuchadrezzar*)

NERIGLISSAR
(*Son-in-law of Nebuchadrezzar*)

LÂBÂSHI-MARDUK
(*Son of Neriglissar*)

NABONIDUS
(*Son-in-law of Nebuchadrezzar?*)

BELSHAZZAR
(*Son of Nabonidus*)

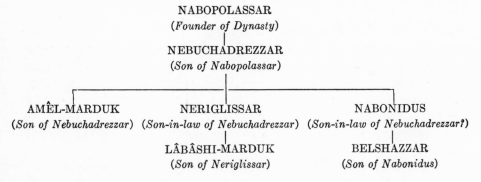

It has been shown that there are circumstances which favor the view that Nabonidus married a daughter of Nebuchadrezzar. With this as a premise we may advance to the following inference. Belshazzar, as the great-grandson of Nabopolassar, the grandson of Nebuchadrezzar, the nephew of Amêl-Marduk and Neriglissar, the cousin of Lâbâshi-Marduk, the son of Nabonidus, and a chief officer of the king in the reign of Neriglissar, would rise to a position of still greater prominence after his father became king. That this was the case will be shown as the discussion develops. Cuneiform inscriptions dated in the reign of Nabonidus reveal Belshazzar (*a*) as a man of affairs, (*b*) as a devotee of the gods, (*c*) as an associate on the throne, and (*d*) as an administrator of government in Babylonia during Nabonidus' absence in Arabia.

VII

BELSHAZZAR'S INTEREST IN MATERIAL AFFAIRS

The recovered literature of the Babylonians is not replete with intimate descriptions of the characters of notable personages. Hence it is necessary to search all the deciphered cuneiform documents of a certain period for every bit of evidence capable of throwing light upon the varied rôle of a particular political leader. This type of investigation has its rewards, for it is often possible to cause a little-known figure to stand forth with conspicuous clarity. Data must be assembled and joined together like the portions of an intricate mosaic. At the conclusion of this painstaking process a completed picture may become available.

Such a course must be pursued with reference to Belshazzar, for nothing in the way of a biographical statement concerning him has been unearthed. Isolated references to him are at hand and these may be used for the reconstruction of a comprehensive view of his activities. An endeavor will be made to weigh each document as carefully as possible so as to determine its true import with reference to the inquiry which is being made.

Six texts, ranging from years one to fourteen of the reign of Nabonidus give information concerning some of the minor aspects of Belshazzar's life. It will be observed that he engaged in business transactions mainly by means of subordinates.

1. Sale of a Tract of Land to Belshazzar's Servant

^{1}*Qanâti*^{meš} *ša* ^{md}*Marduk-êriba apil-šu ša* ^{m}*Ri-mut* ^{2}*apil* ^{m}*Mi-iṣ-ra-a-a pu-ut zitti-šu* ^{3}*ša it-ti* ^{fd}*Ba-ú-e-ṭi-rat aḫâti-šu* ^{4}*ša UŠ-SA-DU* ^{md}*Nabû-aḫê*^{meš}*-iddin apil-šu ša* ^{5} ^{m}*Šú-la-a apil* ^{m}*E-gi-bi u UŠ-SA-DU* ^{6}*bît mâr šarri ki-i pi-i qanâti*^{meš} ^{7}*2/3 ma-na 6 šiqil [kaspi] a-na* ^{md}*Bêl-ri-ṣu-ú-a* ^{8}*a-na šîmi gam-ru-tu id-din ina ḫu-[ud lib]-bi* ^{9}*[ú-il-tim 1/3 ma-na] 7 šiqil kaspi [a-di-i]* ^{10}*ú-il-tim ša 1/3 ma-na 5 šiqil kaspi* ^{11}*maḫ-ru-ú* ^{md}*Marduk-êriba šîm bîti-šu* ^{12}*ina qât* ^{md}*Bêl-ri-ṣu-ú-a* ^{amêl}*qal-la* ^{13}*ša* ^{md}*Bêl-šar-uṣur mâr šarri il-qu-ú* ^{14}*ri-eš qanâti*^{meš} *in-na-aš-šú-ú* ^{15}*kunuk a-pil-tum ik-ka-na-ak-ma* ^{16}*kaspu ma-la it-ti-ru [u i-ma-aṭ-ṭù-ú]* ^{17}*ki-i maḫîri ḫa-sis a-ḫa-meš ip-pa-al.*[283]

[283] *StrNbn* 50: 1–17. See *KB* IV, p. 210f.

[1](As to) the reeds which Marduk-êriba, the son of Rîmût, [2]son of Miṣrâ, corresponding to his share, [3]which (he has jointly) with Bau-êṭirat, his sister, [4]which adjoin (the house of) Nabû-aḫê-iddin, the son of [5]Shulâ, son of Egibi, and (also) adjoin [6]the house of the son of the king, at the proportion of reeds [7]for two-thirds of a mina and six shekels of silver to Bêl-riṣûa [8]at the full price he sold (them), of his own free will [9][the document of one-third of a mina] and seven shekels of silver [together with] [10]the former document of one-third of a mina and five shekels of silver, [11]Marduk-êriba as the price of his house [12]from Bêl-riṣûa, the servant [13]of Belshazzar, the son of the king, received. [14]The best of the reeds shall be brought. [15]The record of the receipt they shall seal and [16]whatever money is in excess [or lacking], [17]according to the stipulated price, they shall compensate one another.

The above document, attested by three witnesses, was written by the scribe Aplâ in Babylon, the twenty-sixth day of Adar, the first year of Nabonidus, the king of Babylon. In brief, it records the sale of a tract of land by Marduk-êriba to Bêl-riṣûa, Belshazzar's servant. It is altogether likely that Bêl-riṣûa negotiated this transfer of property in the interests of Belshazzar whose underling he was.

2. Loan of Money from Belshazzar's Secretary

[1]*Bîtu ša* [md]*Nabû-aḫê*[meš]*-iddin apil-šu ša* [m]*Šú-la-a* [2]*apil* [m]*E-gi-bi ša ita bît* [md]*Bêl-iddin apil-šu ša* [3][m]*Ri-mut apil* [amêl]*di-ki-i a-di 3-ta šanâti*[meš] [4]*a-na* [md]*Nabû-mukîn-aḫi* [amêl]*si-pi-ri ša* [md]*Bêl-šar-uṣur* [5]*mâr šarri a-na 1 1/2 ma-na kaspi a-na i-di bîti* [6]*ia-a-nu ù ḫubulli kaspi ia-a-nu id-din* [7]*u-ri i-ša-an-nu ù bat-qa ša bîti* [8]*i-ṣab-bat ar-ki 3-ta šanâti*[meš] [9]*kaspa-' 1 1/2 ma-na* [md]*Nabû-aḫê*[meš]*-iddin* [10]*a-na* [md]*Nabû-mukîn-aḫi i-nam-din-ma* [11][md]*Nabû-mukîn-aḫi bîta ina pa-ni* [md]*Nabû-aḫê*[meš]*-iddin* [12][a]*ú-maš-ša-ar.*[284]

[1](As to) the house of Nabû-aḫê-iddin, the son of Shulâ, [2]son of Egibi, which adjoins the house of Bêl-iddin, the son of [3]Rîmût, the son of the *dikû* official, for three years [4]to Nabû-mukîn-aḫi, the scribe[285] of Belshazzar, [5,6]the son of the king, for one and one-half minas of silver he gave (it) with the provision that there should be no rent for the house and no interest on the money. [7]The woodwork of the house he shall renew and (any) crack (of the wall) of the house [8]he shall close up. After three years [9]the money, amounting to one and one-half minas, Nabû-aḫê-iddin [10]to Nabû-mukîn-aḫi

[284] *StrNbn* 184: 1–12a. See *KB* IV, p. 222f.

[285] See *JAOS* XLVIII, p. 109–128, where the meaning of 'scribe' for [amêl]*sipîru* is discussed.

shall give and [11,12a]Nabû-mukîn-aḫi shall leave the house at the disposal of Nabû-aḫê-iddin.

The above record, witnessed by three persons, was written by the scribe Bêl-aḫê-iqîsha in Babylon, the twenty-first day of the month Nisan, the fifth year of Nabonidus, the king of Babylon. According to its provisions Nabû-aḫê-iddin obtained a loan of one and one-half minas of silver for three years from Nabû-mukîn-aḫi, the scribe or accountant of Belshazzar. The house of Nabû-aḫê-iddin was given as security for the money, with the stipulation that the house should be kept in good condition throughout the period of three years, at the end of which time the house and money should revert to the original owners, no interest having accrued on the money in the meantime.

3. Transaction of Business by Belshazzar's Officials

[1]*2/3 ma-na 5 šiqil kaspi eš-ru-ú* [2]*ša* ^{d}*Bêl* ^{d}*Nabû* ^{d}*Nergal ù* ^{d}*Bêlit ša Uruk*^{ki} [3]*ra-šú-tu ša* ^{md}*Nabû-ṣa-bit-qâti* ^{amêl}*rab bîti* [4]*ša* ^{md}*Bêl-šar-uṣur mâr šarri ša ina eli* [5] ^{md}*Nabû-mukîn-aḫi . . . .* ^{amêl}*si-pi-ri* ^{amêl}*qal-la* [6]*ša* ^{md}*Bêl-šar-uṣur mâr šarri ša a-na šîm* [7] ^{md}*Nabû-karâbi-ši-me* ^{amêl}*qal-li-šu* [8]*na-ad-nu kaspa-' 2/3 ma-na 5 šiqlê* ^{md}*Nabû-ṣa-bit-qâti* [9] ^{amêl}*rab bîti ša* ^{md}*Bêl-šar-uṣur mâr šarri* [10]*i-na qa-ti* ^{md}*Nabû-aḫê*^{meš}*-iddin* [11]*apil-šu ša* ^{m}*Šú-la-a mâr* ^{m}*E-gi-bi* [12]*a-na eli* ^{md}*Nabû-mukîn-aḫi* [13]*ma-ḫi-ir ina a-ša-bi ša* ^{f}*Di-ki-i-tum* [14]*aššat* ^{md}*Nabû-mukîn-aḫi.*[286]

[1](As to) two-thirds of a mina (and) five shekels of silver, the tithe [2]of Bêl, Nabû, Nergal, and the Bêlit of Erech, [3]the claim of Nabû-ṣâbit-qâti, the steward [4]of Belshazzar, the son of the king, which is (charged) against [5]Nabû-mukîn-aḫi . . . . the scribe (and) servant [6]of Belshazzar, the son of the king, which for the price of [7,8]Nabû-karâbi-šimê, his servant, was given, the money, amounting to two-thirds of a mina (and) five shekels, Nabû-ṣâbit-qâti, [9]the steward of Belshazzar, the son of the king, [10]from Nabû-aḫê-iddin, [11]the son of Shulâ, son of Egibi, [12](as a charge) against Nabû-mukîn-aḫi [13]has received. In the presence of Dikîtum, [14]the wife of Nabû-mukîn-aḫi.

The scribe who wrote the above document was Bêl-aḫê-iqîsha. It was attested by four additional witnesses, one of whom was Arṣa', the son of Antarabi, the servant of Belshazzar, the son of the king. The tablet was written in Babylon, the ninth day of Shebaṭ, the seventh year of Nabonidus, the king of Babylon. The monetary transaction

[286] *StrNbn* 270: 1–14. See Kohler and Peiser, *Aus dem babylonischen Rechtsleben* IV, p. 8. For a similar reference to tithe money see *VS* VI, 67: 5.

described records the receipt of the price of a slave by Nabû-ṣâbit-qâti, the steward of Belshazzar, from tithe funds charged against Nabû-mukîn-aḫi, the scribe of Belshazzar mentioned in the preceding text.

4. Belshazzar Grants a Loan of Money

[1]20 ma-na kaspi šîm šipâte[zun] makkûru [ša] [2][md]Bêl-šar-uṣur mâr šarri ša ina qât [md]Nabû-ṣa-[bit-qâti] [3][amêl]rab bîti ša [md]Bêl-šar-uṣur mâr šarri ù [4][amêl]si-pir[meš] ša mâr šarri ina eli [m]Iddin-[d]Marduk [5]apil-šu ša [m]Iqîša(-ša)-a apil [m]Nûr-[d]Sin ina [araḫ]Addari ša šatti [11[kam]] [6]kaspa-' 20 ma-na i-nam-din bîtu .... [7]amelu-ut-su ù mim-mu-šu ša âli u ṣêri ma-la [8]ba-šú-ú maš-ka-nu ša [md]Bêl-šar-uṣur [9]mâr šarri a-di [md]Bêl-šar-uṣur kaspa-šu [10]i-šal-li-mu kaspa ma-la .... [11]i-ma-ṭu(?) šú-ú ḫubulla i-nam-din.[287]

[1]Twenty minas of silver, the price of wool, the property of [2]Belshazzar, the son of the king, which (are) from Nabû-ṣâbit-qâti, [3]the steward of Belshazzar, the son of the king, and [4]the scribes of the son of the king, (are charged) against Iddin-Marduk, [5]the son of Iqîsha, son of Nûr-Sin. In the month Adar of the eleventh(?) year [6]the money, amounting to twenty minas, he shall pay. The house .... [7]his slave, and whatsoever is his of city and plain, as much as [8]there is, (is) the pledge of Belshazzar, [9,10]the son of the king, until Belshazzar shall be paid his money. On whatsoever money .... [11]is lacking(?)[288] he himself shall pay the interest.

The above document, attested by five witnesses, was recorded in Babylon by the scribe Bêl-aḫê-iqîsha(?),[289] the twentieth day of the month .... the eleventh year of Nabonidus, the king of Babylon. The text indicates that Belshazzar granted a loan of twenty minas of silver to Iddin-Marduk through the agency of his steward and secretaries. The total property of Iddin-Marduk was given as security for the return of the money to Belshazzar at a specified time.

5. Monetary Transaction by Belshazzar's Steward

[1]1 ma-na 16 šiqil kaspi qaqqadu u ḫubullu [2][ra-šú]-tu ša [md]Nabû-ṣa-bit-qâti [amêl]rab bîti [3]ša [md]Bêl-šar-uṣur mâr šarri ša ina muḫ-ḫi [4]Bêl-iddina(-na)

[287] *StrNbn* 581: 1–11.

[288] The text in line 11 has *i-mir*, but the reading *i-ma-ṭu* is suggested as a possibility. See *ContCN* 121: 9; *StrNbn* 715: 17.

[289] The text as copied indicates *[md]Bêl-aḫê[meš]-iddin apil-šu ša [md]Nabû-balâṭsu-iqbi*, but the reading may be emended in view of *[md]Bêl-aḫê[meš]-iqîša .... mâru-šu ša [dm]Nabû-balâṭsu-iqbi*, the scribe mentioned in the preceding text, *StrNbn* 270: 22, 23.

apil-šu ša ^{md}*Bêl-šum-iškun(-un)* [5]*mâr* ^{md}*Sin-tab-ni u* ^{še}*zêru ša bi-rit abullâti*^{meš} [6]*maš-ka-nu ṣa-ab-tum kaspa-' 1 ma-na 16 šiqlê* [7] ^{md}*Nabû-ṣa-bit-qâti ina qât* ^{m}*Itti-*^{d}*Marduk-balâṭu* [8]*apil-šu ša* ^{md}*Nabû-aḫê*^{meš}*-iddin mâr* ^{m}*E-gi-bi* [9]*a-na eli* ^{md}*Bêl-iddina(-na) ma-ḫir.*[290]

[1](As to) one mina and sixteen shekels of silver, principal and interest, [2]the claim of Nabû-ṣâbit-qâti, the steward [3]of Belshazzar, the son of the king, which (are charged) against [4]Bêl-iddina, the son of Bêl-shum-ishkun, [5]son of Sin-tabni, and (for which) the seed field which (is) between the city gates [6]has been taken as a pledge, the money, amounting to one mina and sixteen shekels, [7]Nabû-ṣâbit-qâti from Itti-Marduk-balâṭu, [8]the son of Nabû-aḫê-iddin, son of Egibi, [9]has received (as a charge) against Bêl-iddina.

This tablet was written in Babylon by the scribe Nergal-ushallim in the presence of four witnesses, the twenty-seventh day of second Adar, the twelfth year of Nabonidus, the king of Babylon. It records a monetary transaction on the part of Nabû-ṣâbit-qâti, the steward of Belshazzar mentioned in the two preceding documents. A loan is granted to Bêl-iddina who gives a tract of land as security.

6. *Record of Food Delivered to Belshazzar*

[1]*Ṣi-di-tum ša a-na ....* [2]*u* ^{md}*Šamaš-iqîša(-ša) ša kurummati*^{zun} *ša(?) ....* [3]*a-na pâni mâr šarri [it]-ta-ši(?)* [4]*ûmu 26*^{kam} *šattu 14*^{kam} ^{md}*Nabû-nâ'id šar Bâbili*^{ki} [5]*7 gur suluppi ultu šú-tum-mu šarri* [6]*kurummatu*^{zun} ^{arah}*Nisanni a-di* ^{arah}*Tišrîti šattu 14*^{kam}.[291]

[1]Provisions which (were given) to .... [2]and Shamash-iqîsha, who the food of(?) .... [3]to the son of the king delivered(?), [4]the twenty-sixth day (of the month?), the fourteenth year of Nabonidus, the king of Babylon. [5]Seven *gur* of dates (were given) from the storehouse of the king [6]as food which (is the allowance for) the month Nisan until the month Tishri of the fourteenth year.

The above passage is the introductory portion of a text, the remaining part of which contains a detailed inventory. There is no mention of witnesses or scribe. The broken condition of the tablet makes it difficult to decide whether it was written in Babylon or not. The inscription is a record of payments made to two men who delivered food to the son of the king.

[290] *StrNbn* 688: 1–9.

[291] *StrNbn* 824: 1–6. See p. 137, note 440, for force of *mâr šarri*.

7. *Summary of Data*

It is of no little significance that five of the six texts which have been interpreted as dealing with the interests of Belshazzar represent clearly-described negotiations in the city of Babylon itself. This indicates that Belshazzar was a man of affairs in the metropolis of the empire. However, he did not engage in minor financial activities in person, but delegated the management of monetary matters to subordinates who officiated as his agents. The names of these representatives of Belshazzar were Bêl-riṣûa, his servant, Nabû-mukîn-aḫi, his scribe, and Nabû-ṣâbit-qâti, his steward. Another man prominent in the transactions was Nabû-aḫê-iddin, who seems to have had no official position. The interconnection of the documents is shown by the following facts: No. 1 describes the tract of land bought by Bêl-riṣûa as bordering on property owned by Nabû-aḫê-iddin; No. 2 states that the house of Nabû-aḫê-iddin was given as security for a loan from Nabû-mukîn-aḫi; No. 3 refers to tithe money received by Nabû-ṣâbit-qâti from Nabû-aḫê-iddin as a charge against Nabû-mukîn-aḫi; No. 4 indicates that a loan from Belshazzar was granted by Nabû-ṣâbit-qâti; No. 5 states that money belonging to a son of Nabû-aḫê-iddin was given as a loan by Nabû-ṣâbit-qâti; No. 6 has no connection with the preceding documents. It is clear that Nos. 1–5 represent a related group of archives dealing with the activities of Belshazzar's agents who were commissioned by him to look after affairs which he could not direct with minute attention on account of higher and more important duties. The information given by No. 6 suggests that he had means of support aside from his commercial ventures. Taken together, the texts which have been discussed provide material for a positive appraisal of Belshazzar as a man interested in business, although not dependent upon it for a livelihood. This is true in spite of the limited scope of the texts so far as documentary evidence is concerned.

VIII

BELSHAZZAR'S DEVOTION TO BABYLONIAN DEITIES

The claims of religion were recognized extensively by the Babylonian people. Each city had a temple dedicated to the cult of a patron deity. Kings were especially interested in the erection, renovation, and maintenance of these places of worship. It seems that the Babylonians expected those who exercised sovereign power over them to be exemplars in reverencing the gods.

Six texts, ranging from years five to thirteen of the reign of Nabonidus, show that Belshazzar responded to the needs of Babylonian sanctuaries by making offerings of silver, gold, and sacrificial animals.

1. Belshazzar Presents Silver to the Temple in Erech

[1]*1 ma-na kaspi eš-ru-ú* [2]*ša* ^{md}*Bêl-šar-uṣur mâr šarri* [3]^{m}*Šú-la-*[*a*] *apil-šu ša* ^{md}*Ê-a-šum-iddin* [4]*ina Ê-an-na ma-ḫi-ir* [5]^{arah}*Ulûlu ûmu 29*^{kam} *šattu 5*^{kam} [6]^{d}*Nabû-nâ'id šar Bâbili*^{ki}.[292]

[1]One mina of silver, the tithe [2]of Belshazzar, the son of the king, [3]Shulâ, the son of Êa-shum-iddin, [4]in Êanna received. [5]The twenty-ninth day of Elul, the fifth year [6]of Nabonidus, the king of Babylon.

This brief receipt records the fact that Belshazzar in the fifth year of Nabonidus' reign paid silver amounting to sixty shekels as his tithe-offering to the temple of Êanna in Erech. Light is thrown upon the Babylonian custom of paying tithes. Even members of the royal family participated in the practice.[293]

2. Belshazzar Presents Animals to the Temple in Sippar

[1]*Ištên(-en) alpu šuk-lu-lu* [2]*5 immerê ša mâr šarri* [3]^{md}*Nabû-iddin a-na Ê-babbar-ra* [4]*it-ta-din alpu bîru* [5]*ù ina bît karê*^{meš} [6]^{arah}*Šabâṭu ûmu 12*^{kam} [7]*šattu 7*^{kam} ^{d}*Nabû-nâ'id* [8]*šar Bâbili*^{ki}.[294]

[292] *AENN* 322: 1–6.

[293] See *StrNbn* 2: 1–6 for the following record: *6 ma-na ḫurâṣi eš-ru-ú ša šarri ina abulli ša Ê-babbar-ra id-din-nu* ^{arah}*Simânu ûmu 26*^{kam} *šattu rêštû šarrûti* ^{md}*Nabû-nâ'id šar Bâbili*^{ki}, 'Six minas of gold, the tithe which the king gave in the great gate of the temple Êbabbarra. The twenty-sixth day of Sivan, the accession year of Nabonidus, the king of Babylon.' This is an illuminating instance of tithe paid by Nabonidus to the temple of Shamash at Sippar at the beginning of his reign. Five years later Nabonidus was at Têmâ, and hence Belshazzar was attending to the payment of royal tithes.

[294] *StrNbn* 272: 1–8.

[1]One perfect ox (and) [2]five sheep of the son of the king [3]Nabû-iddin to Êbabbarra [4]gave. The ox (was) young [5]and (was) in the storehouse. [6]The twelfth day of the month Shebaṭ, [7]the seventh year of Nabonidus, [8]the king of Babylon.

This text is a simple statement that Belshazzar in the seventh year of Nabonidus' reign through the agency of Nabû-iddin gave some animals to Êbabbarra, the temple of Shamash in Sippar.

3. Oxen and Sheep Presented as an Offering by Belshazzar

[1]*2 alpê šuk-lu-lu 4-i 33 immerê* [2]*niqê*^{meš} *ša mâr šarri ûmu 11*^{kam} [3]*ša* ^{araḫ}*Ayari ina bâbi rabî(-i) ša Ê-babbar-ra* [4]*ip-ru-us-su immerê*$^{\text{[meš]}}$ *a-na bît [ú-ru-ú]* [5]*it-tal-ka ina qât* ^{md}*Bêl-šar-bul-liṭ ša [kurummat*^{zun}*] šarri* [6]*a-na êkalli šú-bu-ul alpê*$^{\text{[meš]}}$ *ina Ê-babbar-ra* [7]*ina pâni* ^{md}*Šamaš-êriba* ^{araḫ}*Ayaru [ûmu] 22*^{kam} [8]*šattu 9*^{kam} ^{md}*Nabû-nâ'id šar Bâbili*^{ki} [9]*ina lib-bi 10 immerê rabû-ú-tu* [10]*ina bît ú-ru-ú ina pâni* ^{m}*Nûr-*^{d}*Sin.*[295]

[1]Two perfect oxen four years old, thirty-three sheep, [2]the offering of the son of the king, on the eleventh day [3]of the month Iyyar in the great gate of Êbabbarra [4]were apportioned. The sheep to the stable [5]shall go. From Bêl-shar-bulliṭ, (the man in charge) of [the food] of the king, [6]they were brought for the palace. The oxen in Êbabbarra [7]shall be at the disposal of Shamash-êriba. The twenty-second day of the month Iyyar, [8]the ninth year of Nabonidus, the king of Babylon. [9]Of them ten large sheep [10]in the stable shall be at the disposal of Nûr-Sin.

The above record indicates that Belshazzar in the ninth year of Nabonidus' reign made an offering of thirty-five animals to Êbabbarra, the temple of Shamash in Sippar. The document explains that the sheep were brought to the palace from the king's maintenance supply. There is a definite implication in the text that Belshazzar had the right to dispose of animals brought to the palace from the royal store. This may be connected with the fact that Nabonidus, as will be shown, was at Têmâ in Arabia in the ninth year of his reign.

[295] *StrNbn* 332: 1–10. Two partially-obliterated texts, *StrNbn* 265 and 387, dated in the seventh and ninth years of Nabonidus' reign, refer to similar offerings of 'the son of the king.' Their likeness to *StrNbn* 332 makes it unnecessary to quote them in full. See also Speleers, *Recueil des Inscriptions de l'Asie Antérieure des Musées Royaux du Cinquantenaire à Bruxelles*, p. 31, Text 285: 1–3.

4. Belshazzar Presents a Tongue of Gold to Shamash

[1]*Ištênit(-it) li-ša-nu ḫurâṣi* [2]*1 ma-na KI-LAL-šu* [3]*ûmu 11*[kam] *ša* [arab]*Ayari* [4]*mâr šarri a-na* [d]*Šamaš* [5]*it-ta-din.*[296]

[1]One tongue of gold, [2]one mina (being) its weight, [3]on the eleventh day of Iyyar [4, 5]the son of the king gave to Shamash.

This brief statement, recorded on the eleventh day of the month Iyyar, the ninth year of Nabonidus, the king of Babylon, indicates that Belshazzar made a valuable monetary contribution to the sun god. It is interesting that the weight of the tongue of gold presented by him to Shamash was the same as the weight of the silver presented by him to the temple in Erech.

5. Payment for the Transportation of Belshazzar's Offerings to Sippar

[1]*1 šiqil rebût(-ut) kaspi a-na* [2]*i-di* [iṣ]*elippi ša 3 alpê* [3]*ù 24 immerê niqê*[meš] [4]*ša mâr šarri ša ina* [arab]*Nisanni* [5]*a-na* [d]*Šamaš u ilâni*[meš] *Sip-par*[ki] [6]*il-li-ku* [7]*ina manzazi ša* [md]*Bêl-šar-bul-liṭ* [8]*ša kurummat*[zun] *šarri a-na* [9 md]*Šamaš-iddin u* [m]*Dan-nu-*[d]*Adad* [10]*nadin(-in) 1 [gur] 24 [qa] suluppi* [11]*a-na kurummati*[zun]*-šu-nu nadin(-in)* [12 arab]*Nisannu ûmu 9*[kam] *šattu 10*[kam] [13 md]*Nabû-nâ'id šar Bâbili*[ki]*.*[297]

[1]One shekel (and) a quarter of silver for [2]the hire of the ship of the three oxen [3]and twenty-four sheep, the offering [4]of the son of the king, which in the month Nisan [5]to Shamash and the gods of Sippar [6]went, [7]in the presence of Bêl-shar-bulliṭ,[298] [8](the man in charge) of the food of the king, to

[296] *StrNbn* 331: 1–5

[297] *StrNbn* 401: 1–12.

[298] For other references to Bêl-shar-bulliṭ see *StrNbn* 265: 10; 278: 5; 386: 2; 401: 7; 546: 15; 686: 14; 824: 24. *StrNbn* 1043: 1–10 should be quoted in this connection: *1/3 [ma-na] 7 šiqil kaspi KI-LAL . . . . ištênit(-it)*(?) *qa-bu-tu eš-ru-ú ša* [f]*Ina-Ê-sag-ila-ri-mat mârat šarri ina qât* [md]*Bêl-šar-[bul-liṭ]*(?) *ša kurummat*[zun] *šarri a-na* [d]*[Šamaš] ta-ad-din qa-bu-tu . . . . ina bît qâti . . . .* [arab]*Abu ûmu 5*[kam] *šattu 17*[kam] [d]*Na[bû-nâ'id] šar Bâbili*[ki], 'One-third of a [mina], seven shekels of silver, the weight of . . . . one(?) *qabûtu*, the tithe which Ina-Êsagila-rîmat, daughter of the king, gave from Bêl-shar-[bulliṭ](?) of the king's maintenance to [Shamash](?). The *qabûtu* is in the offertory house. The fifth day of the month Ab, the seventeenth year of Na[bonidus](?), the king of Babylon.' The restoration of the name Shamash is based upon the fact that the tablet is supposed to have come from Sippar, where Shamash was the patron deity. See Pinches in *The New York Independent*, August 15, 1889, p. 15. As to *qabûtu*, see *Hwb* p. 578, for the meaning 'Becher.' The name in line 4 was formerly restored to *Bêl-šar-uṣur*, but comparison with the references to Bêl-shar-bulliṭ given above indicates that that person is meant. The expression *ša kurummat*[zun] *šarri* in line 5 may be used as a title similar to *amêlu ša muḫḫi quppi ša šarri*, 'the man who is in charge of the basket of the king.' See *Annual of the American Schools of Oriental Research*, V, p. 25. Evidently Bêl-shar-bulliṭ was an official in charge of the king's maintenance supply at Sippar. Tablet 57002, 1–11, in the British Museum (see *PSBA*, Jan. 1916, p.

[9]Shamash-iddin and Dannu-Adad, [10]were given. One [*gur*] (and) twenty-four [*qa*] of dates [11]for their food were given. [12]The ninth day of the month Nisan, the tenth year [13]of Nabonidus, the king of Babylon.

The salient points in the above document should be noted. Belshazzar made an offering of twenty-seven animals to Shamash and the other gods in Sippar. These animals were transported to Sippar in a vessel in charge of Shamash-iddin and Dannu-Adad. The remuneration consisted of rental for the ship and food for the men. It should be noted that the text is dated in the month Nisan of the tenth year of Nabonidus' reign when, as the discussion of other inscriptions will prove, the king was at Têmâ in Arabia.

6. *Record Referring to the Tithe of Belshazzar*

[1]70 immerê bu-ḫal ù laḫrâti[meš] ša [md]Nabû-na-ṣir [2]apil-šu ša [m]La-qi-pi a-na [amêl]mâr šiprê[meš] ša [m]Zêri-iá [amêl]šatammi Ê-an-na [3]lâ ú-kal-lim-ma lâ iš-mi-it[299] *ù 20 ṣi-e-ni ri-ḫi-it [4]eš-ru-ú ša mâr šarri ša šatti 12[kam] [d]Nabû-nâ'id [5]šar Bâbili[ki] ša ina pa-ni [md]Enurti-iá [amêl]nâqidu [6]ša mâr šarri duppâni[meš] ka-a-an*[300] *[7]napḫaru 90 immerê bu-ḫal ù laḫrâti[meš] makkûr [d]Bêlit ša Uruk[ki] [8]u [d]Na-na-a ina eli [md]Nabû-na-ṣir [9]apil-šu ša [m]La-qi-pi ina [araḫ]Nisanni šattu 14[kam] [10][d]Nabû-nâ'id šar Bâbili[ki] ṣi-e-nu-ám [11]90 it-ti . . . . qa-bu-ut-ti [12]ib-ba-kam-ma ina bâbi*[301] *ša [nâr]Na-aš-ka-pi-ru [13]i-šim-mi-it*[302] *e-lat ri-ḫa-a-nu [14]maḫ-ru-tu.*[303]

---

31) has been interpreted as referring to Belshazzar in line 8. It is highly probable that the name should be read *Bêl-šar-bulliṭ*. The writer's suggested transliteration and translation of the text are as follows: *48 immerê ša bît ri-du-ú-tu ša ina qât [md]Nabû-gamil [md]Šamaš-iddin u [m]Aḫu-'-ú ša kurummat[zun] šarri i-bu-ku-nu a-na Ê-babbar-ra id-dan-na immeru a-na [md]Bêl-šar-[bulliṭ] ša kurummat[zun] šarri nadin(in) [araḫ]Ayaru ûmu 3[kam] šattu 1[kam] [md]Nabû-nâ'id šar Bâbili[ki]*, 'Forty-eight sheep of the administrative palace, which from Nabû-gâmil, Shamash-iddin, and Aḫu'u, who (were in charge of) the food of the king, they brought, unto Êbabbarra they gave. A sheep was given to Bêl-shar-[bulliṭ], who (was in charge of) the food of the king. The third day of the month Iyyar, the first year of Nabonidus, the king of Babylon.'

[299] See notes 390 and 399.

[300] *Ka-a-an* is evidently a permansive of the stem *kânu*, like *dâr* from *dâru*, and *dân* from *dânu*.

[301] *Bâbu*, 'gate,' seems to be used in this context in the sense of the mouth of a stream. See *SBD* p. 46 for another occurrence of this use of the term. Comparison should be made with a similar use of the word *pû*, 'mouth.' Note *ina pî nâri*, 'at the mouth of the river,' etc. Cf. *CD* p. 789. The expression *bâb nâri* may mean 'sluice-gate.' See references in *CD* p. 141 and Ebeling, Meissner, and Weidner, *Die Inschriften der altassyrischen Könige*, p. 8, note 4.

[302] See notes 390 and 399.

[303] *REN* 233: 1–14. See *ContCN* 73: 8.

[1](Concerning) seventy rams and ewes, which Nabû-nâṣir, [2]the son of Lâqîpi, to the messengers of Zêrîa, the administrator of Êanna, [3]did not show and did not brand, and twenty sheep, the balance [4]of the tithe of the son of the king for the twelfth year of Nabonidus, [5]the king of Babylon, which are at the disposal of Enurtîa, the shepherd [6]of the son of the king, the documents are established, [7](and) a total of ninety rams and ewes, the property of the Bêltu of Erech [8]and Nanâ, (are charged) against Nabû-nâṣir, [9]the son of Lâqîpi. In the month Nisan of the fourteenth year of [10]Nabonidus, the king of Babylon, the sheep, numbering [11]90, with . . . . (to) the fold [12]he shall bring and at the gate of the canal Nashkapiru [13, 14]he shall brand (them). In addition, the former remainders.

This document was written in the presence of Zêrîa, the administrator of Êanna, and three witnesses by the scribe Balâṭu on the twenty-seventh day of Tammuz, the thirteenth year of Nabonidus, the king of Babylon. The phrase 'the balance of the tithe of the son of the king for (*i.e.* of) the twelfth year of Nabonidus' reign suggests that Belshazzar was making regular offerings each year and that a strict account of what he presented was kept. That the twenty sheep were given to the Bêltu ('Lady') of Erech and Nanâ for the temple Êanna is indicated by the fact that they were to be branded as sacred property.

7. *Summary of Data*

The above texts depict Belshazzar's interest in the gods of his nation with unquestionable accuracy. They register his zeal in presenting offerings to the deities worshipped in the temples of Erech and Sippar. From his generous attitude towards these sanctuaries it may be concluded that shrines in other Babylonian cities were the beneficiaries of his practical devotion. Belshazzar's gifts were appropriate; they consisted of silver and gold, which could be used as money, and of animals, which could be used in the observance of sacrificial rites.

The provenance of the texts describing Belshazzar's pious contributions is somewhat doubtful, except in the case of No. 6 which was written at Erech. It may be that No. 1 is an Erech text, as it belongs to a collection which came from that site. Since Nos. 2–5 record offerings to Êbabbarra and Shamash, the temple and patron deity of Sippar, it is probable that they are Sippar texts. This partial uncertainty as to the source of most of the above documents does not minimize the value of their contents. The solicitude of Belshazzar for the upkeep of places of worship in Babylonia may be regarded as a proven fact. That such an attitude on his part comported with kingly dignity and responsibility is shown by the offerings of silver, gold, precious stones, and sacrificial animals made by Nabonidus himself.[304] The cuneiform inscriptions which reveal Belshazzar as a devotee of the gods do not detract from the view that he exercised royal authority; they in reality contribute to the exactness of that view. This will appear more plainly in the following chapters.

[304] *NKI* p. 284f, col. IX, lines 50–55. Cf. *RA* XXII, 2, p. 61f, col. I, lines 23–30.

IX

BELSHAZZAR'S ASSOCIATION WITH NABONIDUS ON THE THRONE

Evidences are not wanting that Assyrian and Neo-Babylonian kings afforded their sons opportunity for practical experience in the art of government. It was particularly true that the eldest son of a king was likely to be entrusted with some measure of political responsibility before the end of his father's reign. That this was a policy which produced greater efficiency in the administration of national affairs cannot be doubted. An outcome of this tendency was the occasional elevation of a crown prince to the position of co-regent. Considerations of statesmanship or the requirements of old age might induce a king to recognize the heir apparent as an associate on the throne. Ancient Oriental peoples regarded this as a legitimate act on the part of a sovereign.

There are six lines of proof, representing cross-sections of Babylonian society, which show that Belshazzar was associated with Nabonidus in the administration of affairs during the closing reign of the Neo-Babylonian empire.

1. *Belshazzar Associated with Nabonidus in a Prayer*

Four cylinders found in the ziggurat of Ur contain the following prayer of Nabonidus:

[19]*Ia-ti* ^{md}*Nabû-nâ'id šar Bâbili*^{ki} [20]*i-na ḫi-ṭu ilu-ú-ti-ka* [21]*rabîti(-ti) šú-zib-an-ni-ma* [22]*ba-la-ṭu ū-mu ru-qu-ti* [23]*a-na ši-rik-ti šur-kam* [24]*ù ša* ^{md}*Bêl-šar-uṣur* [25]*mâru reš-tu-ú* [26]*ṣi-it lib-bi-ia* [27]*pu-luḫ-ti ilu-ú-ti-ka rabîti(-ti)* [28]*lib-bu-uš šú-uš-kin-ma* [29]*ai ir-ša-a* [30]*ḫi-ṭi-ti* [31]*la-li-e balâṭi liš-bi.*[305]

[19]As for me, Nabonidus, the king of Babylon, [20, 21]save me from sinning against thy great divinity and [22, 23]grant life unto distant days as a gift. [24]Furthermore, as for Belshazzar, [25]the first son [26]proceeding from my loins,[306]

[305] *KB* III, 2, p. 96f, col. II, lines 19–31. See *NKI* p. 252f.

[306] The expression *mâru reš-tu-ú ṣi-it lib-bi-ia* should be compared with *mâru ṣi-it lib-bi-ia* which is descriptive of Nabonidus as the son of Nabû-balâṭsu-iqbi; see *NKI* p. 290f, col. II, line 4. In the account of Nabonidus' campaign against Têmâ, Belshazzar is referred to as *reš-tu-ú bu-kur-šu,* see *BHT* p. 84, col. II, line 18. The employment of the term *reš-tu-ú* indicates the scribe's purpose to emphasize the fact that Belshazzar was the eldest son of Nabonidus.

[27,28]place in his heart fear of thy great divinity and [29,30]let him not turn to sinning; [31]let him be satisfied with fulness of life.

A variant of the above text occurs twice in a large cylinder of Nabonidus found at Ur, as the following passage indicates:

[23]*[Ia-a-ti]* ^{md}*Nabû-nâ'id šar Bâbili*^{ki} [24]*[pa-liḫ] ilu-ú-ti-ka rabîti(-ti) la-li-e* [25]*ba-la-ṭu lu-uš-bi* [26]*[ù ša]* ^{md}*Bêl-šar-uṣur mâru reš-tu-ú* [27]*[ṣi-it] lib-bi-ia šu-ri-ku ûmê*^{meš}*-šu ai ir-ša-a ḫi-ṭi-ti.*[307]

[23][As for me], Nabonidus, the king of Babylon, [24,25][the venerator of] thy great divinity, may I be satisfied with fulness of life, [26,27][and as for] Belshazzar, the first son proceeding from my loins, lengthen his days; let him not turn to sinning.

Nabonidus, in supplicating the moon god of the temple at Ur in the earnest petitions given above, places Belshazzar in close association with himself. Such association of a royal father and his son in religious entreaty is rare in cuneiform literature. One other instance can be mentioned. This is the association of Cambyses with Cyrus, his father, in the inscription of the latter known as the *Cyrus Cylinder*. The following passage, acknowledging divine favor, should be noted first:

[26b]*A-na ip-še-e-ti-[ia]* ^{d}*Marduk bêlu rabû-ú iḫ-di-e-ma* [27]*a-na ia-a-ti* ^{m}*Ku-ra-aš šarri pa-li-ḫi-šú ù* ^{m}*Ka-am-bu-zi-ia mâri ṣi-it lib-bi-[ia u a]-na nap-ḫar um-ma-ni-ia* [28a]*da-am-qi-iš ik-ru-ub-ma.*[308]

[26b]On account of my deeds Marduk, the great lord, rejoiced and [27,28a]he showed himself gracious to me Cyrus, the king, his venerator, and to Cambyses, the son proceeding from my loins, and to all my troops.

At the close of the text there is a fragmentary part of a prayer in which the king and his son are associated as follows: ^{m}*Ku-ra-aš šarri pa-li-iḫ-ka u* ^{m}*Ka-am-bu-zi-ia mâri-šu,*[309] 'Cyrus, the king, thy venerator, and Cambyses, his son.' This association of Cambyses with Cyrus in a prayer of the latter has special significance because of the following indications that Cambyses acted with authority before the death of his father:

[307] *KB* III, 2, p. 82f, col. II, lines 23–27; p. 88f, col. III, lines 57–61. See *NKI* pp. 244f, 250f.

[308] *KA* pp. 4f, lines 26b–28a.

[309] *KA* p. 6, line 35b.

(1) In Herodotus I, 208, it is stated that Cyrus gave Croesus into the care of Cambyses, whom he had appointed to be his successor on the Persian throne. This is evidence that Cambyses, as crown prince, was entrusted with important administrative affairs.

(2) Cambyses, rather than Cyrus, participated in the first New Year's celebration observed in Babylon during the Persian régime. This is indicated by column III, lines 24–28 of the *Nabonidus Chronicle*.[310] Although these lines are in a fragmentary condition, enough can be deciphered to show the important rôle played by Cambyses.

(3) We know from contract literature that Cambyses was king of Babylon as early as the first year of the reign of Cyrus, *i.e.* soon after the capture of Babylon. The clearest proof of this is a tablet dated as follows: ^{arah}*Sîmânu ûmu 10*^{kam} *šattu 1*^{kam} ^{m}*Ku-raš šar mâtâti* ^{m}*Ka-am-bu-zi-iá šar Bâbili*^{ki},[311] 'the tenth day of the month Sivan, the first year of Cyrus, the king of countries, Cambyses, the king of Babylon.'

The above sources of information prove that Cambyses, the son of Cyrus, was associated with his father in the kingship, Cyrus ruling over the whole Persian empire, while Cambyses had charge of governmental affairs in Babylonia. We can understand, therefore, why Cyrus acknowledged and desired divine guidance for his son as well as for himself.

A similar association of Belshazzar with Nabonidus suggests that an analogous political elevation had come to the former and that Belshazzar had some share in ruling the Babylonian empire. Indeed it is not impossible that the kingship of Cambyses in Babylon during the reign of his father may have been a continuance of the situation which obtained in the time of Nabonidus, when, as will appear, Belshazzar ruled in Babylon during his father's absence in Arabia. Assyrian history furnishes striking precedents for this political procedure. In 699 B. C. Sennacherib placed his son Ashur-nâdin-shum upon the throne in Babylon,[312] and Esarhaddon in 668 B. C. not only made his son Shamash-shum-ukîn king of Babylon but crowned his firstborn son Ashurbanipal king of Assyria.[313]

[310] *BA* II, p. 222f; *BHT* p. 114f.

[311] *StrCyr*. 16: 5–8. See Kugler, *Sternkunde und Sterndeinst in Babel* II, 2, 2, pp. 397–401, where *Das Unterkönigtum des Kambyses* is discussed with reference to the following additional texts: *StrCamb* 36, 42, 46, 72, 81. Cf. *VS* VI, 108; *PSBA* IX, p. 289.

[312] *CAH* III, p. 66.

[313] *CAH* III, p. 87; King, *A History of Babylon*, p. 271.

2. Belshazzar Associated with Nabonidus in Oaths

Cuneiform texts dated in the twelfth year of Nabonidus record oath formulas which are unusual in that Belshazzar is associated with his father on terms of approximate equality. Pinches was the first to publish such an oath formula, the wording of which is as follows:

[1]*^{m}I-ši-^{d}Amurru apil-šu ša ^{m}Nu-ra-nu ina ^{d}Bêl* [2]*^{d}Nabû ^{d}Bêlit ša Uruk^{ki} u ^{d}Na-na-a a-di-e* [3]*^{md}Nabû-nâ'id šar Bâbili^{ki} u ^{md}Bêl-šar-uṣur* [4a]*mâr šarri it-te-me ki-i.*[314]

[1]Ishi-Amurru, the son of Nûranu, by the gods Bêl, [2]Nabû, the Bêltu of Erech and Nanâ, the decrees [3]of Nabonidus, the king of Babylon, and Belshazzar, [4a]the son of the king, took oath as follows.

Two texts in the Yale Babylonian Collection, also dated in the twelfth year of Nabonidus' reign, contain similar oaths, as the following passages indicate:

[18b]*Û ^{md}Marduk . . . .* [19]*ù ^{m}Êriba-^{d}Marduk ina ^{d}Bêl u ^{d}Nabû ^{d}Bêlit ša [Uruk^{ki}]* [20]*u ^{d}Na-na-a a-di-e ša ^{d}Nabû-nâ'id šar Bâbili^{ki}* [21]*ù ^{md}Bêl-šar-uṣur mâr šarri it-mu-ú ki-i.*[315]

[18b]And Marduk . . . . [19]and Êriba-Marduk by the gods Bêl and Nabû, the Bêltu of [Erech] [20]and Nanâ, the decrees of Nabû-nâ'id, the king of Babylon, [21]and Belshazzar, the son of the king, took oath as follows.

[16b]*I-na ^{d}Bêl ^{d}Nabû ^{d}Bêlit ša Uruk^{ki} u ^{d}Na-na-a* [17]*u a-di-e ša ^{d}Nabû-nâ'id šar Bâbili^{ki} u ^{md}Bêl-šar-uṣur mâri-šu* [18a]*it-te-mu-ú ki-i.*[316]

[16b]By the gods Bêl, Nabû, the Bêltu of Erech and Nanâ, [17]and the decrees of Nabonidus, the king of Babylon, and Belshazzar, his son, [18a]they took oath as follows.

These three passages show conclusively that the Babylonian oath formula in the twelfth year of the reign of Nabonidus placed Belshazzar on an equality with his father. Doubtless Neo-Babylonian contract tablets with similar oath formulas, dated in other years of Nabonidus' reign, will come to light. The strength of the oath formula is indicated by the word *adû*. According to *Hwb* p. 232, *adû* means 'Satzung,' 'Gebot,' 'Gesetz,' 'Vertrag.' *CD* p. 17 translates 'agreement,' 'decision,' 'promise,' 'contract.' Streck in *Assurbanipal,* Part 3, p. 431, records the word as *(w)adû,* with the meanings

[314] *PSBA* Jan. 1916, p. 27f; pl. I.
[315] *REN* 225: 18–21.
[316] *REN* 232: 16–18.

given in *Hwb.* See references under *(w)adû* in Streck, *ibid.*, *loc. cit.*, for the following phrases: *a-di-e . . . . aš-kun*, 'I established agreements;' *la na-ṣir a-di-e*, '(who) did not keep the agreements;' *ina a-di-ia iḫ-ṭu-ú*, 'they sinned against my laws (or decrees).' The phrase *ina libbi adê erêbu*,[317] literally, 'to enter into agreements,' hence, 'to bind oneself with an oath,' should be compared with the idiom בוא באלה, as used in Nehemiah 10: 30 and Ezekiel 17: 13.[318] The parallelism between *bêl adî u mamît*, בעל ברית and בעל שבוע should also be noted.[319]

From the time of Hammurabi it was the custom of Babylonians to swear by the gods and the reigning king.[320] There is no other instance in available documents of an oath being sworn in the name of the son of the king. This emphasizes the importance of the oath formula which associates Nabonidus and Belshazzar.[320a] It must be pointed out that two interpretations of the oath formulas containing the name Belshazzar are possible. The word *a-di-e* may be qualified by the remaining part of the formula, or may be construed simply with *mdNabû-nâ'id šar Bâbiliki*. In the former case, the oath would be sworn by the decrees or laws of Nabonidus and those of Belshazzar; in the latter case, by the decrees or laws of Nabonidus and by Belshazzar. Either interpretation would give exalted rank to Belshazzar.

3. *Belshazzar Associated with Nabonidus in an Astrological Report*

In the Yale Babylonian Collection is an astrological report which reads as follows:

1*I-na araḫṬebêti ûmu 15kam šattu 7kam* 2*dNabû-nâ'id šar Bâbiliki mŠum-ukîn* 3*i-qab-bi um-ma kakkabu rabû dDIL-BAT* 4*kakkabu KAK-SI-DI dSin ù*

317 See Zimmern, *Akkadische Fremdwörter*, p. 11.

318 Note the idiom עבר באלה in Deuteronomy 29: 11.

319 See *AJSL* XXX, p. 203f.

320 Mercer, *The Oath in Cuneiform Inscriptions*, *JAOS* XXXIII, pp. 33–50; *AJSL* XXIX, pp. 65–94; XXX, pp. 196–211. In oath formulas of the time of Hammurabi there are two instances of swearing by two kings; *AJSL* XXIX, p. 91.

320a This inference is not absolutely conclusive, since it is based upon a negative rather than a positive premise. It is conceivable that documents which remain to be discovered might furnish qualifying data. However, that there is no instance of an oath sworn in the name of the son of the king in the vast amount of source material investigated by Mercer shows that such an adjuration was extremely uncommon among the Babylonians.

^{d}Šamaš ^{5}ina šú-ut-ti-ia a-ta-mar ù a-na ^{6}dum-qi ša ^{d}Nabû-nâ'id šar Bâbili^{ki} ^{7}bêli-iá ù a-na dum-qi ^{8}ša ^{md}Bêl-šar-uṣur mâr šarri ^{9}bêli-iá uz-ni li-iš-šu-nu-tu ^{10}ûmu 17^{kam} ša ^{arah}Ṭebêti šattu 7^{kam} ^{11}^{d}Nabû-nâ'id šar Bâbili^{ki} ^{m}Šum-ukîn ^{12}i-qab-bi um-ma kakkabu rabû ^{13}a-ta-mar ù dum-qi ^{14}ša ^{d}Nabû-nâ'id šar Bâbili^{ki} ^{15}bêli-iá ù dum-qi ša ^{md}Bêl-šar-uṣur ^{16}mâr šarri bêli-iá uz-ni li-iš.[321]

^{1}In the month Ṭebet, the fifteenth day, the seventh year ^{2}of Nabonidus, the king of Babylon, Shum-ukîn ^{3}says as follows: "The great star Venus, ^{4}the star *KAK-SI-DI*, the moon and the sun, ^{5}in my dream I saw, and for ^{6}the favor of Nabonidus, the king of Babylon, ^{7}my lord, and for the favor ^{8}of Belshazzar, the son of the king, ^{9}my lord, may my ear attend them." ^{10}On the seventeenth day of Ṭebet, the seventh year ^{11}of Nabonidus, the king of Babylon, Shum-ukîn ^{12}says as follows: "The great star ^{13}I saw and (for) the favor ^{14}of Nabonidus, the king of Babylon, ^{15}my lord, and (for) the favor of Belshazzar, ^{16}the son of the king, my lord, may my ear attend."

This valuable astrological document associates the king and his son in a most interesting manner. The presumption is that both Nabonidus and Belshazzar, as political leaders of the people, were in need of the help supposed to be derived through celestial divination. The fact that Nabonidus was at Têmâ in the seventh year of his reign adds to the importance of this text.

4. Belshazzar Associated with Nabonidus in the Salutation of a Letter

The preliminary part of a Neo-Babylonian letter throws further light upon the question under discussion. Although the letter is undated, the personal names mentioned indicate that it was written at Erech, probably in the time of Nabonidus.[322] The salutation of the letter is as follows:

^{1}Ardu-ka ^{m}Ardi-^{d}Na-na-a ^{2}a-na ^{md}Nabû-šar-uṣur ^{3}bêli-ia ū-mu-us-su ^{4}^{d}Bêlit ša Uruk^{ki} ^{5}u ^{d}Na-na-a a-na ^{6}balâṭ napšâti^{meš} ṭu-ub lib-bi ^{7}ṭu-ub šêri la ba-še-e ^{8}mu-ur-ṣu u pa-ni ^{9}ḫa-du-tu ša šarri u mâr šarri ^{10}a-na muḫ-ḫi bêli-ia ^{11}ú-ṣal-lu.[323]

^{1}Thy servant, Ardi-Nanâ, ^{2}unto Nabû-shar-uṣur, ^{3}my lord. Daily ^{4}the Bêltu of Erech ^{5}and Nanâ for ^{6}preservation of life, joy of heart, ^{7}health of

[321] *MI* 39, with discussion on p. 55f.

[322] For instance, Nabû-shar-uṣur, according to *REN* p. 30, was a prominent official at Erech in the reign of Nabonidus, although it must be admitted that he continued until the ninth year of Cyrus, see *RECC* 70: 18.

[323] *NLE* 194: 1–11.

body, that there be no [8]sickness, and (for) a countenance [9]of gladness[324] of the king and the son of the king[325] [10]in behalf of my lord [11]I pray.

Among other things the letter refers to the keeping of the watch of the temple Êanna in Erech. That the phrase 'king and son of the king' refers to Nabonidus and Belshazzar seems reasonably sure. Evidently, the latter, as well as the former, was in a position to bestow favor, and hence it was natural to associate the two in praying for royal good will.

5. Belshazzar Associated with Nabonidus in the Delivery of Royal Tribute

Several texts in the Goucher College Babylonian Collection, dated in the reigns of Nebuchadrezzar and Nabonidus, deal with the delivery of what may be regarded as royal tribute. The texts will be understood best if presented in the following order:

(1) Texts Dated in the Reign of Nebuchadrezzar

(*a*) *[6]1 šiqlu a-na [7]^{m}Nâdina(-na)-aḫu [8]apil ^{md}In-nin-zêr-ibni [9]ša ri-ḫa-a-ta [10]a-na šarri iššû*[326] *na-din.*[327]

[324] Light upon the phrase *pa-ni ḫa-du-tu* is furnished by François Martin, *Lettres Néo-Babyloniennes*, p. 42, no. 53, lines 6–8 and note, where the following occurs: *bu-un-nu pa-ni ša šarri ḫa-du-tu ša it-ti bêli-ia ú-ṣal-la*, '(pour que) les aspects du roi (soient) joyeux a l'égard de mon maitre je prie.' *ContCL* 95: 5–10 reads thus: *a-mur ū-mu-us-su ^{d}Anum u ^{d}Innina a-na balâṭ napšâti^{meš} a-rak ū-mu ṭu-ub lib-bi ṭu-ub šêri u pa-ni ḫa-du-tu ša ilâni^{meš} u šarri a-na muḫ-ḫi bêli-ia ú-ṣal-la.*

[325] See *StrNbk* 381: 2 for *^{m}Mu-še-zib-^{d}Marduk mâr šarri*, 'Mushêzib-Marduk, the son of the king,' and *StrNbk* 382: 5 for *^{md}Marduk-na-din-aḫi mâr šarri*, 'Marduk-nâdin-aḫi, the son of the king.' The texts from which these passages are taken belong to the forty-first year of Nebuchadrezzar's reign. This indicates that *Amêl-Marduk* was not the only son of Nebuchadrezzar who bore the official title *mâr šarri*. There is evidence that Nabonidus had a son called Nebuchadrezzar, but there is no intimation that he ever occupied an important position in the kingdom. See note 236. Hence it is likely that the *mâr šarri* referred to in the above letter was Belshazzar. See note 440.

[326] The ideogram which represents *iššû* is *GIŠ*. For a discussion of *GIŠ* = *našû* see *AENN* p. 20f. Other proofs of the equation *GIŠ* = *našû* are now at hand. In *AJSL* XXXIII, p. 195, col. I, no. 194, of the Chicago Syllabary, there is what Luckenbill explained in a letter to the writer as a *giš te-nu-ú* sign with the value *na-šú-ú*, his restoration in the third column being *giš te-nu-ú*. See *RA* XVII, p. 31, for the restoration *gi-šu te-nu-ú* by Thureau-Dangin. The writer is indebted to Professor Sayce for a reference to *Keilschrifturkunden aus Boghazköi*, Heft III, no. 98, where the *GIŠ* sign

[6]One shekel to [7]Nâdina-aḫu, [8]the son of Innin-zêr-ibni, [9]who delivered *riḫâta* [10]to the king, was given.

(*b*) [1]*19 šiqil kaspi ina 50 šiqil kaspi* [2]*ša* ^{arah}*Du'ûzi šattu 22*^{kam} [3]*a-na* ^{md}*Na-na-a-aḫ-iddin* [4]*apil* ^{m}*Ar-rab* ^{m}*Amêl-*^{d}*Na-na-a* [5]*apil* ^{m}*Balâṭ-su u* ^{m}*Amêl-*^{d}*Na-na-a* [6]*apil* ^{m}*Aḫ-DAGAL-qar ša* [7]*ri-ḫa-a-ta a-na šarri* [8]*is-šú-ú nadnâ(-na)* [9]*a-na makkûri maḫrû(-ú).*[328]

[1]Nineteen shekels of silver, of fifty shekels of silver, [2]which in the month Tammuz, the twenty-second year, [3]to Nanâ-aḫ-iddin, [4]the son of Arrab, Amêl-Nanâ, [5]the son of Balâṭsu, and Amêl-Nanâ, [6]the son of Aḫ-*DAGAL*-qar, who [7]*riḫâta* to the king [8]delivered, were given, [9]for the treasury were received.

(*2*) *Text Dated in the Reign of Nabonidus*

[1]*16 šiqil kaspi a-na ṣi-di-ti-šu-nu* [2]*a-na* ^{md}*Nabû-ušallim apil* ^{m}*Ardi-*^{d}*Nabû u* ^{md}*Bêl-aḫ-êriba* [3]*ša ri-ḫa-a-tu a-na šarri iš-šú-ú* [4]*12 šiqil kaspi a-na ṣi-di-ti-šu-nu* [5]*ša ul-tu* ^{arah}*Abi a-di* ^{arah}*Ṭebêti* [6]*a-na* ^{m}*Nûr-e-a u* ^{m}*Ki-na-a ša ri-ḫa-a-tu* [7]*a-na mâr šarri iš-šú-ú na-din.*[329]

[1]Sixteen shekels of silver for their provisions (were given) [2]to Nabû-ushallim, the son of Ardi-Nabû, and Bêl-aḫ-êriba, [3]who delivered *riḫâtu* to the king. [4]Twelve shekels of silver for their provisions, [5]which (were) from the month Ab to the month Ṭebet, [6]to Nûrêa and Kinâ, who *riḫâtu* [7]to the son of the king delivered, were given.

These three texts indicate that there was the delivery of *riḫâtu* (var. *riḫâta*) to the king in the time of Nebuchadrezzar, and to the king and his son in the fifth year of the reign of Nabonidus. The word *riḫâtu* seems to be a plural form of *rîḫtu*, which means 'rest,' 'remainder.'[330] It can hardly be questioned that the passages deal

---

is represented as having the value *naš* in the sense of 'tree.' As an example note *GIŠ-ERIN*, *i-ri-na*, accompanied by *na-aš ši-ki nu-na-ak-ku*. Further confirmation of *GIŠ* = *našû* is found in IV R^2 13b: 20, where the following equivalence occurs: *GIŠ-ŠIR-IGI* = *ni-iš nu-ur i-ni-šu*. Since *ŠIR* = *nûru* (*Bar* 72) and *IGI* = *înu* (*Bar* 406), *GIŠ* must be represented by *ni-iš*, the whole expression meaning 'the lifting up of the light of his eye.'

[327] *AENN* 72: 6–10. The regnal year has not been preserved.

[328] *AENN* 184: 1–9. Dated in Nebuchadrezzar's twenty-second year.

[329] *AENN* 405: 1–7. Dated in Nabonidus' fifth year.

[330] See note 23 on p. 8 of Lutz, *Neo-Babylonian Administrative Documents from Erech.* Cf. Harper, *Assyrian and Babylonian Letters*, no. 187 (II, p. 184), reverse, lines 1–4, for the following: *ri-ḫa-a-te ša* ^{d}*Nabû a-na mâr šarri bêli-ia ú-si-bi-la*, 'bring the *riḫâte* of Nabû to the son of the king, my lord.' The form *ú-si-bi-la* stands for *uštêbila*.

with the payment of some kind of royal toll or tribute. At any rate there is ample evidence in the third text that Belshazzar was entitled to the same subsidy that was granted to Nabonidus, and this is another proof of the exalted position occupied by him.

6. Belshazzar Placed on an Equality with Nabonidus in the Title of an Official

Professor Theophilus G. Pinches has published a tablet[331] referring to Belshazzar in unusual terms, as the following transliteration and translation indicate:

$^{1\,[m]}$*It-ti-^{d}Nabû-gu-zu ^{amêl}šaqû ša ^{md}Bêl-šar-uṣur* $^{2\,[amêl]}$*mâr šarri a-na ^{md}Nabû-šar-aḫê^{meš}-šu apil-šu ša ^{md}Bêl-ibni* ^{3}*[apil] ^{m}Il-ba-ru-la-bar-ta ki-a-am iq-bi um-ma* $^{4\,[f]}$*Lu-ú-i-di-ia ^{f}Ṭâba-tum ^{f}It-ti-šêpê-šu* ^{5}*mârti(-ti)-šu napḫaru 3 a-me-lut-tum la-ta-ni-ia ši-i-ni* ^{6}*um-ma kaspu itti-ia ḫi-i-ṭu a-na ^{m}Ri-mut apil-šu ša* $^{7\,md}$*Marduk-nâṣir apil ^{m}Il-ba-ru-la-bar-ta a-na lib-bi ši-i-ni* ^{8}*at-ta-din um-ma mi-na-' ina pâni-ka ši-i-ni* $^{9\,md}$*Nabû-šar-aḫê^{meš}-šu ina ^{d}Bêl u ^{d}Nabû u a-di-i ša ^{md}Nabû-nâ'id* ^{10}*šar Bâbili^{ki} it-te-me ki-i a-di-i ûmi 5^{kam} ša ^{arah}Abi* $^{11\,f}$*Lu-ú-i-di-ia ^{f}Ṭâba-tum u ^{f}It-ti-šêpê-šu* ^{12}*la-ta-ni-ka ab-ba-kam-ma a-šar ^{amêl}mâr šarri* ^{13}*a-nam-dak-ka lu-ú ú-il-tim lu-ú ri-ik-ka-sa(?)* ^{14}*lu-ú kanikê^{meš} a-šar ša i-ba-aš-šú-ú* ^{15}*a-na-aš-ša-am-ma a-nam-dak-ka mim-mu ša ni-ik-li* ^{16}*u pi-el-ṣa-tum it-ti-ka ad-da-ab-bu* ^{17}*a-di-i ûmi 5^{kam} ša ^{arah}Abi ^{f}Lu-ú-i-di-ia* $^{18\,f}$*Ṭâba-tum u ^{f}It-ti-šêpê-šu lâ it-tab-kam-ma* $^{19\,md}$*Nabû-šar-aḫê^{meš}-šu a-na ^{m}It-ti-^{d}Nabû-gu-zu* ^{20}*lâ id-dan-nu a-me-lut-tum u man-da-at-ti-šu* $^{21\,md}$*Nabû-šar-aḫê^{meš}-šu a-na ^{m}It-ti-^{d}Nabû-gu-zu* ^{22}*a-šar ^{amêl}mâr šarri i-nam-din ^{amêl}mu-kin-nu* $^{23\,m}$*Pa-ni-^{d}Sin-lu-mur ^{amêl}šaqû ša ^{amêl}mâr šarri* $^{24\,md}$*Nabû-zêr-ukîn apil-šu ša ^{md}Nabû-šarr-a-ni ^{md}Nabû-ta-lim-uṣur* ^{25}*apil-šu ša . . . . lul(?)-du u ^{amêl}dupšarru ^{m}Na-*

This message does not refer to Belshazzar, because the letter seems to belong to the time of Ashurbanipal. In Streck, *Assurbanipal* II, p. 338, (*K* 4457), reverse, lines 3, 4, we find *ri-ḫi-e-ti šarru-ti-ia ú-še-bil-šu ri-ḫi-e-ti ša-a-ti-ma im-ḫur*, 'I (Ashurbanipal) caused him to bring the *riḫêti* of my royalty; he received the same *riḫêti*.' Streck translates *riḫêti* 'Anerbietung.' Another passage in Streck, *ibid.*, II, p. 270f, (col. IV of Cyl. L.^{4}, lines 9, 10), has the following: *ri-ḫa-a-ti il[âni]^{meš} ^{mât}Šumeri*, 'the *riḫâti* of the gods of Sumer.' See *CD* under *riḫtu*, p. 961, for *ri-ḫat ^{d}Bêl ^{d}Nabû ^{d}Nergal lu-ú iš-šu-ni*, 'Verily, they have brought the *riḫâtu* of Bêl, Nabû, (and) Nergal.' Additional references of a similar character are given in *CD* p. 961. These occurrences of *ri-ḫa-a-tu*, *ri-ḫa-a-ti*, *ri-ḫa-a-te*, *ri-ḫa-a-ta*, and *ri-ḫi-e-ti* are sufficient to indicate that the term refers to surplus revenues. There may be some question, however, as to whether *ri-ḫi-e-ti* should be connected with the preceding forms.

331 The caption of Professor Pinches' article is *Tablets Belonging to Lord Amherst of Hackney*. The tablet in question is number 227 of the collection. See *JRAS* Jan., 1926, pp. 105–113.

din apil-šu ša [26]*^{m}Ši-ši-ru ^{âl}Bît šar Bâbili^{ki} ^{arah}Du'ûzu ûmu 14^{kam}* [27]*šattu 10^{kam} ^{md}Nabû-nâ'id šar Bâbili^{ki}.*

[1]Itti-Nabû-gûzu, a chief officer of Belshazzar, [2]the son of the king, to Nabû-shar-aḫêshu, the son of Bêl-ibni, [3]son of Ilbaru-labarta, spoke as follows: [4]"Lû-idîa, Ṭâbatum, (and) Itti-shêpêshu, [5]her daughter,[332] a total of three slaves, (are) my servants of support(?).[333] [6]At present[334] money with me is expended.[335] To Rîmût, the son of [7]Marduk-nâṣir, son of Ilbaru-labarta, for purposes of support(?) [8]I gave (them), saying, 'What is the support(?) (worth) unto thee?' " [9]Nabû-shar-aḫêshu by Bêl and Nabû and the decrees of Nabonidus,[336] [10]the king of Babylon, took oath as follows: "By the fifth day of the month Ab, [11]Lû-idîa, Ṭâbatum, and Itti-shêpêshu, [12]thy servants, I will bring and where the son of the king (is) [13]I will give (them) to thee. Whether there be a document, or bond, [14]or sealed contracts, wherever he is, [15]I will bring and give (them) to thee. Whatever there be of deception[337] [16]or evasion,[338] I will settle with thee." [17](If) by the fifth day of the month Ab Lû-idîa, [18]Ṭâbatum, and Itti-shêpêshu he does not bring and [19]Nabû-shar-aḫêshu to Itti-Nabû-gûzu [20]does not give, the slaves and his hire [21]Nabû-shar-aḫêshu to Itti-Nabû-gûzu [22]where the son of the king (is) shall give. Witnesses: [23]Pâni-Sin-lûmur, a chief officer of the son of the king; [24]Nabû-zêr-ukîn, the son of Nabû-sharrani; Nabû-talîm-uṣur, [25]the son of . . . . lul(?)-du; and the scribe, Nâdin, the son of [26]Shishiru. The city of the house of the king of Babylon, the fourteenth day of the month Tammuz, [27]the tenth year of Nabonidus, the king of Babylon.

The above text records the promise of Nabû-shar-aḫêshu under oath that he will bring back the three female slaves of Itti-Nabû-gûzu, which the latter had placed at the disposal of the cousin of

[332] The masculine pronominal suffix is used for the feminine.

[333] The term *ši-i-ni* may be related to Hebrew שען, 'lean upon,' 'rely upon.' See Gesenius-Buhl[17], p. 853. Pinches treats the word as a feminine, plural pronoun.

[334] Bezold, *Babylonisch-assyrisches Glossar*, p. 5, gives the meanings 'jetzt,' 'nun' for *umma*.

[335] Pinches ascribes the meaning 'expended' to *ḫi-i-ṭu*. See *JRAS* Jan., 1926, p. 111.

[336] It should be noted that Belshazzar is not mentioned in this oath formula, although the record was made in the tenth year of Nabonidus' reign, when the king was at Têmâ, according to the *Nabonidus Chronicle*. See p. 112.

[337] The word *niklu* may mean 'artifice,' 'craftiness,' and hence 'deceit,' 'intrigue.' See *Hwb* p. 462, under נכל.

[338] It is possible that the word *pi-el-ṣa-tum* is related to Hebrew and Aramaic פלט, 'escape.'

the former for a fixed period of time. Uncertainty as to the meaning of the term *ši-i-ni* does not affect the general import of the document. Its salient features, so far as Belshazzar is concerned, are the following:

(1) The position of authority occupied by Belshazzar is indicated in lines 1 and 2 by the expression *amêlšaqû ša mdBêl-šar-uṣur [amêl]mâr šarri*, 'a chief officer of Belshazzar, the son of the king.' In line 23 is found the variant *amêlšaqû ša amêlmâr šarri*, 'a chief officer of the son of the king.' When it is remembered that the usual title is *amêlšaqû šarri*, 'a chief officer of the king,' the full force of the title in the text under consideration can be understood. Belshazzar was high enough in the kingdom to have subordinate officials equal to those of the king.[339]

(2) In lines 12 and 22 occurs the clause *a-šar amêlmâr šarri*, 'where the son of the king (is).' This proves that Belshazzar, in the performance of his administrative duties, went about from place to place and that the important officials of his court accompanied him,[340] which is exactly what we would expect if Belshazzar was entrusted with political responsibility.

(3) The contract recorded in the text was agreed upon in *âlBît šar Bâbiliki*, 'the city of the house of the king of Babylon.'[341] This indicates that Belshazzar's officials were attending to affairs in a royal residence. One of the witnesses, Pâni-Sin-lûmur, was another chief officer of Belshazzar.[342]

7. *Summary of Data*

While there is some difference in their value as documentary proof, the texts which have been discussed demonstrate conclusively that Belshazzar was the co-regent of Nabonidus. Nos. 1, 2, 3, 5, and 6 represent the strongest links in the chain of evidence. As dated inscriptions they may be used for final inferences. No. 4 cannot be

[339] See *JADD* IV, p. 356, for references to *amêlu SAG ša mâr šarri* in Assyrian inscriptions. The *amêlu SAG* (= *amêlšaqû*) functioned in many different capacities. The fact that there were at least two officials bearing this title connected with Belshazzar (lines 1, 2, 23) is evidence which might not have conclusive weight in itself, but its importance is recognized when comparison is made with other data.

[340] See *The Annual of the American Schools of Oriental Research* V, p. 44, note 69.

[341] Cf. *REN* 100: 18.

[342] See line 23 of the text under consideration.

placed as definitely in the reign of Nabonidus, but certain features of the text point with some probability to such a chronological setting. The statements of Nos. 1–3 may be regarded as applying more directly to the deduction drawn, while Nos. 4–6 furnish data of considerable worth even if somewhat indirect in force. In mathematics a point is determined by the intersection of two lines, and 'two or three witnesses' are recognized as satisfactory in establishing truth by testimony. Hence the proofs of the association of Belshazzar with Nabonidus on the throne should be regarded as most convincing.

It must be admitted that the exact amount of regal responsibility placed upon Belshazzar during his father's reign is not indicated by the above texts. One can conceive of a co-regency which would grant far from equal power to the person of lower rank raised to a position of partnership in governing the empire. If there were no other inscriptions throwing light upon this question, our knowledge as to the actual rôle played by Belshazzar would be limited. Happily a highly interesting group of cuneiform tablets containing information of incontrovertible character is available. They establish the fact that Nabonidus, as first ruler in the land, spent a large part of his reign in Arabia, while Belshazzar, with kingship entrusted to him as second ruler in the land, conducted affairs in Babylonia. These texts, whose contents are of far-reaching importance, will now be discussed.

X

BELSHAZZAR'S ADMINISTRATION OF GOVERNMENT IN BABYLONIA DURING NABONIDUS' STAY AT TÊMÂ

That Nabonidus was interested in the western part of his empire during the early years of his reign is indicated by the references to Hamath, Mt. Ammananu, and the Sea of the Westland in the opening fragmentary lines of the *Nabonidus Chronicle*.[343] Former publications of the writer[344] advanced the view that Nabonidus spent the seventh, ninth, tenth, and eleventh years of his reign at the city of Têmâ in Arabia and that Têmâ was the political center from which he ruled the western part of his domain while Belshazzar looked after affairs in Akkad, *i.e.* Babylonia. These inferences were based upon an interpretation of the *Nabonidus Chronicle* in the light of contract tablets dated in the reign of Nabonidus. A cuneiform text in the British Museum, confirming these deductions in the strongest possible manner, has been deciphered by Sidney Smith.[345] His researches, based upon the new text, were published after those of the writer and led to the same general conclusions. The data concerning Nabonidus' stay at Têmâ might be taken up in the order of their discovery, but logical presentation will be served best by discussing the new British Museum text first and then giving a more detailed interpretation of the material formerly published by the writer.

1. *Nabonidus' Conquest of Têmâ in Arabia*

The remarkable inscription published by Sidney Smith under the title *A Persian Verse Account of Nabonidus*[346] cannot be quoted in full in this discussion of Nabonidus' campaign against Têmâ in Arabia. It will be appropriate, however, to summarize the contents of the inscription. Column I condemns the acts of Nabonidus at the beginning of his reign. Emphasis is placed upon the fact that he

343 *BA* II, p. 216f, lines 9b, 10b, 15. See *BHT* p. 111, lines 9, 11, 16. *Ibid.*, *loc. cit.*, line 17 submits the restoration [$^{m\hat{a}t}$*A*]-*du-um-mu*.

344 See *JAOS* XLI (1921), p. 458f; XLII (1922), pp. 305–316; *AENN* (1923), p. 34f.

345 *BHT* ch. III, pp. 27–97. See *ibid.*, pls. V–X. This volume was published in 1924.

346 See references in preceding note.

built a statue of a strange god, designed as the image of the moon in a state of eclipse. Column II records a speech of Nabonidus in which he indicates his purpose to build the temple of Sin at Ḫarrân. The New Year's feast is to cease until the project has been completed. There is a description of the building of the temple. The narrative then indicates that affairs in Babylonia were entrusted to Belshazzar, in order that Nabonidus might proceed against Têmâ. The campaign is described with graphic details. Indications are not wanting in the record that Nabonidus established his residence in Têmâ. Both column III and column IV are very fragmentary. Column V is of special value because it contains a reference to Cyrus, thus indicating that the account has reached the end of Nabonidus' reign. Reference is made to Nabonidus' impiety at the New Year's festival. Column VI chronicles the restoration of the old rites in Babylon and the return of the images of the gods to the cities to which they belonged. The work and name of Nabonidus are destroyed, presumably at the instigation of Cyrus.[347]

The passage which narrates Nabonidus' conquest of Têmâ in Arabia in the third year of his reign, not counting the accession year, is as follows:

[18]*Ka-ra-aš ip-ta-qid a-na reš-tu-ú bu-kur-šu* [19] ^{amêl}*ummani(-ni) ma-ti-tan ú-ta-'-ir itti-šu* [20]*ip-ta-ṭa-ar qât-su ip-ta-qid-su šarru-tam* [21]*ù šú-ú ni-su-ti iṣ-ṣa-bat ḫar-ra-[nu]* [22]*e-mu-qu* ^{mât}*Akkadî*^{ki} *te-bu-ú it-ti-[šu]* [23]*ana* ^{âl}*Te-ma-' qi-rib A-mur-ri-i iš-ta-kan pâni-[šu]* [24]*iṣ-ṣa-bat ḫarrânu ni-su-tu ur-ḫu ul-tu ul-la lâ ina ka-ša-[di]* [25]*ma-al-ku* ^{âl}*Te-ma-' it-ta-a-ru ina* ^{iṣ}*[kakki]* [26]*a-šib âli-[šu?] mât-su kul-li-šu-nu uṭ-ṭa-ab-[bi-ḫu]* [27]*u šú-ú . . . . ir-ta-me šú-bat-su e-muq* ^{mât}*Akkadî*^{ki} *. . . .* [28]*âla [šuâtam?] uš-ta-pi i-te-pu-uš . . . .* [29]*ki-ma [ê]kal Bâbili*^{ki} *i-te-pu-šu . . . .* [348]

[18]He entrusted a camp to his eldest, firstborn son; [19]the troops of the land he sent with him. [20]He freed his hand; he entrusted the kingship to him. [21]Then he himself undertook a distant campaign; [22]the power of the land of Akkad advanced with him; [23]towards Têmâ in the midst of the Westland

[347] Genouillac in *RA* 22, no. 2, p. 75f, presents interesting suggestions concerning the nature of Nabonidus' impiety. It seems that the last Neo-Babylonian king was accused of contempt for both the rites and the myths of the Babylonian religion. Either Nabonidus was badly slandered or he is to be credited with attempting an unpopular religious revolution like that sponsored by Akhenaton in Egypt.

[348] *BHT* pp. 84, 88, col. II, lines 18–29; pl. VII.

he set his face. [24]He undertook a distant campaign on a road not within reach of old. [25]He slew the prince of Têmâ with the [sword]; [26]the dwellers in his city (and) country, all of them they slaughtered. [27]Then he himself established his dwelling [in Têmâ]; the power of the land of Akkad . . . . [28]That city he made glorious; he made . . . . ; [29]they made it like the palace of Babylon . . . .

Although Nabonidus is not mentioned by name in the extant portion of the text from which the above is taken, Smith has been able to prove that it is an account of the reign of Nabonidus. The determining chronological factor is the occurrence of *ᵐKu-ra-aš šar kiš-šat*, 'Cyrus, king of totality,' in column V, line 4,[349] in a context which undoubtedly refers to the fall of Babylon in 539 B. C. Hence Nabonidus must be the Babylonian king whose acts are described. Column II[350] tells of the erection of the temple Êḫulḫul for the moon god at Ḫarrân and then gives the above record of Nabonidus' conquest of Têmâ. Smith has shown conclusively that this Arabian campaign of Nabonidus accords with the events which the *Nabonidus Chronicle* ascribes to the third year of his reign.[351] These explanatory remarks furnish a necessary background for the following comments on the above cuneiform passage dealing with Nabonidus' campaign against Têmâ and his establishment of his abode in that city.

(1) The expression *reš-tu-ú bu-kur-šu* in line 18 possesses strength because the word *bukru* itself means 'firstborn,' and *reštû* means 'first,' 'first in rank,' 'highest.' Hence there can be no doubt that the text refers to Belshazzar, whom Nabonidus elsewhere calls *mâru reš-tu-ú ṣi-it lib-bi-ia*.[352]

(2) Smith interprets line 19 as meaning that the troops 'through the land' accompanied Nabonidus. This translation is based upon the view that the phrase *itti-šu* is reflexive in force. One may suggest, however, that the context allows another interpretation. Lines 18 and 20 refer to the son of the king, *i.e.* Belshazzar, and it seems, therefore, that the pronominal suffix in *itti-šu* ought to refer to him. It is evident that lines 18–20 may be regarded as a unit. Further-

[349] *BHT* pp. 85, 89.
[350] *BHT* pp. 84, 88.
[351] *BHT* pp. 77, 108.
[352] *NKI* p. 252f, col. II, lines 25, 26.

more, the statement of the *Nabonidus Chronicle* that the son of the king was with the troops (*ummanâte*^{meš})[353] in the land of Akkad favors this interpretation.

(3) The verb *ip-ta-ṭa-ar* in line 20 is from *paṭâru*, 'loosen,' 'free.'[354] Smith prefers the meaning 'strike' as indicated by the derivative *paṭru*, 'dagger.'[355] His explanation is that Nabonidus struck the hands of Belshazzar, thus performing an act denoting investiture with authority. This interpretation is possible, but it may be noted that the translation 'he freed his hand,' thus giving him freedom of action, would convey the same idea. Landsberger and Bauer prefer the translation 'Er legte (die Herrschaftsembleme) aus der Hand.'[356]

(4) The bestowal of royal authority upon Belshazzar is indicated further in line 20 by the expression *ip-ta-qid-su šarru-tam*, 'he entrusted the kingship to him.'[357] It is stated in Herodotus VII, 2, 3, that Darius Hystaspes appointed Xerxes to be king over the Persians, 'as he was about to lead forth his levies against Egypt and Athens.' This is a striking parallel to the act of Nabonidus in placing Belshazzar in a position of authority in Babylon on the eve of a military campaign in Arabia.

(5) The words *ù šú-ú*, 'Then he himself,' in line 21 suggest that the succeeding statements refer to what the king did in carrying out his program in Arabia, in contrast with his provisions—as stated in lines 18–20—for a stable government in Babylon during his absence. This is another intimation that lines 18–20 should be treated as a unified section of the text.[358]

(6) The literal meaning of the idiom *ḫarrânu ṣabâtu*, found in lines 21 and 24, is 'take the road,' but derived meanings are 'go on an expedition,' 'undertake a campaign,' since the word *ḫarrânu* means 'road,' 'way,' then 'caravan,' 'campaign.'[359] Comparison should be

[353] *BA* II, p. 218f, lines 5, 10; p. 220f, lines 19, 23. See *BHT* pp. 111f, 115f.

[354] *CD* p. 798f; *Hwb* p. 522.

[355] *BHT* p. 94f.

[356] *ZA* N.F. III (XXXVII), Heft 1, 2, p. 91.

[357] See *BHT* p. 111 for Sidney Smith's reading *te*(?)-*qid* in col. I, line 8, of the *Nabonidus Chronicle*. See *ibid.* p. 119, for a reference to the fact that this expression alludes to Belshazzar's being entrusted with affairs in Babylon before Nabonidus went to Ḫarrân.

[358] Compare with *u šú-ú* in line 27.

[359] *CD* p. 338.

made with *alaktu*, 'road,' 'path,' 'course,'[360] and *girru*, 'road,' 'expedition.'[361] Hebrew ארחה signifies 'road,' 'caravan.'[362]

(7) The difficulty of Nabonidus' expedition is indicated by the term *ni-su-tu* (*ni-su-ti*), 'distant,' in lines 21 and 24. It seems to be emphasized in line 24 by the reading *ur-ḫu ul-tu ul-la lâ ina ka-ša-*[*di*], 'on a road not within reach of old.' Smith argues that these words describe with exactness the remoteness of Têmâ from Babylonia.[363]

(8) The phrase *qi-rib A-mur-ri-i*, 'in the midst of the Westland,' in line 23, is an aid in determining the position of Têmâ with respect to Babylonia. It is evident that *Amurrû* is used in a general geographical sense denoting land extending as far west as Syria and Palestine. The text under consideration is the first to ascribe this descriptive term to a part of Arabia.

(9) That Nabonidus had the backing of Babylonia in this military enterprise is shown in line 22 by the words *e-mu-qu* ^{mât}*Akkadî*^{ki} *te-bu-ú it-ti-*[*šu*], 'the power of the land of Akkad advanced with [him].' No support can be gained from the text for the view that the king invaded Arabia contrary to home sentiment. Neither is there substantiation of the theory that Nabonidus took up his abode in Têmâ as a retired or exiled monarch.

(10) So far as can be determined, Nabonidus did not enter Têmâ at the invitation of inhabitants who sympathized with him racially, religiously or politically. His conquest of the city was a violent one. This is proven by line 25, which begins with the statement *ma-al-ku* ^{âl}*Te-ma-' it-ta-a-ru ina* ^{is}[*kakki*], 'He slew the prince of Têmâ with the [sword].' There is a lack of agreement as to how line 26 should be translated,[364] but it cannot be regarded as indicating peaceful occupation of the city.

(11) Smith translates *u šú-ú . . . . ma ir-ta-me šú-bat-su*, in line

[360] *Hwb* p. 68.

[361] *CD* p. 230f.

[362] See Job 6: 19, for ארחות תמא, 'The caravans of Têmâ.'

[363] *BHT* p. 77.

[364] The translation given by the writer is that of Sidney Smith, *BHT* p. 88. See *ZA* N.F. III (XXXVII), Heft 1, 2, p. 91, for the following rendition of the line: *a-šib âli* [*u*] *mâti su-gul-li-šu-nu uṭ-ṭa-ab-*[*bi-iḫ*], 'den Bewohnern von Stadt und Land schlachtet er die Viehherden.'

27, 'But he set the god (Sin?) in his dwelling,'[365] restoring ^{d}*EN-ZU* in the text. The writer would suggest provisionally that the original form of the text may have been *u šú-ú* [*ina* ^{âl}*Te*]-*ma ir-ta-me šú-bat-su*, 'Then he himself established his dwelling [in the city of Têmâ].' A vertical wedge, which may be regarded as the last part of the *te* sign, is legible before *ma*. Several things make this restoration plausible. In the first place, ^{âl}*Te-ma-a* in the *Nabonidus Chronicle* has the variant reading ^{âl}*Te-ma* in Col. II, line 19.[366] Furthermore, the idiom *ir-ta-me šú-bat-su*, 'he established his dwelling,' requires an accompanying phrase such as *ina* ^{âl}*Te-ma*, 'in the city of Têmâ.' This restoration is in harmony also with the context. In the preceding lines there is a reference to the conquest of the city of Têmâ; in the following lines there is a reference to the fact that the city was adorned and made like the palace of Babylon. What more natural, then, that the intervening line should contain a statement that Nabonidus established his dwelling in the city of Têmâ?[367]

(12) The rest of the text dealing with the conquest and occupation of Têmâ is mutilated, but enough remains in lines 28 and 29 to establish the fact that Nabonidus regarded Têmâ with considerable interest. Though speculation as to his purpose is inevitable, we know that he beautified the city and erected a royal residence in it, as the words *ki-ma* [*ê*]*kal Bâbili*^{ki} *i-te-pu-šu*, 'they made it like the palace of Babylon,' indicate.

To recapitulate, the cuneiform passage which has been discussed presents the following historical facts: (*a*) Nabonidus before starting on his campaign against Têmâ in Arabia divided the rule of his empire between himself and Belshazzar, entrusting 'kingship' (*šarrûtam*) to the latter; (*b*) He then set out on a long and arduous journey to Têmâ, a strong military force from Babylonia accompanying him; (*c*) Upon reaching his objective Nabonidus captured Têmâ, established his dwelling there, and adorned the city with the glory of Babylon.

[365] *BHT* p. 89.

[366] *BA* II, p. 220; *BHT* p. 112, pl. XII.

[367] The writer submitted the above restoration to Sidney Smith and received a reply from him, dated Jan. 3, 1927, in which he held to the view that the vestiges of signs on the original tablet favor his restoration as published in *BHT*, p. 95, note on the break in line 27 of col. II. Luckenbill, *AJSL* XLII, 4, p. 280, suggested *âla šú-ma* as the restoration for the lacuna of line 27 and translated 'and he made that city his abode.'

The historical situation presented by this text is so unexpected that there is a natural desire for corroborative data if its implications are to be accepted *in toto*. Why should a king of Babylon establish his court in the land of Arabia at a great distance from the capital of his empire? Why should he live in apparent exile while his son played a royal rôle in the homeland? If Nabonidus lived in Arabia during a large part of the time when he was king, there should be some evidence of his sojourn there in the numerous published documents of his reign. A consistent silence or a lack of intimation with reference to the Arabian adventure of Nabonidus would weaken confidence in the accuracy of the information contained in the tablet published by Sidney Smith. This dilemma need not be faced. The following array of cuneiform testimony indicates that Nabonidus' stay at the oasis of Têmâ was an important episode in his life.

2. Data Furnished by the Nabonidus Chronicle

Of supreme importance is the fact that the *Nabonidus Chronicle* records that Nabonidus was in a city called Têmâ in the seventh, ninth, tenth, and eleventh years of his reign. The exact statements are as follows:

Šattu 7^{kam} *šarru ina* $^{\hat{a}l}$*Te-ma-a mâr šarri* $^{am\hat{e}l}$*rabûti*$^{me\check{s}}$ *ummanâte*$^{me\check{s}}$*-šu ina* $^{m\hat{a}t}$*Akkadî*^{ki}.[368]

In the seventh year the king (was) in the city of Têmâ. The son of the king, the princes (and) his troops (were) in the land of Akkad.

Šattu 9^{kam} ^{md}*Nabû-nâ'id šarru* $^{\hat{a}l}$*Te-ma-a mâr šarri* $^{am\hat{e}l}$*rabûti*$^{me\check{s}}$ *u ummani(-ni) ina* $^{m\hat{a}t}$*Akkadî*^{ki}.[369]

In the ninth year Nabonidus, the king, (was in) the city of Têmâ. The son of the king, the princes and the troops (were) in the land of Akkad.

[368] *TSBA* VII, p. 156, col. II, line 5. Cf. *KB* III, 2, p. 130f; *BA* II, p. 218f; *BHT* p. 111, pl. XII.

[369] *TSBA* VII, p. 157, col. II, line 10. Cf. *KB* III, 2, p. 130f; *BA* II, p. 218f; *BHT* p. 112, pl. XII. A part of a text in the Goucher College Babylonian Collection, *AENN* 355, 1–3; *ibid.*, p. 37, should be mentioned in this connection. The passage is as follows: *2 šiqil kaspi a-na* ^{md}*Dan-nu-aḫê*^{me}*-šu-ibni apil* ^{md}*Nergal-uballiṭ(-iṭ) ša a-na pa-ni mâr šarri šap-ru*, 'Two shekels of silver (were given) to Dannu-aḫêshu-ibni, the son of Nergal-uballiṭ, who was sent to the son of the king.' This text is dated in the ninth year of Nabonidus' reign and indicates that a man was sent with a message, not to the king, but to the son of the king, *i.e.* Belshazzar.

Šattu 10^{kam} *šarru ina* ^{âl}*Te-ma mâr šarri* ^{amêl}*rabûti*^{meš} *u ummani(-ni)-šu ina* ^{mât}*Akkadî*^{ki}.[370]

In the tenth year the king (was) in the city of Têmâ. The son of the king, the princes and his troops (were) in the land of Akkad.

Šattu 11^{kam} *šarru ina* ^{âl}*Te-ma-a mâr šarri* ^{amêl}*rabûti u ummanu-šu ina* ^{mât}*Akkadî*^{ki}.[371]

In the eleventh year the king (was) in the city of Têmâ. The son of the king, the princes and his army (were) in the land of Akkad.

It should be stated that the above passages are the initial statements for the years mentioned. On account of the mutilated condition of the text there is no complete record for the first, second, third, fourth, fifth, sixth, twelfth, thirteenth, fourteenth, fifteenth, and sixteenth years of the reign of Nabonidus. At the place where the record of the eighth year ought to be the words *Šattu 8*^{kam}[372] occur, followed by an unwritten space equal to two lines. The last part of the record gives an account of the events of the seventeenth year of Nabonidus' reign.

Each of the above initial statements for the seventh, ninth, tenth, and eleventh years of the reign of Nabonidus is supplemented by the following comment:

Šarru ana ^{arah}*Nisanni ana Bâbili*^{ki} *lâ illiku(-ku)* ^{d}*Nabû ana Bâbili*^{ki} *lâ illiku(-ku)* ^{d}*Bêl lâ ittaṣâ(-a) i-sin-nu a-ki-tu ba-ṭil*.[373]

The king for the month Nisan did not come to Babylon; Nabû did not come to Babylon; Bêl did not go forth (from Êsagila); the New Year's festival ceased (*i.e.* was not celebrated).[374]

The passages of the *Nabonidus Chronicle* quoted above indicate that Nabonidus was in the city of Têmâ during the years mentioned and that the son of the king, *i.e.* Belshazzar, was with the princes and

[370] *TSBA* VII, p. 160, col. II, line 19. Cf. *KB* III, 2, p. 132f; *BA* II, p. 220f; *BHT* p. 112, pl. XII.

[371] *TSBA* VII, p. 161, col. II, line 23. Cf. *KB* III, 2, p. 132f; *BA* II, p. 220f; *BHT* p. 112, pl. XII.

[372] *TSBA* VII, p. 157, col. II, line 9. Cf. *KB* III, 2, p. 130f; *BA* II, p. 218; *BHT* p. 112, pl. XII.

[373] *TSBA* VII, p. 156f, col. II, lines 5, 6; 10, 11; 19, 20; 23, 24. Cf. *BA* II, p. 218f; *BHT* p. 111f, pl. XII.

[374] See *NKI* p. 284f, col. IX, lines 41f, for a reference to the observance of the New Year's festival. An allusion to the fact that Nabonidus ordered its cessation is found in *BHT* p. 49 and pp. 84, 88, col. II, line 11.

troops in the land of Akkad. The non-observance of the New Year's festival was a natural result of Nabonidus' prolonged sojourn at a great distance from Babylon.

In this connection it should be noted that Pinches endeavored to connect ^{âl}*Te-ma-a* with *Te-e*^{ki} *ša qi-ir-ba Bâbili*^{ki} and *Tu-ma*^{ki}.[375] This was natural in the absence of evidence as to the real identity of ^{âl}*Te-ma-a*. There is phonetic difficulty in equating ^{âl}*Te-ma-a*, *Te-e*^{ki}, and *Tu-ma*^{ki} for the purpose of proving that a section of the city of Babylon is meant by ^{âl}*Te-ma-a*. Another explanation is demanded by the *Nabonidus Chronicle*, in which the statement that Nabonidus was in ^{âl}*Te-ma-a* is followed almost immediately by the declaration that the king did not go to Babylon. Hence the conclusion is warranted that ^{âl}*Te-ma-a* was not a part of the city of Babylon. Furthermore, it is intimated that ^{âl}*Te-ma-a* was outside the land of Akkad, for the statement that Nabonidus was in ^{âl}*Te-ma-a* is opposed by the affirmation that the son of the king (*i.e.* Belshazzar), the princes, and the troops were in ^{mât}*Akkadî*^{ki} (*i.e.* the land of Akkad). The term Akkad was used often for the whole of Babylonia by both the Assyrians and the Babylonians.[376] Thus it is apparent that the ^{âl}*Te-ma-a* of the *Nabonidus Chronicle* must be sought without the bounds not only of the city of Babylon but of Babylonia itself. The fact that important religious ceremonies were not performed in the seventh, ninth, tenth, and eleventh years of Nabonidus' reign may be adduced as corroborative evidence. It is difficult to believe that the king failed to function at these exalted rites while within easy reach of his capital.

Another piece of evidence from the *Nabonidus Chronicle* is the record of the death of Nabonidus' mother in the ninth year of his reign. The chronicle runs as follows:

^{arah}*Nisannu ûmu 5*^{kam} *ummu šarri ina Dûr-Ka-ra-šu ša kišâd* ^{nâr}*Puratti e-la-nu Sip-par*^{ki} *im-tu-ut mâr šarri u ummanâte*^{meš}*-šu 3 ū-mu šú-du-ru bikitu*

[375] *TSBA* VII, p. 171, with illustration on p. 152, shows a plan of the city of Babylon mentioning the district *Tu-ma*^{ki}.

[376] According to King, *A History of Sumer and Akkad*, p. 12, the Assyrians used the term Akkad loosely for the whole of Babylonia. It is probable that there was similar employment of the term in Neo-Babylonian times. See Halévy, *Mélanges de critique et d'histoire*, p. 2, note 2.

šitkunat(-at) ina ^{arah}*Sîmâni ina* ^{mât}*Akkadî bi-ki-tu ina eli ummi šarri šit-kunat(-at)*.[377]

On the fifth day of the month Nisan the king's mother died at Dûr-Karâshu on the bank of the Euphrates above Sippar. The son of the king and his troops mourned three days; a weeping took place. In the month Sivan in the land of Akkad a weeping for the king's mother took place.

The death of Nabonidus' mother occurred almost at the very beginning of the ninth year of his reign, a year when he is mentioned as being at Têmâ. We must note that two periods of mourning took place. One period of three days was observed by Belshazzar and his troops. The second period was observed during the month Sivan throughout the land of Babylonia. Nabonidus is not mentioned as taking part in either period of mourning, although it is conceivable that word could have been sent to him at Têmâ outside of Babylonia and that he could have returned in time for the mourning observed during the month of Sivan. His mother died on the fifth of Nisan which was almost two months before the beginning of the general lamentation, the month Iyyar intervening between Nisan and Sivan. The plain intimation of the text is that he was absent during both periods of mourning, and we may infer, therefore, that the city of Têmâ at which Nabonidus sojourned was at a considerable distance from Babylon and that the interests which took him there were of no little importance.

3. *Food for Nabonidus Taken to Têmâ*

Another link in the chain of evidence is a tablet in the Yale Babylonian Collection dated in the tenth year of Nabonidus when he was in the city of Têmâ. The record reads as follows:

[1]*Ina ū-mu* ^{amêl}*mu-kin-nu it-tal-kam-ma* [2]*a-na* ^{md}*Bêl-tuk-lat-ú-a* ^{amêl}*qal-la ša* ^{md}*Nabû-mukîn-zêr* [3]*uk-tin-nu ša* ^{imêr}*A-AB-BA ša kurummat*^{zun} *šarri* [4]*it-ti-šu a-na* ^{mât}*Te-ma-a iš-šú-ú* [5]*ul-tu* ^{mât}*Te-ma-a ú-tir-ra-am-ma* [6]*a-na kaspi id-di-nu uk-tin-nu-uš* [7]*ištêneš(-eš)* ^{imêr}*A-AB-BA a-na* ^{d}*Bêlit ša Uruk*^{ki} [8]*i-nam-din*.[378]

[1]When a witness has come and [2]for Bêl-tuklatûa, the slave of Nabû-

[377] *TSBA* VII, p. 158f, col. II, lines 13–15. Cf. *KB* III, 2, p. 130f; *BA* II, p. 218; *BHT* p. 112, pl. XII.

[378] *REN* 134: 1–8.

mukîn-zêr, [3-6]has testified that he brought back from the land of Têmâ and sold a camel[379] which carried the food of the king with him to the land of Têmâ, (and) has established it, [7,8]he (*i.e.* Bêl-tuklatûa) shall at once give a camel to the Bêltu of Erech.

The interesting part of this record is the reference to a camel which bore the food of the king to the land of Têmâ. The temple in Erech furnished food for the king and means for its transportation to the land of Têmâ, at the same time protecting itself against the possible loss of a camel by the above legal document. We may imagine that similar contributions for the king came from different parts of Babylonia and that the caravans conveying royal supplies to Têmâ consisted of many camels.

It should be noted that the word for camel occurs rarely in cuneiform literature. Thompson in *Late Babylonian Letters*, p. XIV, says, "It is a curious thing that the camel is not mentioned in these letters, nor in any of the enormous collection of contract tablets published by Strassmaier, and it is rarely spoken of in the Assyrian texts proper save in lists of captured booty or tribute. Its name ^{imêr}*A-AB-BA*, 'Beast of the Sea,' would imply that it first came into Mesopotamia by way of the Persian Gulf."[380] This being the case, the above Yale text mentioning the camel is most important. It indicates that the city

[379] In lines 3 and 7 of the text ^{imêr}*A-AB-BA* should have been copied instead of *biltu AB-BA*. There are various Semitic equivalents for the ideogram ^{imêr}*A-AB-BA*. That it may be read *gammalu*, 'camel,' is indicated by V *R* 8, 114; 9: 5, 42, 46, 48, 52, the text being a description of Ashurbanipal's campaign against the Arabians. In 9: 46 of the text ^{imêr}*A-AB-BA*^{meš} has the variant ^{imêr}*GAM-MAL*^{meš}. In III *R* 9, no. 3, 56, occurs ^{imêr}*A-AB-BA*^{meš}, followed in 57 by $^{\text{f imêr}}$*a-na-qa-a-te*, ^{imêr}*ba-ak-ka-ri*. Cf. also III *R* 10, no. 2, 36 and II *R* 67, 55. The expression ^{amêl}*rîd* ^{imêr}*A-AB-BA*^{meš} occurs in II *R* 31, 54, followed in 55 by ^{amêl}*rîd* ^{imêr}*GAM-MAL*^{meš}, which may indicate that there was some difference, in the minds of certain scribes at any rate, between the *A-AB-BA* beast and that which was called *gammalu*. In *Hwb* p. 30, under *udru*, there is a suggestion that ^{imêr}*A-AB-BA*^{meš} may be read *udrâte*. See Delitzsch, *Assyrische Lesestücke*, 5th edition, p. 18, no. 139. For the possible derivation of *udru* from Avestan *uštra* (*ušdru*) see *JAOS* XXXVI, p. 227. In *RA* 14, p. 79, Langdon corrects *B* 4990 to read ^{imêr}*AB-BA* = *i-bi-lu*. *DlSGl* p. 14, under *anšu* (*a*)-*ab-ba* quotes *CT* 14, 11d: 11 (= 93080), which is also given in *M* 3410 as $^{[\text{imêr}]}$*A-AB-BA* = *i-bi-lu*. See also *M* 3397. There are indications, therefore, that ^{imêr}*A-AB-BA* may have stood for the Semitic equivalents *gammalu*, *ibilu*, and *udru*, all of which refer to the camel.

[380] For an additional discussion of the introduction of the camel into Babylonia see *CAH* I, p. 501.

of Têmâ, where Nabonidus dwelt at the time, could be reached only by crossing desert terrain.

A small but very important Goucher tablet, showing that travel must have been common between Erech and the land of Têmâ in the time of Nabonidus, contains the following record:

[1]*50 šiqil kaspi a-na* [2]*1* ^{imêr}*A-AB-BA* [3]*ù a-na qîmi-šu* [4]*a-na* ^{md}*Nabû-mušêtiq-urra* [5]*apil* ^{md}*Ištar-na-din-aḫi* [6]*ša a-na* ^{mât}*Te-ma-a* [7]*šap-ra na-din* [8] ^{arah}*Addaru ûmu 5*^{kam} *šattu 5*^{kam} [9] ^{d}*Nabû-nâ'id šar Bâbili*^{ki}*.*[381]

[1]Fifty shekels of silver for [2]one camel[382] [3]and his flour[383] [4]to Nabû-mushêtiq-urra, [5]the son of Ishtar-nâdin-aḫi, [6,7]who was sent[384] to the land of Têmâ, were given. [8]The fifth day of the month Adar, the fifth year of [9]Nabonidus, the king of Babylon.

This inscription is all the more remarkable because it contains an additional reference to traveling by camel from Babylonia to the land of Têmâ. It furnishes interesting corroboration of the close relation between the two countries in the sixth century B. C. That there was communication between Têmâ and the land of Akkad in the time of Nebuchadrezzar is shown by the following text:

[381] *AENN* 294: 1–9. This text furnished the clue which enabled the writer to prove that Nabonidus spent certain years of his reign at Têmâ in Arabia. See *JAOS* XLII, p. 305. Nabonidus received his usual subsidy in his fifth year. See p. 100.

[382] In *JAOS* XLII, p. 305, note 2, and in *AENN* p. 34, the writer transliterated and translated this text upon the basis of the inexactly copied text *AENN* 294, reading *A-GUB-BA* instead of *A-AB-BA*. Upon a suggestion from Professor Langdon, the original tablet was examined more carefully and it was found that the Babylonian scribe really wrote *A-AB-BA*. This correction of the reading adds interest to the document, which has special significance in view of *REN* 134.

[383] Flour was generally supplied for the use of human beings. See *StrNbn* 1065: 3, 6, 9. Cf. Thomas, *With Lawrence in Arabia*, p. 178, for the following interesting statement: "Although 'the camel is an intricate animal and calls for skilled labor in handling,' according to Colonel Lawrence, 'she yields a remarkable return. We had no system of supply: each man was self-contained and carried on the saddle from the sea-base, at which the raid started, six weeks' food for himself. The six weeks' ration for ordinary men was a half-bag of flour, forty-five pounds in weight. Luxurious feeders carried rice also for variety. Each man baked for himself, kneading his own flour into unleavened cakes and warming it in the ashes of a fire.'" As to the camels, Lawrence says, *ibid.*, p. 179, "They lived on grazing as we marched (we never gave them grain or fodder)."

[384] The primary meaning of *šapâru*, 'send with a message,' 'charge with a mission,' indicates that Nabû-mushêtiq-urra was dispatched upon an official errand, probably to the king's court, which remained at Têmâ after that city was captured by Nabonidus.

^{1}*1 pi 24 qa ŠE-BAR* ^{2}*ina kurummati*^{zun}*-šu* ^{3}*ša* ^{arah}*Tišrîti* ^{m}*Ri-mut* $^{4\,amêl}$*Te-ma-a-a iššî(GIŠ)* $^{5\,arah}$*Ulûlu ûmu 30*^{kam} ^{6}*šattu 7*^{kam} $^{7\,d}$*Nabû-kudurri-uṣur* ^{8}*šar Bâbili*^{ki}.[385]

^{1}One *pi,* twenty-four *qa* of barley, ^{2}of his sustenance ^{3}of the month Tishri, Rîmût, ^{4}the Têmaean (*i.e.* man of Têmâ) received. ^{5}The thirtieth day of the month Elul, ^{6}the seventh year of ^{7}Nebuchadrezzar, ^{8}the king of Babylon.

The three texts which have just been discussed supply a background of intercourse between Babylonia and the land of Têmâ during the Neo-Babylonian régime and particularly during the reign of Nabonidus. Two of the inscriptions indicate that contact was maintained by means of camels, thus suggesting that the land of Têmâ was in Arabia.

4. Light on the Situation from Two Leases of Land

The Yale Babylonian Collection contains two royal leases of land issued during the reign of Nabonidus. One, dated in the first year of his reign, was obtained from Nabonidus himself; the other, dated in the eleventh year of his reign, when he was at the city of Têmâ, was obtained from Belshazzar. In order to contrast the provisions of these leases more carefully the full text of each is presented.

(1) *Lease of Land from Nabonidus*

$^{1\,m}$*Šum-ukîn(-na) apil-šu ša* ^{m}*Bêl-zêr apil* ^{m}*Ba-si-ia u* ^{m}*Kal-ba-a apil-šu ša* ^{m}*Iqî[ša(-ša)]* ^{2}*a-na* ^{d}*Nabû-nâ'id šar Bâbili*^{ki} *šarri bêli-šu-nu ú-ṣa-al-lu-ú um-ma* ^{3}*6000 gur* ^{še}*zêri pi-i šul-[pu] e-lat* ^{še}*zêri Bît-*^{iṣ}*Gišimmari* ^{4}*400* ^{amêl}*ikkarâtu*^{meš} *400 alpê*^{meš} *ù 100 liâti rabâti*^{me} *a-na pít-qa* ^{5}*ša 400 alpê*^{me} *šarru bêlu-a-ni lid-di-na-an-ši-ma ina šatti 25000 gur ŠE-BAR* ^{6}*gamrûti(-ti) ù 10000 gur suluppi gam-ru-tu ina muḫ-ḫi me-e* ^{7}*a-na* ^{d}*Bêlit ša Uruk*^{ki} *ni-id-din*[386] ^{d}*Nabû-nâ'id šar Bâbili*^{ki} *šarru bêlu-šu-nu* ^{8}*im-gur-šu-nu-ti-ma 6000 gur* ^{še}*zêri a-di na-bal-kat-tu*[387] ^{9}*ša ina šatti mi-šil* ^{še}*zêri ú-pa-aš-ša-ḫa*[388] *400* ^{amêl}*ikkarâtu*^{me} *400*

[385] Sidney Smith called the writer's attention to this unpublished tablet, 117520 of the British Museum. Dr. H. R. Hall of the British Museum kindly gave permission to publish the text in this volume. See pl. I, 2, opposite p. 68.

[386] See Ungnad, *Babylonisch-assyrische Grammatik*, 2nd edition, p. 40.

[387] *Nabalkattu*, from *balkatu*, has been given various meanings, such as 'revolt,' 'rebellion,' 'destruction,' 'adjoining land,' etc. Apparently a more primary meaning must be sought for the above context. The verb *balkatu* has the meaning 'tear,' 'rend,' in certain passages. See *CD* p. 165. See following note.

[388] The root *pašaḫu* means 'appease,' 'quiet.' Hence *a-di na-bal-kat-tu ša ina šatti mi-šil* ^{še}*zêri ú-pa-aš-ša-ḫa* may be translated 'including the tearing (or rending)

alpê^{me} ^{10}*ù 100 liâti rabâti*^{me} *a-na pít-qa ša 400 alpê*^{me} *a-na* ^{m}*Šum-ukîn(-na)* ^{11}*apil-šu ša* ^{m}*Bêl-zêr apil* ^{m}*Ba-si-ia u* ^{m}*Kal-ba-a apil* ^{m}*Iqîša(-ša) id-din* ^{12}*alpê*^{me} *ù liâti rabâti*$^{[meš]}$ *ina lib-bi ul i-mut-ti mâr liâti rabâti*^{meš} *ma-la* ^{13}*im-mal-la-du*[389] *a-na* ^{amêl}*mâr šipri ša šarri ú-kal-la-mu-ú-ma* ^{14}*ina šin-du*[390] *parzilli ša* ^{d}*Bêlit ša Uruk*^{ki} *i-šim-mi-ti ù* ^{15}*ú-tar-ma a-na* ^{m}*Šum-ukîn u* ^{m}*Kal-ba-a i-nam-din-ma pít-qa* ^{16}*ša* ^{iṣ}*APIN*^{meš} *ina lib-bi i-ṣab-ba-ti* ^{17} ^{m}*Šum-ukîn(-na) u* ^{m}*Kal-ba-a ina šatti 25000 gur ŠE-BAR gamrûti(-ti) ù* ^{18}*10000 gur suluppi gam-ru-tu napḫaru 35000 gur ŠE-BAR u suluppi* ^{19}*ina eli me-e*[391] *ina* ^{iṣ}*ma-ši-ḫu ša* ^{d}*Bêlit ša Uruk*^{ki} *a-na* ^{d}*Bêlit ša Uruk*^{ki} ^{20}*i-nam-di-nu ištênit(-it) šattu maḫ-ri-tu 3000 gur SE-BAR a-na* ^{še}*zêri* ^{21}*ù 10 bilat parzilli ul-tu Ê-an-na i-nam-di-nu-niš-šu-nu-tum* ^{22}*eqlê*^{meš} ^{iṣ}*kirî ḫal-lat ša* ^{d}*Bêlit ša Uruk*^{ki} *ša pâni* ^{amêl}*[rab bânî]*^{meš} ^{m}*Šum-ukîn(-na)* ^{23}*u* ^{m}*Kal-ba-a i-mit-ti ul im-mi-du*[392] *ù a-na muḫ-ḫi ul i-šal-la-ṭu*[393] ^{24} ^{m}*Šum-ukîn u* ^{m}*Kal-ba-a mimma ma-la [ip-pu]-šu-' ištên(-en) pu-ut šanî(-i) na-šu-u*[394]

---

which in a year appeases half the seed field.' This might refer to some kind of agricultural operation for reclaiming land. It should be noted that the root פשח in cognate Semitic languages means 'tear,' 'diminish,' etc. In the absence of a clearer context it is difficult to interpret the passage with certainty.

[389] *Im-mal-la-du* represents *iwwalladu* from *alâdu*, 'bear,' 'beget.' See *REN* 150: 18.

[390] *Šin-du* is a derivative from the verb *šamâtu* which appears in *i-šim-mi-ti* in the above context. The idiom *ina šin-du šamâtu* means 'brand (mark) with a mark.' See discussion in *SBD* pp. 81–85.

[391] *Ina eli me-e* should be compared with *ina muh-hi me-e* in line 6 and with *ina eli maš-qat-tum*, *REN* 150: 10. See note in *ŠBD* p. 73 indicating that *mašqattum*, from *šaqû*, 'to water' refers to some canal or stream like an irrigating ditch. It may also refer to a more extensive body of water caused by general inundation. *Mê rabûti* should be compared with מים רבים, Jeremiah 41: 12; Ezekiel 27: 26. The word *maškattu*, 'warehouse,' 'threshing-floor,' should not be overlooked. See Bezold, *Babylonisch-assyrisches Glossar*, p. 273. It would seem, however, that *ana eli* or *ana muḫḫi* would be used with *maškattu* instead of *ina eli* or *ina muḫḫi*. A Neo-Babylonian passage (*REN* 26: 3–6) favors the reading *mašqattum*, 'watered region,' in the sense of a canal full of water or an extensively irrigated district. Iqîsha, the son of Nanâêresh, the shepherd of the Bêltu of Erech, said to temple officials in Erech as follows: *2000 ṣi-e-nu 500 [liâti rabâti*^{meš} *ša] qa-bu-ut-ti ša* ^{d}*Bêlit ša Uruk*^{ki} *ina pa-ni-ia maš-qat-ti ša* ^{d}*Bêlit ša Uruk*^{ki} *ina pa-ni-ia ia-a-nu ṣi-e-ni-ia ù liâti rabâti*^{meš}*-ia ina ṣêri us-saq-qa-am-[ma]*, 'Two thousand sheep (and) five hundred [mature cows of] the fold of the Bêltu of Erech are at my disposal. A watered region of the Bêltu of Erech is not at my disposal. I have apportioned my sheep and my mature cows in the plain (or desert).' It is evident that *maš-qat-ti* and *ṣêri* are contrasted. Note Arabic *masqâtun*, *locus quo aqua continetur;* Freytag, *Lexicon Arabico-Latinum*, 1833, II, p. 331.

[392] In contract tablets the idiom *imitti emêdu* means 'impose the impost.' Hence it conveys the idea of taxing or assessing.

[393] The literal meaning of *a-na muḫ-ḫi ul i-šal-la-ṭu* is 'they shall not have power over it,' hence 'they shall not claim it.'

[394] *REN* 11: 1–24.

[1]Shum-ukîn, the son of Bêl-zêr, son of Basîa, and Kalbâ, the son of Iqîsha, [2]Nabonidus, the king of Babylon, the king, their lord, besought as follows: [3]"Six thousand *gur* of seed field, uncultivated land, in addition, the seed field of Bît-Gishimmari, [4]four hundred husbandmen, four hundred oxen, and one hundred mature cows for the *pitqa*[395] [5]of the four hundred oxen, may the king, our lord, give us and yearly twenty-five thousand *gur* of barley [6]in full and ten thousand *gur* of dates in full upon the water [7]to the Bêltu of Erech let us deliver." Nabonidus, the king of Babylon, the king, their lord, [8]was gracious unto them and six thousand *gur* of seed field, including the *nabalkattu* [9]which yearly appeases half the seed field, four hundred husbandmen, four hundred oxen, [10]and one hundred mature cows for the *pitqa* of the four hundred oxen to Shum-ukîn, [11]the son of Bêl-zêr, son of Basîa, and Kalbâ, the son of Iqîsha, gave. [12]No oxen and mature cows among them shall be killed (literally, die). The offspring of the mature cows, as many as [13]are born, they shall show to the messenger of the king and [14]he shall brand (them) with the iron mark of the Bêltu of Erech and [15]return and give (them) to Shum-ukîn and Kalbâ. Furthermore, the construction [16]of the cultivating instruments in it they shall assume. [17]Shum-ukîn and Kalbâ yearly twenty-five thousand *gur* of barley in full and [18]ten thousand *gur* of dates in full, a total of thirty-five thousand *gur* of barley and dates, [19]upon the water, according to the measure of the Bêltu of Erech, to the Bêltu of Erech [20]shall deliver. For the first year three thousand *gur* of barley for the seed field [21]and ten talents of iron from Êanna they shall give them. [22]The orchard lands, the fief of the Bêltu of Erech which is at the disposal of the [*rab bânî*], Shum-ukîn [23]and Kalbâ shall not assess and shall not claim. [24]Shum-ukîn and Kalbâ in whatever they do shall bear a mutual responsibility.

The names of nine witnesses and the scribe follow, and the document is dated at Larsa, the twenty-eighth day of the month Nisan, the first year of Nabonidus, the king of Babylon.

(2) *Lease of Land from Belshazzar*

[1] *^{m}Ib-ni-^{d}Innina apil-šu ša ^{m}Ba-la-ṭu ^{amêl}širku ša ^{d}Bêlit ša Uruk^{ki} ^{md}Bêl-šar-uṣ[ur]* [2] *mâr šarri bêla-šu ú-ṣa-al-li um-ma 625 gur ^{še}zêri Bît-Me-ri-šu* [3] *ina ^{še}zêri pi-i šul-pu ša ^{d}Bêlit ša Uruk^{ki} ša ina ^{tâmirtu}Su-man-dar 100*

[395] *Pitqa* is a noun derived from *patâqu*, 'form,' 'build,' 'make.' *CD* p. 856. The statement 'one hundred mature cows for the *pitqa* of four hundred oxen' suggests that the cows were to be used for breeding purposes. This interpretation harmonizes with the special provision of the lease with reference to the offspring of the cattle. The word *pitqa* in line 15 may be read *batqa* as construed with *ṣabâtu*. Cf. *CD* p. 207.

^{amêl}*ikkarâtu*^{meš} ^{4}*100 alpê*^{meš} *ù 50 liâti rabâti* $^{\text{[meš]}}$ *mâr šarri bêlu-a lid-din-namma i-na šatti* ^{5}*5000 gur ŠE-BAR ga-mir-tum ina* ^{iṣ}*ma-ši-ḫu ša šarri ina Ê-an-na lud-[din]* $^{6\,\text{md}}$*Bêl-šar-uṣur mâr šarri bêlu-šu iš-me-šu-ma 625 gur* ^{še}*zêri Bît-[Me-ri-šu]* ^{7}*ina* ^{še}*zêri pi-i šul-pu ša ina* ^{tâmirtu}*Su-man-dar 100* ^{amêl}*ikkarâtu*^{meš} *100 alpê* $^{\text{[meš]}}$ *um . . . .* ^{8}*ù 50 liâti rabâti*^{meš} *a-na* ^{m}*Ib-ni-*^{d}*Innina apil-šu ša* ^{m}*Ba-la-ṭu id-din i-na šatti* ^{9}*5000 [gur] ŠE-BAR ga-mir-tum ina* ^{iṣ}*ma-ši-ḫu ša šarri ina Ê-an-na i-nam-din* ^{10}*3000 ma-ak-ṣa-ru ša ti-ib-nu ina eli maš-qat-tum i-nam-din* ^{11}*ù 2081 gur* ^{še}*zêri Bît-Me-ri-šu nak-kan-du*[396] *ša* ^{d}*Bêlit ša Uruk*^{ki} ^{12}*ša ina pa-ni-šu* ^{še}*zêru ma-la ib-ba-lak-ki-tu-ú-ma*[397] *ina* ^{iṣ}*APIN*^{meš} *ša ina pa-ni-šu ina lib-bi ir-ri-šu* $^{13\,\text{še}}$*zêru ma-la* ^{še}*zêru ul-tu* ^{še}*zêri ša ina pa-ni-šu a-na nak-kan-du ša* ^{d}*Bêlit ša Uruk*^{ki} ^{14}*[ú-maš]-šar ù* ^{še}*zêra-ám 2081 gur nak-kan-du pi-i šul-pu* ^{15} *. . . . GIŠ-BAR-šu at-ru* ^{amêl}*ir-ri-še-e ina lib-bi ir-ri-šu* ^{16}*[*^{amêl}*e-mi-di]-e ša Ê-an-na im-mi-du*[398] *ù zitta a-na Ê-an-na i-nam-di-nu* ^{17} *. . . .* $^{\text{[amêl]}}$*ikkarâtu*^{meš} *ša ina pa-ni-šu alpê*^{meš} *ù liâti rabâti*$^{\text{[meš]}}$ *ina lib-bi ul i-mut-tum* ^{18} *. . . . šu-nu mârê*^{meš} *liâti rabâti*^{meš} *ša* ^{d}*Bêlit ša Uruk*^{ki} *ša ina pa-ni-šu im-mal-la-du* ^{19}*[a-na]* ^{md}*Nabû-šar-uṣur* ^{amêl}*šaqî šarri ù* ^{amêl}*šangê*^{meš} *ša Ê-an-na ú-kal-lam-ma* ^{20}*[ina] šin-du parzilli ša* ^{d}*Bêlit ša Uruk*^{ki} *i-šim-mi-tum*[399] *ù ú-tar-ru-ma* ^{21}*i-nam-di-nu-niš-šim-ma pít-qa ša* ^{iṣ}*APIN*^{meš}*-šu ina lib-bi i-ṣab-bat* ^{22}*šattu maḫ-ri-tum 625 gur ŠE-BAR a-na* ^{še}*zêri 5 bilat 20 ma-na parzilli* ^{23}*ù 120 gur ŠE-BAR a-na kurummati*^{zun} *ša 30* ^{amêl}*ikkarâtu . . . . a-na* ^{24}*šul-lu-mu ša 25* ^{iṣ}*APIN*^{meš} *a-na* ^{m}*Ib-ni-[*^{d}*Innina apil-šu ša* ^{m}*Ba]-la-ṭu na-ad-nu*[400] ^{25}*ul-tu Ê-an-na ab*[401] *. . . .* ^{26}*i-na 1 gur 1 pi 6 qa ŠE-BAR a-na kurummati*^{zun} *ša* ^{amêl}*šangê*^{meš} ^{amêl}*man-[di-di]*^{meš} *e-lat 1 pi 6 qa . . . . SES.*[402]

^{1,2}Ibni-Innina, the son of Balâṭu, a *širku*[403] of the Bêltu of Erech, besought

[396] *Nakkandu* is a form of *nakamtu, nakantu*, from *nakâmu*, 'heap up.' Although *nakamtu* means 'treasure,' derived meanings such as 'property,' 'possession,' are possible.

[397] The verb *ib-ba-lak-ki-tu-ú-ma* in this lease should be compared with the term *nabalkattu* in the Nabonidus lease, line 8. See notes 387 and 388. The occurrence of the verb in the Belshazzar lease does not seem to throw additional light upon the meaning of the stem in these contexts.

[398] Compare with *i-mit-ti ul im-mi-du* in line 23 of the Nabonidus lease. See note 392.

[399] Compare with *i-šim-mi-ti* in line 14 of the Nabonidus lease. See note 390. Animals branded with the iron mark of the Bêltu of Erech, *i.e.* Ishtar, were no doubt marked with Ishtar's symbol, a star. The term describing the branded state of such animals is *kakkabtu šindu*. See *REN* 123: 1, 9; 156: 5, 15, 16; 169: 1, 15; 231: 1, 17, 18. For additional references see *SBD* p. 83, note 98.

[400] The permansive form of *nadânu*, 'give,' should be compared with *i-nam-di-nu-niš-šu-nu-tum*, 'they shall give,' in line 21 of the Nabonidus lease.

[401] The sign *ab* suggests the permansive form of the verb *abâku*, 'bring.'

[402] *REN* 150: 1–26.

[403] The term *širku* denotes that the individual was a temple servant dedicated to a special deity. See a summary of the characteristics of the order in *SBD* pp. 88–91.

Belshazzar, the son of the king, his lord, as follows: "Six hundred and twenty-five *gur* of the seed field Bît-Mêrishu [3]from the uncultivated land of the Bêltu of Erech which is in the vicinity of Sumandar, one hundred husbandmen, [4]one hundred oxen and fifty mature cows may the son of the king, my lord, give me and yearly [5]five thousand *gur* of barley in full, according to the measure of the king, in Êanna let me give." [6]Belshazzar, the son of the king, his lord, heard him and six hundred and twenty-five *gur* of the seed field Bît-Mêrishu [7]from the uncultivated land which is in the vicinity of Sumandar, one hundred husbandmen, one hundred oxen . . . . [8]and fifty mature cows to Ibni-Innina, the son of Balâṭu, gave. Yearly [9]five thousand *gur* of barley in full, according to the measure of the king, in Êanna he shall give. [10]Three thousand bundles of straw upon the water (?)[404] he shall deliver. [11]Furthermore, (as for) the two thousand and eighty-one *gur* of the seed field Bît-Mêrishu, the property of the Bêltu of Erech, [12]which is at his disposal, as much seed field as they shall tear up and with the cultivating instruments at his disposal they shall cultivate in it, [13]seed field for seed field, from the seed field which is at his disposal, for the possession of the Bêltu of Erech [14]he shall leave, and the seed field, *i.e.* the two thousand and eighty-one *gur* of uncultivated property [15]. . . . his surplus tax (according to what) the farmers shall cultivate in it, [16]the tax officials of Êanna shall assess and give the share to Êanna [17]. . . . the husbandmen which are at his disposal. The oxen and the mature cows in it shall not be slaughtered (literally, shall not die). [18]. . . . The calves that are born of the mature cows of the Bêltu of Erech which are at his disposal [19]he shall show to Nabû-shar-uṣur, the chief officer of the king, and the priests of Êanna and [20]they shall brand (them) with the iron mark of the Bêltu of Erech, and shall return and [21]give (them) to him. He shall assume the construction of his cultivating instruments in it. [22]For the first year six hundred and twenty-five *gur* of barley for the seed field, five talents and twenty minas of iron, [23]and one hundred and twenty *gur* of barley for the food of thirty husbandmen . . . . for [24]the completion of the twenty-five cultivating instruments to Ibni-Innina, the son of Balâṭu, are to be given. [25]From Êanna (they are to be brought), ... [26]including one *gur*, one *pi*, and six *qa* of barley for the food of the priests (and) the sur[veyors]. In addition one *pi*, six *qa* . . . .

The names of seven witnesses and the scribe follow. The date of the document is partially illegible, but the unmutilated part of the date indicates that the lease was issued in the eleventh year of the reign of Nabonidus.

[404] For a discussion of the meaning of *mašqattum* see note 391. Cf. *VS* III, 56: 5.

(3) *Comparison of the Nabonidus and Belshazzar Leases*

The two leases of land presented above are extremely interesting. Similar provisions exist in them, but there are essential differences. The lease from Nabonidus was obtained by two men for six thousand measures of ground, four hundred husbandmen, four hundred oxen and one hundred mature cows at a proffered yearly rental of twenty-five thousand measures of barley and ten thousand measures of dates. The lease from Belshazzar was obtained by one man—a consecrated servant of Ishtar—for six hundred and twenty-five measures of ground, one hundred husbandmen, one hundred oxen, and fifty mature cows at a proffered yearly rental of five thousand measures of barley. The following comparisons may be made.

(*a*) In both leases the scribes and petitioners use the same terms of royal address. The formula of the scribe in the first lease (line 2) is *a-na* ^{d}*Nabû-nâ'id šar Bâbili*^{ki} *šarri bêli-šu-nu ú-ṣa-al-lu-ú*, 'they besought Nabonidus, the king of Babylon, the king, their lord.' The formula of the scribe in the second lease (lines 1, 2) is ^{md}*Bêl-šar-uṣur mâr šarri bêla-šu ú-ṣa-al-li*, 'he besought Belshazzar, the son of the king, his lord.' The verb *ṣalû* is construed either with or without *ana*.[405] The two petitioners in the first lease refer to Nabonidus as *šarru bêlu-a-ni*, 'the king, our lord.' The petitioner in the second lease refers to Belshazzar as *mâr šarri bêlu-a*, 'the son of the king, my lord.'

(*b*) The attitude of Nabonidus (line 8) towards his petitioners is expressed by *im-gur-šu-nu-ti*, 'he hearkened unto them,' 'he was gracious unto them.' The attitude of Belshazzar (line 6) is expressed by the term *iš-me-šu*, 'he heard him,' 'he hearkened unto him.' Both terms are used to describe the attitude involved in granting petitions or answering prayers.

(*c*) Nabonidus granted his lease at the proffered rental, whereas Belshazzar required an additional rental (line 10) to be paid in the form of three thousand bundles of straw (*3000 ma-ak-ṣa-ru ša ti-ib-nu*). There is no reference to the delivery of straw in the lease obtained from Nabonidus.

(*d*) In the Nabonidus lease (line 19) there is the provision that the

[405] See *CD* p. 874; *Hwb* p. 567.

rent shall be paid according to the measure of the Bêltu of Erech (*i-na* ^{is}*ma-ši-ḫu ša* ^{d}*Bêlit ša Uruk*^{ki}), whereas in the Belshazzar lease (line 9) it is provided that the rent shall be paid according to the measure of the king (*ina* ^{is}*ma-ši-ḫu ša šarri*). The import of this difference cannot be determined since the volume of these measures is unknown.

(*e*) In the lease obtained from Nabonidus there is a stipulation (line 19) that the rental shall be delivered upon the water (*ina eli me-e*), *i.e.* upon some canal or submerged area permitting transportation by water. In the lease obtained from Belshazzar no such inclusive provision appears. However, in the latter document there is a clause stating that three thousand bundles of straw are to be delivered upon the water of an irrigated section (*ina eli maš-qat-tum*).[406]

(*f*) There is no difference between the two leases as to the provision for branding the offspring of the cattle placed at the disposal of the lessees, beyond the fact that in the lease from Nabonidus (line 13) the messenger of the king is to inspect and brand, whereas in the lease obtained from Belshazzar (line 19) these functions are to be performed by a chief officer of the king and the priests of Êanna. After the animals have been inspected and branded with a star mark—the symbol of Ishtar—as a sign that they belong to the temple, the contracts provide that they shall be returned to the lessees.

(*g*) The numerical proportion of husbandmen and animals allowed with the leases varies considerably. In the lease obtained from Belshazzar the proportion is more than double that of the lease obtained from Nabonidus,[407] and much greater in the case of the mature cows.

(*h*) With reference to the making of the cultivating instruments needed in increasing the fertility of the leased land no difference seems to exist. In both leases the responsibility for their construction or repair is placed upon the lessees.[408]

(*i*) As to the amount of barley to be advanced to the lessees from

[406] It is probable that this means that the delivery was to be made at the time of year when travel was facilitated by full canals and extensive areas of submergence. See *The Annual of the American Schools of Oriental Research*, VII, p. 66.

[407] See Nabonidus lease, line 4; Belshazzar lease, lines 3, 4.

[408] See Nabonidus lease, line 16; Belshazzar lease, line 21.

the temple during the first year, as an aid in getting the crops started, there is considerable difference. In the Nabonidus lease (line 20) three thousand measures of barley are apportioned for six thousand measures of land, *i.e.* one-half a *gur* of barley for each *gur* of land. In the Belshazzar lease (line 22) six hundred and twenty-five measures of barley are apportioned for six hundred and twenty-five measures of land, *i.e.* one *gur* of barley for each *gur* of land.

(*j*) There is a greater difference as to the amount of iron to be dispensed to the lessees from the temple. In the Nabonidus lease (line 21) ten talents (= 600 minas) are to be given for six thousand measures of land, *i.e.* one-tenth of a mina for each measure of land. In the Belshazzar lease (line 22) five talents and twenty minas (= 320 minas) are to be given for six hundred and twenty-five measures of land, *i.e.* slightly more than one-half a mina for each measure of land.

(*k*) In the lease obtained from Nabonidus (lines 22, 23) there is a provision that the lessees are to have no claim upon the landholdings of the temple which are for the particular use of certain temple officials. There is no specific reference to this in the lease obtained from Belshazzar, although there may be something similar in the stipulation concerning the *nakkandu* (lines 11, 13) of the Bêltu of Erech.

(*l*) In the Nabonidus lease no provision is made for the food of the workmen, etc., whereas such provision is made with evident care in the Belshazzar lease (line 26).

All the factors involved in the granting of the above leases of land are not known. It is conceivable that there were differences between the two tracts of land that were leased. Fertility of soil, stage of cultivation, and topographical position could vary extensively in different regions. Hence final conclusions cannot be reached with reference to the authority assumed by Belshazzar as compared with that of Nabonidus. However, it may be that the deviation of these two leases of land represents independence of action on the part of Belshazzar. Whatever uncertainty may exist along some lines, we may feel sure that the lease obtained from Belshazzar in the eleventh year of the reign of Nabonidus fits perfectly into the picture of the king's absence at Têmâ during that year.

5. *Administrative Matter Attended to by Belshazzar*

The Yale Babylonian Collection contains the record of a most important administrative act performed by Belshazzar with reference to a controversial matter at Erech in the sixth year of Nabonidus' reign. Fortunately the record is preserved in duplicate texts, *REN* 71 and 72, so that it is possible to restore the mutilated sections and omitted portions of one text from the corresponding legible and fully-written passages in the other, and thus a complete text is available. The following transliteration and translation use the verse notation of *REN* 71:

1 ^{md}*Nabû-šar-uṣur* ^{amêl}*šaqû šarri* ^{amêl}*bêl pi-qit-ti Ê-an-na* 2 *a-na* ^{md}*Bêl-uballiṭ(-iṭ) apil-šu ša* ^{m}*Mušallim-*^{d}*Marduk apil* ^{m}*Gimil-*^{d}*Na-na-a* 3 ^{m}*Ba-la-ṭu apil-šu ša* ^{m}*Šú-ma-a apil* ^{m}*Iddin-*^{d}*Papsukal* 4 ^{md}*Marduk-šum-iddin apil-šu ša* ^{md}*Nabû-aḫê*^{meš}*-bul-liṭ apil* ^{m}*Ba-la-ṭu* 5 ^{m}*Ša-du-nu apil-šu ša* ^{m}*Mu-še-zib-*^{d}*Bêl apil* ^{m}*Nûr-*^{d}*Sin* 6 ^{md}*Nabû-êṭir-napšâti*^{meš} *apil-šu ša* ^{m}*Ardi-*^{d}*Bêl apil* ^{m}*E-gi-bi* 7 ^{m}*Na-di-nu apil-šu ša* ^{m}*Ap-la-a apil* ^{m}*Aḫê*^{meš}*-ia-ú* 8 ^{m}*Mušallim-*^{d}*Marduk apil-šu ša* ^{m}*Ardi-*^{d}*Nabû apil* ^{amêl}*šangû* ^{d}*Nabû* 9 ^{md}*Nabû-êṭir-napšâti*^{meš} *apil-šu ša* ^{md}*Bêl-iqîša(-ša) apil* ^{md}*Bêl-apal-uṣur* 10 ^{m}*Ibni-*^{d}*Ištar apil-šu ša* ^{md}*Nabû-zêr-ukîn apil* ^{amêl}*ašlaku* 11 ^{md}*In-nin-šum-uṣur apil-šu ša* ^{m}*Iddin-*^{d}*Nabû apil* ^{m}*Ki-din-*^{d}*Marduk* 12 ^{m}*A-ḫu-lap-ia apil-šu ša* ^{md}*Bêl-šum-iškun(-un) apil* ^{md}*Bêl-apal-uṣur* 13 ^{m}*Bêl-šu-nu apil-šu ša* ^{md}*Nabû-aḫê*^{meš}*-iddin apil* ^{m}*E-gi-bi* 14 ^{md}*Nabû-bâni-aḫi apil-šu ša* ^{md}*Nabû-balâṭ-su-iq-bi apil* ^{md}*Sin-lîq-unnînni* 15 ^{md}*Šamaš-šum-ukîn apil-šu ša* ^{m}*Šú-la-a apil* ^{amêl}*man-di-di* 16 ^{m}*Ina-Ê-sag-ila-zêr apil-šu ša* ^{m}*Ša-pî-*^{d}*Bêl apil* ^{m}*Amêl-*^{d}*Êa* 17 ^{md}*Nabû-mušêtiq-urra apil-šu ša* ^{md}*Bêl-ri-man-ni apil* ^{m}*E-gi-bi* 18 ^{amêl}*Bâbili*$^{ki\ meš}$ ^{amêl}*Uruk*^{ki}*-a-a* ^{amêl}*IGI*^{meš}[409] ^{amêl}*TU-Ê*[410]

[409] Primary meanings of *IGI* are 'see,' 'look,' and hence the ^{amêl}*IGI*^{meš} may have been temple inspectors or overseers. See *Bar* 406.

[410] See *RA* VIII, p. 54, note 18, for the suggestion that ^{amêl}*TU-Ê* should be read ^{amêl}*ṣâbit bîti* instead of ^{amêl}*êrib bîti*. See *LSS* II, 1, p. 69. Comparison is made with *νεωκόρος*, the term used in Greek for 'temple caretaker'. Note Latin *aedituus*, 'temple custodian.' In *MI* 45, col. II, line 28, occurs ^{amêl}*ti-ir-bit*. Since *TU* has the value *târu*, 'turn,' 'return,' it is possible that ^{amêl}*ti-ir-bit*, better ^{amêl}*ti-ir bîti*, is the Semitic rendering of ^{amêl}*TU-Ê*, although the exact meaning of this title as applied to a temple official is not easy to determine. It should be noted that in the above text ^{amêl}*TU-Ê* is mentioned in connection with ^{amêl}*ki-na-al-tu* and this is the case with ^{amêl}*ti-ir bîti* in *MI* 45, for in col. II, line 30, occurs ^{amêl}*ki-ni-iš-tu* which is a variant of ^{amêl}*ki-na-al-tu*. Cf. *NLE* 152: 7, 8, for a similar association. There is good evidence, therefore, that ^{amêl}*TU-Ê* and ^{amêl}*ti-ir bîti* are equivalent. See Tallqvist, *Neubabylonisches Namenbuch*, p. 106, under *Mu-še-zib-*^{d}*Marduk*, for a reference to ^{amêl}*TU ša bît* ^{d}*Šamaš*.

u ^{amêl}ki-na-al-tu[411] ^{19}*ša Ê-an-na iq-bi um-ma mâr šarri ši-pir-ti il-tap-ra* ^{20}*um-ma ^{ṣubât}kusâti^{meš}-ši-na šittâ(-ta) ša ul-tu eli ^{d}Na-na-a* ^{21}*ša Ê-zi-da ur-ra-da-nim-ma*[412] *a-na eli ^{d}Bêlit ša Uruk^{ki} u ^{d}Na-na-a* ^{22}*il-la-ka*[413] *ki-i iq-bu-nu aš-ša it-tar-da-a-nu ištênit(-it) ina lib-bi-ši-na* ^{23}*a-na ^{d}Bêlti a-šib-ti Uruk^{ki} ta-an-na-an-din* ^{24}*ù en-na ka-la-a-ta*[414] *ak-ka-a-'-i ki-i ka-la-a-ta* ^{25}*ḫur-ṣa-am-ma šup-ra qi-ba-a-nim-ma a-na mâr šarri lu-uš-pur* ^{26}*^{amêl}Bâbili^{ki} ^{meš}ù ^{amêl}Uruk^{ki}-a-a ^{amêl}IGI^{meš} ^{amêl}TU-Ê u ^{amêl}ki-na-al-[tu]* ^{27}*ša Ê-an-na a-na ^{md}Nabû-šar-uṣur ^{amêl}šaqî šarri ^{amêl}bêl pi-qit-ti Ê-an-na* ^{28}*iq-bu-ú um-ma na-da-a-nu ša ^{ṣubât}kusîti ul-tu [Ê-an-na] a-na ^{âl} ^{d}Bêlti-ia* ^{29}*ia-a-nu al-la*[415] *ištên-šu*[416] *a-na tar-ṣi ^{d}Nabû-kudurri-uṣur ^{m}Êṭir-^{d}Marduk* ^{30} *^{amêl}paqdu Êkurâti^{meš} ki-i id-di-nu-uš ṭi-ir-du*[417] *ina muḫ-ḫi ki-i iš-šak-nu* ^{31} *^{md}Nabû-kudurri-uṣur [ki-i] iš-mu-ú ik-*

[411] The variant in *REN* 72: 26 is *^{amêl}ki-na-al-ti*. In *REN* 71: 26 it occurs as *^{amêl}ki-na-al* which is no doubt an error of the scribe. See *NLE* 57: 6 for *^{amêl}ki-na-aš-ti* which represents the original form of which *^{amêl}ki-na-al-ti* is a modification. Note also *NLE* 86: 8, 14 for *^{amêl}ki-na-al-tum*. *RECC* 16: 10 preserves the form *^{amêl}ki-na-aš-tum*. The forms *^{amêl}ki-ni-iš-tum*, *MI* 45, col. II, line 30, and *^{amêl}ki-niš-ti*, *NLE* 6: 18; 152: 8, are variants of the same term. See *NLE* 51: 17. Cf. *SBD* p. 68, note 74. It is evident that Babylonian *kiništu*, *kinaštu*, and *kinaltu* are related to Aramaic **כנשתא**. See Meissner, *Babylonien und Assyrien* II, p. 67, for *kiništu* = Priester Kollegium. Of interest in this connection is *^{amêl}puḫru; REN* 92: 22; 240: 20.

[412] The terms *ur-ra-da-nim-ma* in line 21 and *it-tar-da-a-nu* in line 22 indicate that temple vestments were brought from the temple Êzida in Borsippa to the temple Êanna in Erech. Note the following in *REN* 229: 26: *5 gur a-na ^{amêl}ṣâbê^{me} ša ^{iṣ}elippa ša ^{ṣubât}kusîti il-du-ud*, 'Five *gur* (of dates) for the soldiers (or workmen) who drew the *kusîtu* ship.' See *AENN* 350: 1–3 for a reference to hired laborers drawing (*i.e.* towing) a ship to Sippar. Doubtless these texts refer to men on the bank of a canal or river towing a ship by means of a rope. The same method of towing vessels is used in 'Irâq today. See *The Annual of the American Schools of Oriental Research* VII, p. 66f. For other references to the *^{iṣ}elip kusîti* see *AENN* 73: 2; 298: 2; 384: 2, 3; 386: 1; 404: 2. Evidently the ship which carried temple vestments or religious paraphernalia brought in quite a revenue. The vestments of the images of the gods were used, it seems, in different temples. Cf. *NLE* 62.

[413] There is a reference to the process of adorning the image of Ishtar in Erech with vestments and ornaments in the words *a-na eli ^{d}Bêlit ša Uruk ^{ki}u ^{d}Na-na-a il-la-ka*. An interesting parallel to this practice of decorating the image of a god is given by Mrs. Sinclair Stevenson in *The Heart of Jainism*, p. 251.

[414] *Ka-la-a-ta* may be regarded as permansive, feminine, singular, from *kalû*, 'withhold,' 'forbid.'

[415] For evidence that *al-la* has the meaning 'except' see *AENN* p. 24, note 1.

[416] For the meaning of *ištên-šu* see Streck, *Assurbanipal* II, p. 62, line 54, note g; Böhl, *Die Sprache der Amarnabriefe*, *LSS* V, 1, p. 38; Ungnad, *Babylonsich-assyrische Grammatik*, 2nd edition, p. 39, g.

[417] *Ṭi-ir-du* is from *ṭarâdu* 'drive away,' 'drive off.' Arabic *ṭard* means 'expulsion,' 'repudiation.'

te-liš[418] *a-na tar-ṣi* ^{md}*Nergal-šar-uṣur* ^{32}*ištên-šu ki-i ta-an-na-ad-nu* ^{md}*Nergal-šar-uṣur ki-i iš-mu-ú ik-te-liš* ^{33}*ù ina šatti 1*^{kam} ^{md}*Nabû-nâ'id šar Bâbili*^{ki} ^{amêl} ^{âl} ^{d}*Bêlti-ia-a-a*[419] ^{34}*[ina] Larsa*^{ki} *a-na šarri bêli-i-ni ki-i iq-bu-ú šarru bêlu-a-ni* ^{35}*[amêlu] ša a-na muḫ-ḫi iq-ba-aš-šu iṭ-ṭi-ru ù šarru bêlu-a-ni* ^{36}*[ul iq]-bi um-ma in-na*[420] ^{amêl}*dupšarru* ^{m}*Na-di-nu* ^{37}*[apil-šu ša]* ^{md}*Bêl-aḫê*^{meš}*-iqîša(-ša) apil* ^{m}*E-gi-bi Uruk*^{ki} ^{araḫ}*Araḫsamnu* ^{38}*ûmu 23*^{kam} *šattu 6*^{kam} ^{d}*Nabû-nâ'id šar Bâbili*^{ki}.

^{1}Nabû-shar-uṣur, the chief officer of the king (who is) the chief guardian of Êanna, ^{2}to Bêl-uballiṭ, the son of Mushallim-Marduk, son of Gimil-Nanâ, ^{3}Balâṭu, the son of Shumâ, son of Iddin-Papsukal, ^{4}Marduk-shum-iddin, the son of Nabû-aḫê-bulliṭ, son of Balâṭu, ^{5}Shadûnu, the son of Mushêzib-Bêl, son of Nûr-Sin, ^{6}Nabû-êṭir-napshâti, the son of Ardi-Bêl, son of Egibi, ^{7}Nâdinu, the son of Aplâ, son of Ahê-iau, ^{8}Mushallim-Marduk, the son of Ardi-Nabû, son of the priest of Nabû, ^{9}Nabû-êṭir-napshâti, the son of Bêl-iqîsha, son of Bêl-apal-uṣur, ^{10}Ibni-Ishtar, the son of Nabû-zêr-ukîn, son of the fuller, ^{11}Innin-shum-uṣur, the son of Iddin-Nabû, son of Kidin-Marduk, ^{12}Aḫulâpîa, the son of Bêl-shum-ishkun, son of Bêl-apal-uṣur, ^{13}Bêlshunu, the son of Nabû-aḫê-iddin, son of Egibi, ^{14}Nabû-bâni-aḫi, the son of Nabû-balâṭsu-iqbi, son of Sin-lîq-unnînni, ^{15}Shamash-shum-ukîn, the son of Shulâ, son of the surveyor, ^{16}Ina-Êsagila-zêr, the son of Sha-pî-Bêl, son of Amêl-Êa, ^{17}Nabû-mushêtiq-urra, the son of Bêl-rimanni, son of Egibi, ^{18}Babylonians, Erechians, *IGI* officers, the *TU-Ê* officer, and the assembly ^{19}of Eanna spoke as follows: "The son of the king has sent a message, ^{20}saying, '(As to) their two vestments which from upon the Nanâ ^{21}of Êzida come down and upon the

[418] The verb *ik-te-liš* is evidently from *kalû*, the verbal root from which *ka-la-a-ta* in line 24 is derived The final sibilant is the pronominal suffix. For *kalû*, 'verweigern,' 'verwehren,' see *Hwb* p. 328.

[419] The term ^{amêl} ^{âl} ^{d}*Bêlti-ia-a-a* should be compared with ^{d}*Bêlti a-šib-ti Uruk*^{ki} in line 23. The latter term seems to be contrasted with ^{d}*Bêlit ša Uruk*^{ki} *u* ^{d}*Na-na-a* (line 21), the common designation for Ishtar who was worshipped in Êanna. Thus there is evidence that two rival cults of Ishtar existed in Erech. One was represented by the temple Êanna; the other was represented by the group who worshipped 'the Bêltu dwelling in Erech.' That there was a similar divergent cult of Ishtar in Larsa is indicated by the expression ^{amêl} ^{âl} ^{d}*Bêlti-ia-a-a ina Larsa*^{ki}. The term ^{âl} ^{d}*Bêlti-ia*, 'the city of My Lady,' in line 28 should be noted. See *LCE* 153: 15 for a reference to three ^{âl} ^{d}*Bêlti-ia*. These intimations of a secondary Ishtar cult are interesting. Its devotees wished to use the vestments belonging to the main Ishtar cult, probably for the purpose of gaining greater prestige. Our text indicates that this religious schism was brought to the attention of three Neo-Babylonian kings and that Belshazzar also had to deal with it. It seems fairly certain that heterodox Ishtar worship did not meet with royal favor.

[420] In Neo-Babylonian letters the imperative of *nadânu*, 'give,' is written *in-na-'*, *in-ni-i*, as well as *i-din*. See Martin, *Lettres Néo-Babyloniennes*, p. 180.

Bêltu of Erech and Nanâ [22]go, according to what they say with reference to the fact that they come down, one of them [23]shall be given to the Bêltu dwelling in Erech. [24]But, behold! it has been held back; how is it that it has been held back?'[421] [25]Investigate and send word letting me know and I shall send (the message) unto the son of the king." [26]The Babylonians and Erechians, *IGI* officers, the *TU-Ê* officer, and the assembly [27]of Êanna to Nabû-shar-uṣur, the chief officer of the king, the chief guardian of Êanna, [28]spoke as follows: "(There has been) no giving of a vestment from Êanna to the city of Bêltîa, [29]but the first time[422] in the time of Nebuchadrezzar, when Êṭir-Marduk, [30]the keeper of the temples, gave it, the repudiation concerning the matter was established thus: [31]Nebuchadrezzar, when he heard, held it back. In the time of Neriglissar, [32]when it was given the first time, Neriglissar, when he heard, held it back. [33]Furthermore, in the first year of Nabonidus, king of Babylon, when the residents of the city of Bêltîa [34]in Larsa spoke to the king, our lord, the king, our lord, [35]spared the man who addressed him concerning the matter, but the king, our lord, [36]did not say 'Give' " Scribe: Nâdinu, [37]the son of Bêl-aḫê-iqîsha, son of Egibi. Erech, the month Marchesvan, [38]the twenty-third day, the sixth year of Nabonidus, the king of Babylon.

The above text shows that an important inquiry concerning the use of temple paraphernalia in Erech was made by Belshazzar in the sixth year of the reign of Nabonidus. The inquiry was addressed to the chief officer of the king, Nabû-shar-uṣur, who communicated it to the prominent officials of the temple represented by sixteen persons mentioned by name. As a result the records were investigated for the purpose of determining the precedents set by Nebuchadrezzar, Neriglissar and Nabonidus. A decision made by Nabonidus in the first year of his reign is recorded. The whole document is meaningless if Nabonidus was present in Babylon at the time. The implications of the record can be explained best by the supposition that the king

[421] It may be that the words 'But, behold! it has been held back; how is it that it has been held back?' do not belong to the message of the son of the king. They may be construed as a part of the message of Nabû-shar-uṣur. This uncertainty has little effect upon the interpretation of the text, although the message of the son of the king is stronger with the words added. It is also possible that the message of the son of the king ended with the words 'But, behold! it has been held back,' and that the words 'How is it that it has been held back?' belong to the message of Nabû-shar-uṣur. In any case the import of the document is clear.

[422] See note 416.

was at a distance from the central seat of Babylonian government. Only in this way can we understand why such a weighty administrative matter was attended to by Belshazzar and why a precedent established by his father, the reigning monarch, was quoted impersonally along with those of Nebuchadrezzar and Neriglissar. These facts furnish evidence that Nabonidus was absent from Babylonia in the sixth[422a] as well as in the seventh, ninth, tenth, and eleventh years of his reign.

The authority possessed by Belshazzar is indicated by this text. His message was received with deference by the chief officer of the king at Erech. The highest officials of the city, described as Babylonians, Erechians, the assembly of the temple, etc., when apprised of Belshazzar's communication, made a careful investigation of all precedents in order that a thorough report might be made. This means that he was accorded the obedience due to royal command. The following cuneiform passages furnish additional instances of Belshazzar's power to issue orders.

6. Records of Commands Given by Belshazzar

Two cuneiform records in the form of commercial documents and three in the form of letters show that Belshazzar gave independent

[422a] Further indication of Belshazzar's position in the sixth year of Nabonidus is furnished by *VS* VI, 70: 1–8. The passage is as follows: ^{md}*Nabû . . . .* [*apil*] *-šu ša* ^{md}*Nabû-muk-e-lip a-na* ^{md}*Nabû . . . . apil-šu ša* ^{m}*Ṭâb-šar-Ê-sag-ila* ^{amêl}*mâr šipri ša* ^{amêl}*mâr šarri ù* ^{md}*Nabû-zêr-iddin apil-šu ša* ^{md}*Nabû-êriba* ^{amêl}*di-ku-ú ša* ^{amêl}*BAN*$^{[\text{meš}]}$ *ša eš-še-ti ša bît ri-du-tu ki-a-am iq-bi um-ma il-ku ul al-lak . . . .* ^{amêl}*BAN šu-ṭur-a-in-ni-ma* [*il*]*-ki ša* ^{amêl}*mâr šarri lil-lik*, 'Nabû . . . . , the son of Nabû-muk-elip, to Nabû . . . . , the son of Ṭâb-shar-Êsagila, the messenger of the son of the king, and Nabû-zêr-iddin, the son of Nabû-êriba, the enlistment officer of bowmen who (are on duty in connection with) the renovation of the administrative palace, spoke as follows: "I am not engaged in any service. . . . . Enroll me as a bowman and I shall enter upon the service of the son of the king." ' Since Meissner has presented good reasons (*ZA* X, p. 75) that *bît ri-du-tu* denotes 'Regierungspalast' and not 'Harem,' the above text, which was written on the twenty-fourth day of Tishri in the sixth year of Nabonidus' reign, may be interpreted as intimating very strongly that Belshazzar was occupying the royal palace in Babylon in that year. See, however, *ZA* X, p. 243, for Jensen's opposition to Meissner's explanation of *bît ri-du-tu*. Nevertheless, the meaning 'administrative palace' is quite possible. At any rate the record under consideration accords with the view that Nabonidus was in Têmâ in the sixth year of his reign. That a Babylonian, whose name has not been preserved, volunteered to serve Belshazzar as a bowman is interesting.

orders that certain things should be done. It must be admitted that these orders, so far as we are able to judge them, appear to deal with commonplace matters. In this respect they do not reveal much of statesmanship, but the fact that very high officials received and executed the commands of Belshazzar is not without significance.

(1) *An Action Performed at the Command of Belshazzar*

[1][md]*Bêl-uballiṭ(-iṭ) apil-šu ša* [m]*Mušallim-*[d]*Marduk apil* [m]*Gimil-*[d]*Na-na-a* [2][m]*A-a-i-ga-a-šu* [amêl]*šaqû šarri* [md]*In-nin-zêr-ušabši(-ši)* [3]*apil-šu ša* [m]*Ap-la-a apil* [md]*Sin-lîq-unnînni* [m]*Êṭir-*[d]*Marduk* [4]*apil-šu ša* [md]*Bêl-uballiṭ(-iṭ) apil* [m]*Amêl-*[d]*Ê-a* [m]*Kal-ba-a* [5]*apil-šu ša* [m]*Aḫê*[meš]*-ša-a* [amêl]*mârê*[meš]*bânî-ia ša ina manzazi-šu-nu* [6][md]*A-num-aḫê*[meš]*-uṣur* [amêl]*mâr šipri ša mâr šarri* [7]*a-na* [md]*Nabû-šar-uṣur* [amêl]*šaqî šarri* [amêl]*bêl pi-qit-tum* [8]*Ê-an-na iq-bu-ú um-ma 2 liâti rabâti* [[meš]] [9]*1 littu ṣiḫirtu napḫaru 3 liâti alpê*[zun] *ša ina qa-bu-ut-tum* [10]*ša* [d]*Bêlit ša Uruk*[ki] *ša ina pâni* [m]*Ba-ni-ia* [11]*apil-šu ša* [md]*Marduk-êriba* [md]*Ba-ú-êṭir* [12]*apil-šu ša*[m]*Ba-ni-ia ki-i ú-kal-li-man-nu*[423] [13]*ina a-mat mâr šarri ki-i a-bu-ku a-na* [14][md]*Ba-ú-êṭir ap-te-qi-id* [15]*u* [md]*Ba-ú-êṭir a-na* [md]*Nabû-šar-uṣur iq-bu-ú* [16]*um-ma liâti rabâti-ám 3-ta ša* [md]*A-num-aḫê*[me]*-uṣur* [17][amêl]*mâr šipri ša mâr šarri ip-qi-du* [m]*Ap-la-a* [18]*apil-šu ša* [md]*Nabû-tab-ni-uṣur a-na ši-gi-il-tu*[424] [19]*ina qâti-ia i-ta-bak* [20][amêl]*dupšarru* [m]*Na-din apil-šu ša* [md]*Bêl-aḫê*[meš]*-iqîša(-ša)* [21]*apil* [m]*E-gi-bi Uruk*[ki] [araḫ]*Araḫsamnu* [22]*ûmu 16*[kam] *šattu 10*[kam] [d]*Nabû-nâ'id šar Bâbili*[ki].[425]

[1]Bêl-uballiṭ, the son of Mushallim-Marduk, son of Gimil-Nanâ, [2]Âigâshu, a chief officer of the king, Innin-zêr-ushabshi, [3]the son of Aplâ, son of Sin-lîq-unnînni, Êṭir-Marduk, [4]the son of Bêl-uballiṭ, son of Amêl-Êa, Kalbâ, [5]the son of Aḫê-shâ, *mârê bânîa*, in whose presence [6]Anum-aḫê-uṣur, the messenger of the son of the king, [7]to Nabû-shar-uṣur, the chief officer of the king (who is) chief guardian [8]of Êanna, spoke as follows: "(As to) the two large cows [9](and) one small cow, a total of three cows, which are of the fold [10]of the Bêltu of Erech, which are at the disposal of Bânîa, [11]the son of Marduk-êriba, when Bau-êṭir, [12]the son of Bânîa, showed (them), [13]at the command of the son of the king I took (them, and) to [14]Bau-êṭir I entrusted (them)." [15]Then Bau-êṭir spoke to Nabû-shar-uṣur [16]as follows: "(As to) the three large cows which Anum-aḫê-uṣur, [17]the agent of the son of the king,

[423] It seems that the verb *ú-kal-li-man-nu* ought to end with *ni* instead of *nu*, as one would expect the pronominal suffix of the first person, singular, but the cuneiform text has been copied correctly.

[424] The form *šigiltu* stands for *šigištu* from the root *šaqâšu*, 'slay.' See *CD* p. 1103.

[425] *REN* 131: 1–22.

entrusted (to me), Aplâ, [18]the son of Nabû-tabni-uṣur, for slaughtering [19]took (them) from me." [20]Scribe: Nâdin, the son of Bêl-aḫê-iqîsha, [21]son of Egibi. Erech, the month Marchesvan, [22]the sixteenth day, the tenth year of Nabonidus, the king of Babylon.

This tablet, more by its general tone than by its contents, reveals the position of authority occupied by Belshazzar in the tenth year of Nabonidus' reign, at a time when Nabonidus was at Têmâ. The text records a statement of the official messenger of Belshazzar to the same chief officer of the king referred to in the preceding document, in the presence of five prominent persons, one of whom was another chief officer of the king. It is apparent that the inscription deals with a transaction which was under the jurisdiction of Belshazzar and which it was necessary to submit to him for his approval. The phrase *ina amât mâr šarri*, 'at the command of the son of the king,' should be compared with *ina amât šarri*, 'at the command of the king,' the usual Babylonian phrase denoting royal command. The official ^{amêl}*mâr šipri ša mâr šarri*, 'the messenger of the son of the king,' is additional evidence that Belshazzar was a man who had control of affairs.

(2) Belshazzar Issues an Order with Reference to the Shepherding of Sheep

[6]*Ina qi-ba-a-tum* ^{md}*Bêl-šar-uṣur mâr šarri* ^{m}*Zêri-ia* ^{amêl}*šatammu Ê-an-na* [7]*apil-šu ša* ^{m}*Ib-na-a apil* ^{m}*E-gi-bi ù* ^{amêl}*šangê*^{meš} *Ê-an-na* [8]*ṣi-e-ni-ám 2036 a-na ri-'-i-tum* [9]*a-na* ^{md}*Na-na-a-aḫ-iddin apil-šu ša* ^{m}*La-a-qi-pi id-di-nu.*[426]

[6]At the command of Belshazzar, the son of the king, Zêrîa, the administrator of Êanna, [7]the son of Ibnâ, son of Egibi, and the priests of Êanna, [8, 9]gave sheep, numbering two thousand and thirty-six, to Nanâ-aḫ-iddin, the son of Lâqîpi, for shepherding.

This cuneiform passage is part of an extensive record dealing with the rental of sheep and goats. The above lines indicate that Belshazzar ordered the supreme temple officials at Erech to give a large number of sheep to a certain individual for pasturing. Belshazzar's position of authority is shown by the fact that they obeyed. The phrase *ina qibâtum* has the same force as *ina amât* in the preceding text.

[426] *REN* 155: 6–9. This text is dated in the twelfth year of Nabonidus' reign.

(3) *Belshazzar Sends a Letter Containing an Order*

[1]*Duppi* ^{d}*Bêl-šar-uṣur mâr šarri a-na* [2]^{md}*Nabû-šar-uṣur ilâni*^{meš} [3]*šú-lum-ka liq-bu-ú a-na eli* [4]*ḫurâṣi šú-ú ša aš-pur-rak-ka* [5]*um-ma i-ša-am-ma a-na dul-lu* [6]*ša Ê-kur šú-kun a-mur* ^{md}*Bêl-uballiṭ(-iṭ)* [7]^{amêl}*za-zak-ku a-na pâni-ka al-tap-ra* [8]*ḫurâṣa ma-la ir-ri-šú-ka* [9]*in-na-aš-šim-ma*[427] [10]*dul-lu li-pu-uš.*[428]

[1]Letter of Belshazzar, the son of the king, unto [2]Nabû-shar-uṣur. May the gods [3]decree thy prosperity! With reference to [4]that gold concerning which I sent thee a message [5]as follows: "Hold (it) and for the work [6]of the temple deposit (it)," behold, Bêl-uballiṭ, [7]the *zazakku,*[429] I have sent unto thee. [8]As much money as he asks of thee [9]give him and [10]let him do work.

The remaining section of the letter, lines 11 to 19, contains additional references to gold, but the complete sense is difficult to determine. One may feel reasonably certain, however, that the letter with its specific directions was addressed to the Nabû-shar-uṣur who was the chief officer of the king at Erech.

(4) *A Letter which Quotes an Order from Belshazzar*

[1]*Duppi* ^{md}*Nabû-šar-uṣur a-na* [2]^{amêl}*ša-ku abi-iá* ^{d}*Nabû u* ^{d}*Marduk* [3]*ana abi-iá liq-ru-bu* [4]*ši-pir-tum ša mâr šarri* [5]*a-na pâni-iá ta-at-tal-ku* [6]*um-ma 20 ma-na ḫurâṣi* [7]*ḫi-ri-i-ma a-na dul-lu* [8]*ina Ê-an-na e-pu-uš* [9]*ù 1 ma-na ḫurâṣi* [10]*ša* ^{d}*Bêlit ša Uruk*^{ki} *ina muḫ-ḫi* [11]^{m}*Ki-na-a apil-šu ša* ^{m}*Ra-ḫaṣ* [12]*ina lib-bi ša ana šu-a-šu* [13]*a-na muḫ-ḫi* [14]*a-na bêli-iá aq-bu-ú* [15]*ki-i a-na mâr šarri* [16]*a-na muḫ-ḫi lâ aš-pu-ru* [17]*en-na a-ki* ^{md}*Bêl-ibni* [18]*ù* ^{md}*Marduk-šum-lîšir* [19]*a-na bêli-iá al-tap-ra* [20]*ḫurâṣa-ám 1 ma-na* [21]*ul-tu bît* ^{m}*Ki-na-a* [22]*bêl liš-šam-ma a-na* [23]*Ê-an-na bêl lu-še-bi-la.*[430]

[1]Letter of Nabû-shar-uṣur unto [2]the *šaku* officer, my father. May Nabû and Marduk [3]be gracious unto my father! [4]A message of the son of the king [5]has come unto me [6]as follows: "Twenty minas of gold [7]divert (from the treasury) and for the work [8]in Êanna perform service." [9]However, one mina of gold [10]of the Bêltu of Erech (is charged) against [11]Kinâ, the son of Raḫaṣ. [12]Out of that which (is) for him [13]concerning it [14]I said unto my

[427] The form *in-na-aš-šim-ma* is not derived from *našû,* 'bring,' etc., but from *nadânu,* 'give.' The form is the imperative with the pronominal suffix. See Martin, *Lettres Néo-Babyloniennes,* p. 146, no. 215, lines 12–14, for the following: *ŠE-BAR ma-la i-riš-šú-ú-ka in-na-aš-šu,* 'tout le grain qu'il te demandera, donne-lui.'

[428] *ContCL* 136: 1–10.

[429] Exact meaning unknown.

[430] *ContCL* 132: 1–23.

lord [15]that unto the son of the king [16]concerning it I did not send (word). [17]Now, accordingly, Bêl-ibni [18]and Marduk-shum-lîshir [19]I have dispatched unto my lord. [20]The gold, amounting to one mina, [21]from the house of Kinâ, [22]may (my) lord take and unto [23]Êanna may (my) lord deliver (it)!

That the above letter is a document from Erech is indicated by the following: (*a*) mention of Êanna, the temple in Erech, and (*b*) reference to the Bêltu of Erech. In addition, the personal names are in harmony with this provenance of the text. Hence one is driven to the inference that the Nabû-shar-uṣur of this cuneiform record represents the person by that name who was chief officer of the king and chief guardian of the temple in Erech in the reign of Nabonidus. This suggests that the son of the king mentioned in the letter was none other than Belshazzar.[431] He sent an order to Nabû-shar-uṣur that twenty minas of gold should be used for work in the temple of Êanna. It seems that one mina of this amount had been placed at the disposal of Kinâ without informing the son of the king. Hence Nabû-shar-uṣur requested that it be removed from the house of Kinâ and brought to Êanna.

(*5*) *Belshazzar Sends a Letter Containing an Urgent Command*

[1]*Duppi* [md]*Bêl-šar-uṣur* [2]*a-na* [md]*Nabû-šar-uṣur* [3]*ilâni*[meš] *šú-lum-ka* [4]*liq-bu-ú* [5]*ū-mu ši-pir-ta-a* [6]*ta-mu-ra nu-bat-tum* [7]*lâ ta-ba-a-tum* [8]*u* [amêl]*ṣabê*[meš] *TU-Ê* [9][amêl]*AB-BA*[meš] [10]*ša mil-ki* [11]*ša lâ man-zal-la-ti-šu-nu* [12]*it-ti-ka* [13]*ab-ka* [14]*ù kab-du* [15]*al-ka.*[432]

[1]Letter of Belshazzar [2]unto Nabu-shar-uṣur. [3, 4]May the gods decree thy prosperity! [5–7]On the day when thou seest my message do not observe a holiday, [8]but[433] the *TU-Ê*[434] staff,[435] [9, 10]the advisory elders,[436] [11]without their *manzallâti*,[437] [12, 13]bring with you [14, 15]and come quickly.

431 It should be noted, however, that Nabû-shar-uṣur kept his position as chief officer of the king until the eighth year of Cyrus. See *RECC* 70: 18. There may be some uncertainty, therefore, as to whether the *mâr šarri* of the text refers to Belshazzar.

432 *ContCL* 137: 1–15.

433 The sign *u* also means 'ten.' It may be that it is used in this sense in the text.

434 See note 410.

435 The [amêl]*ṣâbê*[meš] of a particular kind of work would constitute a staff of workers.

436 Literally 'elders of advice.' See *B* 3821.

437 The word *manzallâti* seems to be the plural of *manzaltu*, 'station,' 'position,' 'office.' The sense in which the term is used in the text is obscure.

That the above letter was written to the same Nabû-shar-uṣur mentioned in the previous letters seems certain. The tone of the message sent by Belshazzar indicates that some important emergency impelled him to send a communication to the chief officer of the king at Erech. It is possible that political affairs required the help of Êanna's board of counselors at the center of jurisdiction where Belshazzar happened to be. There is nothing in the letter opposed to the view that Nabû-shar-uṣur and the temple's elders were summoned to Babylon. If this interpretation is correct, the letter may represent an administrative crisis involving aggressive initiative on the part of Belshazzar, and at the same time requiring extensive deliberative action.

7. *Summary of Data*

Inscriptions of varied type have been adduced as proof that Belshazzar was an administrator of government in Babylonia during Nabonidus' absence in Arabia. The historical texts quoted are of fundamental importance, since the two inscriptions available for interpretation, viz., *A Persian Verse Account of Nabonidus* and the *Nabonidus Chronicle*, contain statements which are not contradictory, but which lead to the same conclusion. One of the records is a descriptive account; the other is an annalistic chronicle. This difference in their character as literature adds significance to the fact that they supplement and corroborate one another so adequately. The former indicates that Nabonidus conquered Têmâ and made it his residence in the third year of his reign; the latter shows that Nabonidus was in the Westland soon after he became king and that he was at Têmâ in the seventh, ninth, tenth, and eleventh years of his reign. Each inscription, unsupported by the other, is sufficient to demonstrate Belshazzar's administrative position in Babylonia during the period when Nabonidus was interested in Têmâ. Their combined testimony is authentic evidence of the highest value.

Another type of Neo-Babylonian literature, viz., records of business transactions dated in the reign of Nabonidus, have been found to reveal the same historical situation. The validity of the contents of contract tablets is unquestioned. Coming from ancient archives, these documents are genuine and reliable. Each tablet represents a transaction which occurred at a certain time and place. The interested persons are mentioned by name, temple officials often participating in the agreement which is recorded. These considerations emphasize the worth of the two texts which show that there was contact by means of camel transportation between Erech and Têmâ during the reign of Nabonidus. A Neo-Babylonian sphere of influence in the heart of Arabia is indicated. The inscription which refers to the fact that food for the king was taken to Têmâ in the tenth year of Nabonidus is direct corroboration of the information conveyed by the *Nabonidus Chronicle*. Data presented by the two leases of land, one from the king himself in the first year of Nabonidus' reign and one from Belshazzar in the eleventh year of his father's reign, may be regarded as throwing a great deal of light upon the period. Belshazzar is portrayed as exercising a jurisdiction which was Nabonidus' prerogative before he went to Têmâ. Very suggestive are the two texts which record orders issued by Belshazzar in the tenth and twelfth years of Nabonidus' reign, but they do not possess as much weight as if the commands dealt with general administrative matters. On the whole, the contract tablets which have been quoted authenticate what has been learned from historical sources concerning Nabonidus' stay in Arabia and Belshazzar's consequent position of authority in Babylonia.

The duplicate texts dealing with the use of religious paraphernalia at Erech represent a third type of reliable cuneiform inscriptions containing information having an important bearing upon the rôles played by Nabonidus and Belshazzar. It must be remembered that a Babylonian wielding sovereignty over the nation was the representative of the gods and the religious head of the people. There are strong indications that the ultimate appeal in any controversy as to the ceremonial of worship or the employment of cult objects was to the throne. In the sixth year of the reign of Nabonidus such an appeal was made to Belshazzar. He referred the matter to the assembly of Êanna, although Larsa as well as Erech was interested in the question at stake. The right of Belshazzar to investigate and to demand an explanation is recognized in the detailed record of the affair. A reasonable interpretation of the document requires the assumption that Nabonidus was not in Babylonia at the time when the religious crisis in two of the most important cities of his kingdom arose. If he had been, it would not have been appropriate for Belshazzar to give attention to the settlement of the contention. Therefore, this administrative record, of which two copies are available, confirms that which is revealed by the above-mentioned historical and commercial documents.

Letters comprise a fourth type of cuneiform literature connected intimately with the present inquiry. The value of personal messages as criteria of individual experiences and political situations is recognized. At the same time, this class of inscriptions is generally characterized by terseness of language, inasmuch as a great deal is taken for granted by the writer of a letter. Obtuseness in meaning often results. In spite of this handicap Babylonian literature of the epistolary type yields much information. If considered apart from other data, the three letters quoted above, two from Belshazzar and one possibly referring to him, could not prove very much. Linked with the other Belshazzar texts, they gain new meaning and are therefore valuable as auxiliary proof. The urgent message in which Belshazzar summons the temple elders of Erech along with a prominent Babylonian, proved by other texts to have been a chief officer of the king, is exceptionally capable of an interpretation entirely in harmony with the exalted position occupied by the eldest son of Nabonidus.

Hence the different types of cuneiform literature, which deal in any way with the question of Belshazzar's participation in governmental administration during Nabonidus' absence in Arabia, are in complete agreement. It should be noted, however, that no cuneiform text applies the term *šarru* to Belshazzar. His title remains *mâr šarri*, 'the son of the king.' The title *šarru*, 'king,' is ascribed to Nabonidus as the real sovereign. A text in the Yale Babylonian Collection indicates that Belshazzar was subject to the commands of Nabonidus. The pertinent passage is as follows:

[1] *[še]Zêru ša [d]Bêl ša ina [araḫ]Nisanni šattu 7[kam] [d]Nabû-nâ'id* [2] *šar Bâbili[ki] [md]Bêl-šar-uṣur mâr šarri* [3] *ina a-mat šarri a-na [amêl]rabûti[meš] GIŠ-BAR[meš] ú-za-'-i-zu.*[438]

[438] *REN* 103: 1–3. See line 7 of this text for an additional occurrence of *mâr šarri.*

[1]The seed field of the god Bêl, which in the month Nisan of the seventh year of Nabonidus, [2]the king of Babylon, Belshazzar, the son of the king, [3]at the command of the king divided for the tax-masters.

It is specifically stated in the *Nabonidus Chronicle* that Nabonidus was in Têmâ in the seventh year of his reign and that he did not come to Babylon for the festival in the month of Nisan.[439] Hence the passage just quoted shows that Nabonidus while in Têmâ issued a command to Belshazzar in Babylonia and that this command was carried out. It is very evident that Nabonidus, although absent from Babylonia, did not relinquish his position as first ruler in the empire. All the fully-dated documents of his reign specify him as king. Furthermore, when Nabonidus and Belshazzar are mentioned together, precedence is never given to the latter. This detracts in no wise, however, from the royal rôle played by Belshazzar. Nabonidus himself states that he entrusted *šarrûtam*, 'the kingship,' or 'the kingdom,' to his eldest son.[440] Belshazzar was undoubtedly the second ruler in the land.

[439] See p. 111f.

[440] See p. 106. Although cuneiform inscriptions do not refer to Belshazzar as *šarru*, it is worthy of note that the title *mâr šarri* as applied to the firstborn son of the king seems to have had special significance. If a king had more than one son, each was designated *mâr šarri*. However, the title by itself does not appear to have been ascribed to a second or third son. In such instances the name of the son appears with the title. See note 325. On the other hand, the firstborn son of the King was referred to as *mâr šarri* without the mention of his name, and this indicates the independent force of the title as applied to him.

XI

CONJECTURAL REASONS FOR NABONIDUS' STAY AT TÊMÂ

No deciding statement concerning the purpose of Nabonidus' extended stay at Têmâ in Arabia is furnished by any of the inscriptions which deal with this historical episode. Conjecture holds full sway in attempts to determine the motive which actuated a Babylonian king in making an emporium of Arabia his official residence during a large part of his reign. Discussion of the various theories which have been propounded should be introduced by a summary of what is known concerning Têmâ.

1. *The Oasis of Têmâ in Arabia*

The location of the city of Têmâ, where Nabonidus, as has been demonstrated, had his court during a large part of his reign, requires consideration. A site outside of Babylonia at some distance from the capital of the empire, with intervening desert terrain, is suggested by the cuneiform inscriptions which have been discussed. The famous oasis of Têmâ in Arabia is the sole spot capable of satisfying all the demands of the situation.

So far as records indicate, no attempt to identify the *^{al}Te-ma-a* of the *Nabonidus Chronicle* with the city of Têmâ in Arabia was made prior to 1921.[441] Tiele in 1886 saw that *^{al}Te-ma-a* must be sought outside the bounds of Akkad, but came to the conclusion that it could not be regarded as the Arabian city by that name, although he suggested no proof for the latter inference beyond its apparent improbability.[442] At the same time he recognized the historical enigma presented by the absence of Nabonidus from Babylonia. Hagen in 1894 decided against the identification of the *^{al}Te-ma-a* of the *Nabonidus Chronicle* with Têmâ in Arabia. He advanced the theory that *^{al}Te-ma-a* was the favorite residence of Nabonidus in Babylonia outside the capital city, adducing the fact that it was customary for Babylonian kings to have special living quarters from which they

[441] See references in note 344 to the writer's publications dealing with this question. Note 345 refers to Sidney Smith's publication of the same conclusion.

[442] Tiele, *Babylonisch-assyrische Geschichte* I, p. 470f.

would depart for Babylon only at the time of the New Year's festival.[443] However, it has already been shown that the direct intimation of the record is that ^{al}*Te-ma-a* was not in Babylonia and that Nabonidus did not go to Babylon for the usual ceremonies at the beginning of the years during which he was at ^{al}*Te-ma-a.* This must mean that Nabonidus was at a considerable distance from the political center of his kingdom. Furthermore, Hagen concluded that ^{al}*Te-ma-a* must have been located in Babylonia on account of the building operations which Nabonidus credits to himself at Sippar, Ḫarrân, etc., during the years when he seems to have dwelt continuously at ^{al}*Te-ma-a.*[444] It is true that the building inscriptions of Nabonidus are very detailed in their accounts of operations, but it is not necessary to suppose that everything was done under direct royal supervision. It is probable that the work was in charge of special officers who made reports to the king from time to time. Nabonidus, even at Têmâ in Arabia, could have kept in touch with all the affairs of his domain, as an elaborate messenger service was maintained in ancient times. It is also likely that royal building inscriptions were written by trained scribes who could compose documents characterized by traditional standards of accuracy and excellence, even if the king were too far away to dictate in person.

The inscriptions of Tiglathpileser III (745–727 B. C.) are an aid in determining the geographical position of Têmâ, for the gentilic terms ^{al}*Te-ma-a-a,* $^{[al]}$*Ma-as-'-a-a,* and ^{al}*Sa-ba-'-a-a* are linked together in that part of the record dealing with Arabia.[445] The list of the sons of Ishmael in Genesis 25: 13–15 includes תימא and משא, and ^{al}*Sa-ba-'-a-a* may possibly be a gentilic expression related to שׁבא, Genesis 10: 7; 25: 3; Job 1: 15; 6: 19. No doubt need be felt concerning the identification of ^{mât}*Te-ma-a* with ארץ תימא, Isaiah 21:14. As early as 1881 Delitzsch associated the ^{al}*Te-ma-a-a* of Assyrian inscriptions with Biblical תימא and Arabic تَيْمَاء, *Teimâ,* a city in Arabia of known importance in the middle of the first milliennium

[443] *BA* II, p. 236f.

[444] *BA* II, p. 236f, note.

[445] III *R* 10, no. 2, 38; *KB* II, p. 20, line 53; Delitzsch, *Wo lag das Paradies?* p. 301f; Schrader, *KAT*³, p. 58. *Sebâ,* Gen. 10: 7, etc., has thus far been located in Africa.

B. C.[446] It is called Θαῖμα on Ptolemy's map of Arabia Felix. Thus the equivalence of Assyrian and Babylonian *[al]Te-ma-a,* Hebrew תימא, Greek Θαῖμα and Arabic تَيْمَاء is established with definiteness.

A convincing proof of the ancient culture and central position of Têmâ, half-way between Damascus and Mecca and equidistant from Babylonia and Egypt, is a monument known as the Têmâ Stone, bearing an early Aramaic inscription.[447] Cooke says, "Caravans (Job 6: 19) on their way to Egypt or Assyria halted here (*i.e.* at Têmâ); and the influence of commerce with these two countries is evident in this stone: the name of the priest's father is Egyptian, the figures of the god and his minister are Assyrian."[448] Another suggestion of Mesopotamian influence upon Têmâ is seen in certain words in the inscription supposed by some to have been borrowed from the Babylonians.[449] It is thought that the Têmâ stele belongs to the sixth century B. C.[450] and that the city enjoyed a high degree of civilization at that time, with its life colored largely by Babylonian and Egyptian influence.

We are indebted to modern explorers and archaeologists for detailed accounts concerning the city and its environs. Wallin's report of his visit to Têmâ in 1848 makes note of its favorable location, its mode of irrigation, and its excellent products.[451] Doughty, a generation later, reveals its attractive appearance, its prosperous condition, its good water supply, its valuable salt deposits, its height of 3400 ft. above sea level, its healthful climate, its extensive ruins, its ancient inscriptions, and its old importance as the center of a large province.[452] Hogarth emphasizes the fact that Têmâ was "on the old route from the Gulf of Akaba to the Persian Gulf" and that it was "a dividing point of roads from Petra to Gerra (on the Persian Gulf) in the east and Sheba in the south."[453]

[446] Delitzsch, *op. cit.*, p. 303.

[447] Cooke, *North Semitic Inscriptions*, pp. 195–199. See note 166.

[448] Cooke, *op. cit.*, p. 197. See Job 6:19.

[449] *BHT* p. 79f; *JAOS* XLII, p. 309.

[450] *Corpus Inscriptionum Semiticarum* II, Tome I, pp. 107–115.

[451] *Cyclopaedia of Biblical Literature* X, p. 242f.

[452] See *JAOS* XLII, p. 307f, notes 9–20 for the required references to Doughty, *Travels in Arabia Deserta*.

[453] Hogarth, *The Penetration of Arabia*, p. 280. See map on plate II.

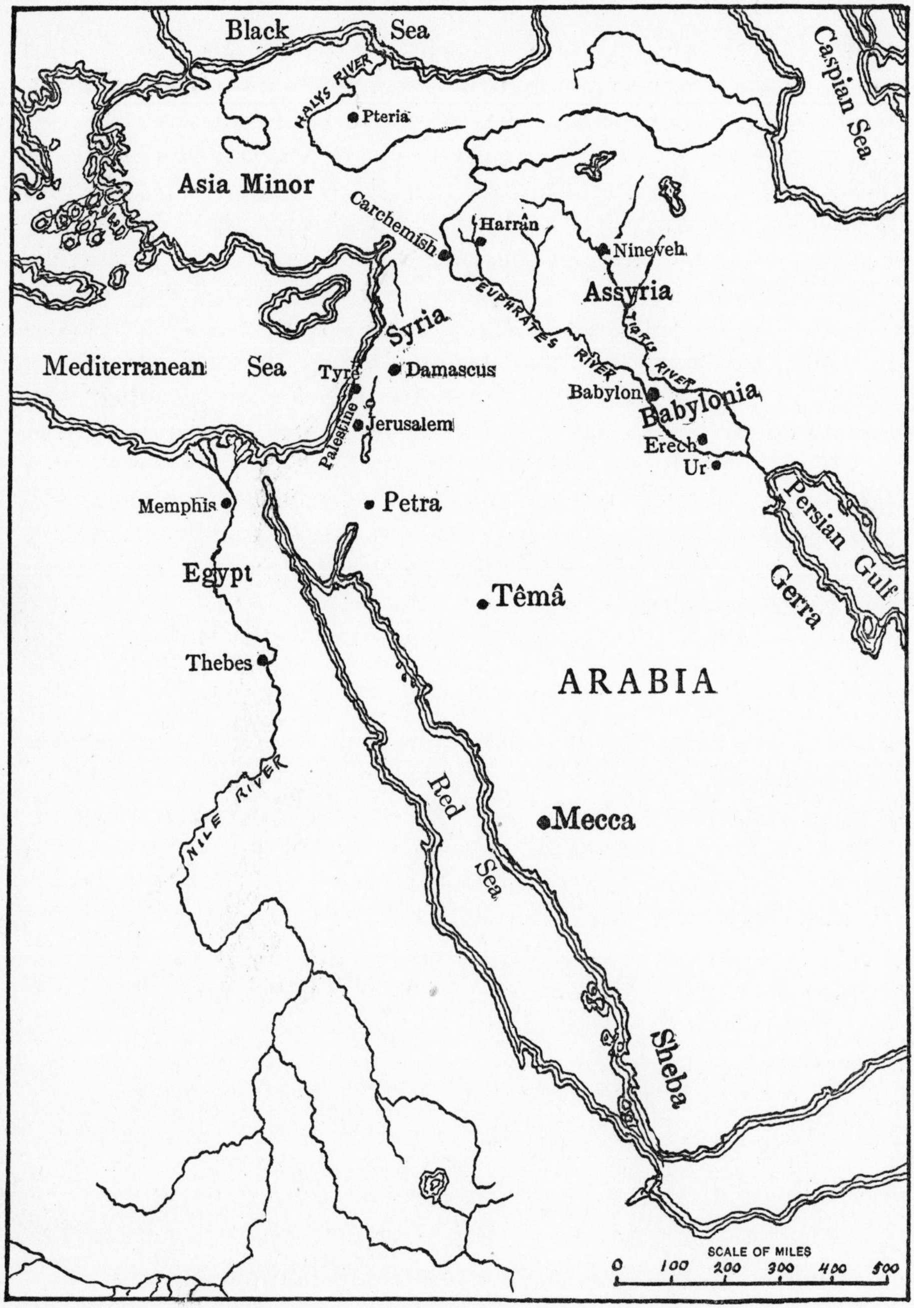

Map Showing Strategic Importance of Têmâ

The most recent contribution to our knowledge (*a*) of the ruins of Têmâ and (*b*) of the present condition of the oasis has been furnished by Jaussen and Savignac in *Mission Archéologique en Arabie.* A section of this scientific publication describes a visit to the site of ancient Têmâ in the spring of 1909.[454] The explorers found three centers of population in a wide valley extending from southeast to northwest. The greatest length of the whole settlement at that time was two or three kilometers, with an extreme width of four or five hundred meters.[455] The perimeter of the old encircling walls, now in ruins, was estimated by Doughty to be about three English miles, but Jaussen and Savignac came to the conclusion that it did not exceed three kilometers.[456] According to the two French investigators just quoted, the walls originated in the Aramaean, or pre-Arab period.[457] The *tumuli*, of which there are interesting examples, are regarded as pre-Islamic.[458] The modern condition of the oasis is extremely attractive. Flourishing gardens and groves furnish a wide variety of products, such as dates, peaches, figs, oranges, lemons, barley, and wheat.[459] Dates of superior quality are the main article of diet. The oasis is still one of the main trade centers of interior Arabia.[460] Its commercial prestige arises from the fact that it continues as the intersection of important caravan routes from north to south and from east to west. At the beginning of the Mohammedan era, in the time of Abû Bekr, Têmâ was a rendezvous for the troops which Khâlid ibn-Saʿîd assembled for the invasion of Palestine and Syria.[461] This is an indication that it was recognized at that time

[454] Consult volume II, pp. 109–165, of the publication by Jaussen and Savignac, quoted above, for *Excursion à Teïma.* Alois Musil was unable to visit Teima in 1909 (see Musil, *American Geographical Society, Oriental Explorations and Studies* I, p. 155; II, pp. 142f, 179f). Miss Gertrude L. Bell did not quite reach Teima in her journey across Arabia in 1913 (see map at end of volume I of *The Letters of Gertrude Bell*). The inhospitable disposition of the dwellers in Teima and its environs has been known for a long time.

[455] Jaussen and Savignac, *op. cit.*, p. 148.

[456] *Ibid.*, p. 151.

[457] *Ibid.*, p. 153.

[458] *Ibid.*, p. 155.

[459] *Ibid.*, p. 149f.

[460] *Ibid.*, p. 144. The king of the Hejâz at one time lived in Têmâ. See Moritz, *Arabien-Studien zur physikalischen und historischen Geographie des Landes*, p. 25.

[461] Jaussen and Savignac, *op. cit.*, p. 147.

as a notable city and that it was looked upon as the most suitable place for the concentration camp of the Arab army. These judgments harmonize with the rôle it played a thousand years earlier and explain the position which it occupies at the present time. Geographical facts and historical data agree in ascribing great importance to the city of Têmâ. Many reasons for Nabonidus' stay at Têmâ have been advanced. These will now be discussed.

2. The Influence of Military Strategy

It is natural to surmise, first of all, that Nabonidus' invasion of Arabia was inspired by imperial ambitions. For centuries the countries of the Westland had felt the tread of Assyrian and Babylonian armies. Cuneiform historical inscriptions, ranging in date through a large part of the initial half of the first millennium B. C., describe campaigns of conquest in Syria, Palestine, and Arabia.[462] There can be no doubt that a military interest in these lands became traditional in Mesopotamia. Nabonidus was by no means the originator of a new policy when he headed his troops westward. That this forceful encroachment by king after king constituted not an end in itself but a means to an end may be taken for granted. The general aim of obtaining revenue from tribute is implied by many texts. At the same time ability to carry out aggressive schemes of far-reaching importance was not lacking in ancient Oriental monarchs.

Nabonidus seems to have had plans for an expedition into Syria almost as soon as he became king. There is cuneiform proof that he levied his troops in the first year of his reign, but the text, because of its mutilated condition, has not preserved a statement with reference to his objective.[463] However, that he was in Syria in the second year of his reign is certain, and this suggests the goal which he had in mind when he mustered his forces during the previous year. It is of no little significance that Nabonidus began his reign with definite designs upon the Westland. His policy cannot be said to have been weak and flabby, for he exhibited energy and decision when he had once embarked upon it. Whether it was his original purpose to extend his operations to include the land of Têmâ cannot be deter-

[462] Luckenbill, *Ancient Records of Assyria and Babylonia*, I and II.
[463] *Nabonidus Chronicle*, col. I, line 7. See *BHT* pp. 111 and 114.

mined. He must have regarded Syria and Palestine as thoroughly mastered or else he would not have ventured into the heart of Arabia in the third year of his reign.

Nabonidus did not proceed to Têmâ upon a peaceful mission. That he subdued the city by force of arms is indicated by definite cuneiform statements. The military power of Babylonia accompanied him. He could hardly have advanced otherwise in a strange and difficult land even if ruthless conquest had not been his avowed intention. Very suggestive are the words: 'Towards Têmâ in the midst of the Westland he set his face.'[464] There was nothing haphazard or aimless in the Arabian campaign of Nabonidus. For some reason or other Têmâ attracted his attention; the wresting of its oasis from local control dominated his plans; the thorough vanquishment and virtual annihilation of its inhabitants were deemed necessary by him. 'He slew the prince of Têmâ with the [sword]; the dwellers in his city (and) country, all of them they slaughtered.'[465] When all this had been accomplished, Nabonidus did not leave Têmâ and return to Babylon. He established his residence in the garden-spot which he had acquired by warfare, the language of the text indicating that he changed Têmâ into a Babylonian city.[466] This sequel to his Arabian expedition suggests that some important motive dominated the mind of Nabonidus.

(1) Could Nabonidus have been influenced by the realization that *a necessity for protection against Egypt* faced his empire? Was he merely trying to implant his rule in the region of Têmâ or was he endeavoring to establish a strong center in Arabia for the purpose of curbing any tendency on the part of Egypt to strike at Babylonia? Only twelve years before Nabonidus became king, according to the Strassmaier text already quoted, Nebuchadrezzar in the thirty-seventh year of his reign felt it necessary to make an expedition against Amasis, king of Egypt.[467] This same Pharaoh governed Egypt during the whole of Nabonidus' reign. Might not the Babylonian king have thought of using Têmâ as a base from which he could threaten any Egyptian army that attempted to invade his domain?

[464] *BHT* pp. 84 and 88, col. II, line 23.
[465] *Ibid.*, col. II, lines 25 and 26.
[466] *Ibid.*, col. II, lines 27–29.
[467] *StrNbk* 329. See note 221.

It has been noted that Têmâ was used as a concentration camp by the Arabs in the time of Abû Bekr for the army that was to move against Palestine and Syria.[468] The feasibility of employing similar strategy in the sixth century B. C. must be recognized. An Egyptian army seeking to check Babylonian prestige would naturally pass through Palestine and Syria, thus exposing itself and its line of communication with the homeland to attack from any body of hostile troops that might be maintained in Arabia. If Nabonidus' plan of action was based upon such considerations, the accepted estimate of his character must be set aside, for it would appear that he was a man of resourcefulness and energy in the scheme which he devised for the protection of his empire. However, unless other discoveries are forthcoming, there is no way of proving with absolute certainty that Nabonidus felt the impulse of such a farseeing purpose.

(2) The possibility that Nabonidus was guided in what he did by *a desire for allies against Cyrus* must be taken into account. Luckenbill has stated this phase of the question in the following words: "Were the prolonged stays[469] of Nabonidus in Têmâ an indication of his belief in the adage that discretion is the better part of valor? Or was Nabonidus making a desperate attempt to gather together a few allies to help him in the desperate situation that was obviously developing? We know that Assyria before the fall of Nineveh (612 B. C.) had the Egyptians fighting at their side. Was Nabonidus looking to the West for help?"[470] The factor of an alliance between Nabonidus and Cyrus should not be overlooked. According to available records an agreement was made between the two kings in the accession year of Nabonidus.[471] It seems that, in harmony with

[468] See note 461.

[469] Luckenbill evidently believed that Nabonidus did not stay at Têmâ continuously. He thought of the Babylonian king as indulging in a number of "prolonged stays" at the Arabian city.

[470] *AJSL* XL, p. 222. Landsberger and Bauer have advanced the view that Nabonidus' sojourn in Têmâ was for the purpose of allying Babylonians, Aramaeans, and Arabs as a counter-weight against "den indogermanischen Ansturm." Cf. *ZA* N. F. III (XXXVII), Heft 1, 2, p. 97f. Shamash-shum-ukîn made a similar alliance against Assyria. See note 183. Meissner, *Könige Babyloniens und Assyriens*, p. 300, note 10, says, "Ich glaube dass diese Auffassung der politischen Weisheit Nabonids zu viel Ehre antut." Cf. Kittel, *Geschichte des Volkes Israel* III, 1st half, p. 18f.

[471] *BHT* pp. 44f, 100. See *NKI* p. 220f, col. I, lines 26–31.

its terms, Nabonidus was to advance against Syria at once, while Cyrus was to revolt from Astyages three years later. There are indications that both sovereigns kept their word, which means that Cyrus broke with Astyages about the time that Nabonidus undertook his campaign against Têmâ. Hence it is hardly possible that the inception of Nabonidus' expedition into Arabia was due to his distrust of Cyrus. An exceedingly complex situation, involving plot within plot, would have to be presumed in order to conclude that Nabonidus and Cyrus were working against one another at the same time that they were meeting the requirements of an alliance. Luckenbill's hypothesis does not include the view that Nabonidus' *invasion* of Arabia hinged upon his desire for Egyptian allies; it seeks to find a reason for Nabonidus' prolonged *sojourn* at Têmâ. Some ground for this theory that the Babylonian king had his eyes upon Egypt in the years which followed his choice of Têmâ as his residence may be found in the fact that Nabonidus entered into a compact with the Lydians and the Egyptians against Cyrus in the ninth year of the former's reign, at a time when he lived in Têmâ according to cuneiform texts.[472] The Egyptians could not have viewed the rising power of Persia without alarm. It is credible that they were willing to ally themselves with the Babylonians against the new menace which was looming upon the eastern horizon. This much may be admitted, but, in the absence of specific data, it cannot be asserted that Nabonidus sought such an alliance.

(3) One may surmise that Nabonidus' venture into Arabia was due to *an ambition to secure imperial expansion.* Every ancient monarch wished to extend his rule and thus make his dynasty more stable. This policy characterized the reigns of Assyrian and Babylonian kings for many centuries. At times a situation arose in the related group of nations of Western Asia which prevented opportunities for much spread of power, or limited a particular nation to development only in one direction. To a large extent this was the lot of Babylonia during the reign of Nabonidus. The preëmpted claims of Cyrus left nothing to Nabonidus except the Westland, which included Arabia as well as Syria and Palestine. There was no disposition on the part

[472] Herodotus I, 77.

of the Babylonian king or his son to precipitate a conflict with Persia. That was to come soon enough. Nabonidus seems to have sensed, for some reason or other, that his rôle as a sovereign could be best filled by efforts on his part to consolidate the West as a sphere of Neo-Babylonian influence. It may be that it was for this purpose that he relinquished the greater personal prestige which would have accrued if he had remained in Babylon to receive the acclaim of those who were loyal and to win the homage of those who were disaffected. At any rate he entrusted the management of home affairs to Belshazzar, his eldest son, and then launched upon a singular career in Arabia, where, one may suppose, he endeavored through the larger part of his reign to organize the Arabian province which he had added to his empire, at the same time keeping in close touch with all parts of the nation by means of a constant messenger service.[473] Under such circumstances Têmâ must have been the real capital of the Neo-Babylonian empire, for the king lived there in a palace which equalled that of Babylon. From it Nabonidus must have issued his commands and decrees, and because of this the major portion of Arabia must have felt a strong impact of Babylonian political and cultural life. However, it is easier to estimate the probable results of an imaginary course of events than to determine the main motive responsible for a known line of action. Hence no final conclusion can be drawn from the survey which has been presented.

3. The Demands of Political Expediency

The problem may be approached from another angle. A consideration of all the data at our disposal indicates that an unusual political situation existed during the last reign of the Neo-Babylonian empire. The meaning of events may be comprehended by comparing the reign of Neriglissar with that of Nabonidus. There is documentary evidence that Neriglissar gained the throne by means of a conspiracy which resulted in the death of Amêl-Marduk.[474] Neriglissar's wife

[473] *AENN* 294, which indicates that a man was sent with a message to Têmâ in the fifth year of Nabonidus' reign, represents in all probability a typical occurrence of the time. The treaty made in the ninth year of Nabonidus' reign suggests that the king was keeping in touch with all the affairs of his kingdom, in spite of the fact that he was residing at Têmâ.

[474] Josephus, *Contra Apionem* I, 20.

was the daughter of Nebuchadrezzar, but nothing is recorded concerning any share in public affairs on her part. Neriglissar had a son of whom little is known except that he was a puerile king for a few months.[475] Neriglissar himself was a colorless monarch who ruled no longer than four years. On the other hand, an entirely different state of affairs characterized the reign of Nabonidus, who likewise became king because of a plot which the Babylonians fomented against his predecessor, although, as has been pointed out, there is no proof that Nabonidus was a leader in the conspiracy.[476] It is of consequence, however, that there were two other persons of forceful influence in the domain of Nabonidus. The plain import of Herodotus' account is that the wife of Nabonidus was Nitocris, an energetic queen who may have been the daughter of Nebuchadrezzar.[477] Belshazzar, the firstborn son of Nabonidus, seems to have been prominent in the nation even before his father ascended the throne.[478] Eliminating all suppositions, we still have to reckon with a queen of unusual ability and a crown prince of extraordinary efficiency who played important rôles during the last reign of the Neo-Babylonian empire. Does this furnish a clue as to the reason why Nabonidus spent so much time away from Babylonia? Did an opposition party arise and become powerful soon after Nabonidus became king? On the basis of such a theory one may consider a number of possibilities.

(1) Before the Têmâ where Nabonidus resided was identified with the Arabian city by that name, *forced abdication from the throne* was presented as a reason for his long absence from Babylon.[479] It was thought that only a deposed king or one who was a virtual prisoner would fail to perform his rightful functions in connection with the New Year's festival at the capital of the empire. The idea that a Babylonian king spent a large part of his reign in the normal activities of his office without living in Babylon seemed so incredible that a cessation of kingly authority was deemed the only rational explanation. Hence the hypothesis was advanced that Nabonidus was com-

[475] See pp. 71ff.
[476] See pp. 72ff.
[477] See pp. 51–63.
[478] See pp. 67ff.
[479] Cf. Goodspeed, *A History of the Babylonians and Assyrians*, p. 372.

pelled to vacate the throne in favor of Belshazzar who thus became the real ruler of the nation. All that has come to light concerning the reign of Nabonidus is against this view. Every fully-dated cuneiform document of the period in question mentions Nabonidus as king. Complete royal authority is not ascribed to Belshazzar by any record upon clay. In contract tablets belonging to the twelfth year of Nabonidus' reign there are instances of oaths sworn by the laws or decrees of Nabonidus,[480] the king of Babylon, and Belshazzar, the son of the king. The historical text published by Sidney Smith indicates that Nabonidus 'entrusted' the oversight of affairs in Babylonia to Belshazzar, but there is no evidence of coercion in this delegation of authority.[481] Belshazzar never became the sole sovereign of Babylonia, for, if he had possessed full kingly power, the non-performance of metropolitan rites and ceremonies would not have resulted during the absence of Nabonidus.[482] Hence the theory that Nabonidus found asylum at Têmâ as a deposed monarch is far from the truth.

(2) If Nabonidus was not forced to abdicate, may not *voluntary retirement from the kingship* be a sufficient explanation for his stay at Têmâ? It must be remembered that royal succession in Babylonia had been attended with factional strife on two occasions since the time of Nebuchadrezzar.[483] Although the records intimate that Nabonidus received universal acclaim when he ascended the throne,[484] there are evidences that he was not regarded with favor by all Babylonians as his reign progressed. An antagonistic attitude towards him on the part of an influential section of the nation might easily have found a rallying center in the crown prince, especially if the latter was a descendant of Nebuchadrezzar. Do the facts warrant such a reconstruction of the historical situation? Was the defection from Nabonidus strong enough to cause deliberate relinquishment of sovereignty on his part? The arguments against forced abdication apply here also. No corroboration of the view that Nabonidus actually gave up the throne has been found. Estrangement between

[480] See p. 96f.
[481] See p. 106f.
[482] See p. 112f.
[483] Josephus, *Contra Apionem* I, 20.
[484] See p. 72f.

him and his consort cannot be proven; neither is there any evidence that Belshazzar was his political rival. The command which Nabonidus gave to Belshazzar in the seventh year of his reign shows that the latter remained amenable to the authority of his father.[485] Nabonidus did not cease to be king in power or in name until Babylon was captured by Cyrus in 539 B. C.[486]

(3) The possibility that Nabonidus decided upon *tactful withdrawal from Babylonia,* with supreme authority continuing in his possession, remains to be considered. He may have felt that his position would be more secure if he was engaged outside of Babylonia in an enterprise for the strengthening of the empire. The element in the homeland opposed to him would be mollified by such a step on his part, particularly if he made Belshazzar co-regent. Those in favor of Nabonidus could not raise serious objections inasmuch as his title and jurisdiction were not nullified. Under such circumstances the factor of political expediency would operate with good results. One hesitates to intimate that Nabonidus feared assassination, a fate which overtook two of his predecessors in the Neo-Babylonian dynasty. He seems to have had a real objective in the Westland. That his course may have been influenced by a critical situation in Babylonia is within the range of possibility. To what extent this was the case cannot be determined from information now at our disposal. It may be asserted, however, that Nabonidus does not appear to have abandoned entirely any of his royal prerogatives during his extended stay at Têmâ in Arabia.

4. The Incentive of Commercial Interests

A commercial motive, representing an interest in trade relations and a desire for new sources of revenue, has been ascribed to Nabonidus. As Sidney Smith has pointed out, Assyrian kings from the time of Tiglathpileser endeavored to gain more complete control of "the trade routes through Edom and the lands to the south."[487] The strategic location of Têmâ for a program of commercial expansion in Arabia has also been noted by the same author.[488] Professor W. F.

[485] See p. 136f.
[486] See p. 170f.
[487] *BHT* p. 81.
[488] See also *JAOS* XLII, p. 308.

Albright is inclined to the view that the energy of the Minaean empire in the sixth century B. C. added greatly to the commercial prosperity of Arabia and that this increased wealth affected the fortunes of Adummu and Têmâ.[489] He mentions Nabonidus' building operations as enterprises which required funds too enormous for Babylonia itself to supply. To secure such funds was the reason for the extended stay of Nabonidus in Arabia. The plausibility of these opinions is supported by many facts. Arabia was closely associated with Babylonia geographically, racially, and economically. Of all the countries of the Westland it alone bordered on the real land of Babylonia. There were no intervening districts between its territory and the lower Euphrates region. Intimate points of contact drew the two lands together and resources of a supplementary character induced a certain degree of intermingling of peoples. This close relationship should not be overlooked in attempting to interpret events in southwestern Asia in the sixth century B. C. It may well be that overpowering commercial interests exerted a determining influence upon the course of history. Various phases of this question will now be discussed.

(1) The heart of the problem may be approached by a consideration of the *main trade routes of Arabia*. The peninsula of Arabia, called by its inhabitants *Jezîrat el-'Arab*, 'The Island of the Arabs,' was no inconsiderable part of the region which was occupied by the ancient Semitic world. A study of the map indicates that it was many times larger than the combined area of the regions inhabited by Babylonians, Assyrians, Amorites, Phoenicians, Hebrews, etc. Caravans, traveling well-defined routes, traversed this vast land for intertribal barter and for trade with other countries. Ancient authorities indicate that spices and gold were the main products of Arabia. Herodotus states that frankincense, myrrh, cassia, cinnamon, and resinous gum were to be obtained only in Arabia,[490] a land whose atmosphere was laden with perfume.[491] Diodorus Siculus enumerates balsam, myrrh, frankincense, and other aromatic plants as the peculiar exports of Arabia, the very soil of which was supposed to

[489] *JRAS* April, 1925, p. 294f.
[490] Herodotus III, 107.
[491] Herodotus III, 113.

possess odoriferous qualities.[492] Strabo presents the same view of Arabia as a spice-producing country and numbers fragrant palms and scented reeds among its gifts to the world.[493] The extensive gold deposits of Arabia were equally famed. This valuable metal was found in the whole western half of the peninsula, from Midian to Yemen, and gold was not wanting in the center of the land.[494] That the gold of Ophir was of Arabian origin has been clearly demonstrated by Moritz.[495] The mountains of central Arabia also yielded precious stones.[496] Spices, gold, and gems were in great demand in countries which bordered upon Arabia, and fixed caravan routes were employed in conveying these products to marts of exchange. The chief artery of trade from the south consisted of a main track as far as Têmâ which was a central emporium. From Têmâ commercial transportation proceeded in three principal directions, viz., towards Egypt, Syria, and Babylonia.[497] This emphasizes the extreme importance of Têmâ in the international trade movements of Arabia.

(2) A study of *Babylonia's need for imports from Arabia* assists in weighing the question more carefully. The land of Akkad was self-supporting so far as the necessities of life were concerned. Its broad area of intense irrigation culture yielded rich returns in barley[498] and dates, while enormous flocks and herds were supported by its fertile pasture lands. However, the full expression of Babylonian civilization required commodities not produced in the homeland. Two

[492] See Booth, *The Historical Library of Diodorus the Sicilian*, p. 79.

[493] Strabo 16, 4, 19.

[494] See Moritz, *Arabien-Studien zur physikalischen und historischen Geographie des Landes*, p. 89. The gold of Ophir was described as ἄπυρος, 'without fire,' 'untouched by fire,' *i.e.* unsmelted. See Moritz, *ibid.*, p. 85. Diodorus asserts that Arabia possessed mines of pure gold, called ἄπυρος χρυσός, which it was unnecessary to purify by melting in fire. Cf. Vogel, *Diodori Bibliotheca Historica*, I, p. 250.

[495] See Moritz, *op. cit.*, pp. 63–117.

[496] See Schoff, *The Ship "Tyre,"* p. 118; Booth, *op. cit.*, p. 80.

[497] See Moritz, *op. cit*, p. 30f, note 7, quoting Hamdâni; Jaussen and Savignac, *op. cit.*, p. 144, note 3, quoting Muqaddasi. Cf. Hartmann, *Die arabische Frage* in *der islamische Orient* II, p. 35f. See map of ancient trade routes in *CAH* I, p. 224. O'Leary, *Arabia before Mohammed*, p. 103f, discusses the old land routes through Arabia. See references under Tejma and Têmâ in Musil, *The Northern Heǧâz* and *Arabia Deserta*, Nos. 1 and 2 of *Oriental Studies and Explorations* of the American Geographical Society. Cf. Montgomery in *Proceedings American Philosophical Society*, LXVII, p. 212.

[498] Other grains were produced, but barley took precedence.

phases of highly-developed society—religion and industry—had to be maintained with lavish contributions from abroad. Incense[499] was used in the worship of the gods, and when one remembers that each Babylonian city had its own temple, the rites of which required faithful attention, some idea can be gained of the amount of incense which had to be imported. In the time of Darius the Arabians supplied Persia with "a thousand talents' weight of frankincense yearly."[500] The Neo-Babylonian empire must have been the recipient of a comparable amount of aromatic materials from Arabia. Furthermore, gold was needed for the paraphernalia used in sanctuaries.[501] Costly vestments, ceremonial utensils, and sacred images were not made of the commoner metals. The renovation and, in certain cases, the rebuilding of temples created a demand for a plentiful store of wealth. An abundance of gold found in Arabia could not have been unrelated to this paramount Babylonian need. In addition, the general industrial activities of the land exacted an ample supply of the basic metals, which had to be obtained from other countries. Numerous references to the goldsmith and to gold itself in contract tablets indicate that a good stock of gold was a necessity in Babylonian industrial life. That Arabia possessed great potentiality as a contributor to Babylonia's accumulation of gold has already been shown. Precious stones were used extensively in Babylonia as objects of adornment, the highest art of the jeweler being devoted especially to the making of brilliant temple vestments.[502] The Arabian city which Nabonidus made his residence was a distributing center in the traffic maintained by caravans, and hence it must have had a great deal to do with trade in spices, gold, and precious stones. That Têmâ was a distinct factor in Babylonian prosperity can hardly be doubted.

(3) It is not impossible that *Egyptian competition for Arabian products* had some influence upon the course of history. The early domination of Palestine and Syria by Egypt is one of the outstanding facts of ancient history. Under these circumstances it is inconceivable that Arabia should have been untouched by Egyptian in-

[499] See *qutrinnu CD* p. 940; *mazḫatu*, Bezold, *Babylonisch-assyrisches Glossar*, p. 167.

[500] Herodotus III, 97.

[501] See *REN* p. 13.

[502] The extensive use of engraved seal cylinders increased the demand for different kinds of hard stones.

fluence. There is no lack of data proving that Egypt took a deep interest in the land east of the Red Sea. The fact that the part of North Arabia adjoining Egypt is referred to as *Muṣur* or *Muṣri* in Assyrian inscriptions is at least an intimation that the region was under the sway of Egypt.[503] Additional evidence is furnished by the efforts taken by Egypt to maintain connections with the Red Sea. From early times a much-used road through the Wadi Hammâmât joined the Nile and the Red Sea.[504] Later a canal was built between the most eastern branch of the Nile in the Delta region and the northern part of the Red Sea.[505] All this indicates that the development of culture in the Nile Valley depended to a large extent upon intensive navigation of the Red Sea. A paramount object of all this traffic by ships was the securing of spices, which were produced extensively in South Arabia, for the Egyptians needed aromatic materials not only for use in the services of their temples but also for the proper embalming of the dead.[506] That the Egyptians also sought Arabian gold need not be questioned. Hence there is abundant reason for believing that Egypt was a real rival of Babylonia for the control of Arabia's exports. However, it is problematical whether these facts concerning the importance of the commerce of Arabia are sufficient in themselves to explain Nabonidus' long stay at Têmâ.

5. *The Stimulus of Religious Zeal*

Deep religious fervor was regarded as an essential characteristic of Babylonian and Assyrian kingship. This is disclosed by a survey of the royal inscriptions of those who ruled at Babylon and Nineveh.[507] In reality the ideal priest-king may be traced back to Sumerian times. Sovereignty upon earth included submission to the gods and loyalty to righteousness as well as support of justice and punishment of evil. The true king was a shepherd of the people in all things, including veneration towards accepted deities. Nabonidus may be adjudged as

[503] Cf. Hommel, *Ethnologie und Geographie des alten Orients*, p. 600f.

[504] O'Leary, *Arabia before Mohammed*, p. 29.

[505] Herodotus II, 158; Pliny, *N. H.* 6, 29, 33; Diodorus 1, 33. See O'Leary, *op. cit.*, p. 31f.

[506] Consult O'Leary's discussion of the Egyptian use of incense, *op. cit.*, p. 38f.

[507] Note especially the descriptive titles assumed by Nabonidus, *NKI* p. 252f, no. 6, col. I, lines 1–9. See pp. 16ff of this monograph.

one who was strongly moved by feelings of religious piety. The contents and tone of his long inscriptions reveal an attitude of reverence and obedience on his part.[508] This may have been innate in his being, for both his father and mother are described as sincere venerators of divinity.[509] A strong influence towards religion came from his mother, who, according to a reasonal interpretation of cuneiform data, was high priestess of the moon god at Ḫarrân. It is doubtless true, therefore, that Nabonidus was conscientiously addicted to the worship of Babylonian deities long before he became king. Thus he brought to the throne a background of religious training and a firmness of religious principle which must have had some effect upon his career as a monarch. All the impulses which took their rise from Nabonidus' pious convictions cannot be estimated with exactness, but an attempt may be made to determine the play of religious motive in the attention which he gave to Arabia.

(1) Account should be taken, first of all, of *Nabonidus' devotion to the cult of the moon god.* One of the main deities in the Babylonian pantheon was Sin, whose worship amounted to an exaltation of lunar influence in human affairs. Throughout the history of Babylonia Sin was revered as a great god, at first at Ur and then at other cities until the cult became practically universal.[510] However, the sanctuaries Êgišširgal at Ur and Êḫulḫul at Ḫarrân were the chief centers for the veneration of the moon god in the time of Nabonidus. That his mother served long years as a high priestess of this deity at Ḫarrân is the clear intimation of the Eski-Ḫarrân text.[511] It seems that this parental example influenced Nabonidus considerably, although he was interested in other gods aside from Sin, as is shown by his restoration of temples at Sippar and Larsa as well as at Ur and Ḫarrân.[512] With a building program on hand involving the renovation of important places of worship—a seeming prominence being accorded to sacred edifices dedicated to the glorification of the moon god—Nabonidus

[508] *NKI* pp. 218–295.

[509] See pp. 18, 23ff.

[510] Cf. references to Sin in Hehn, *Die biblische und die babylonische Gottesidee*, listed on p. 427. See Jastrow, *Religion of Babylonia and Assyria*, p. 77, note.

[511] See pp. 23ff.

[512] E.g. *NKI* pp. 224ff, col. II, lines 47–65; col. III, lines 1–21; *NKI* pp. 234ff, col. I, lines 31–55; col. II, lines 1–60; col. III, lines 1–30

may have penetrated Arabia under the impulse of a consuming aim to spread the worship of his favorite deity. To what extent should acceptance be given to this view? Some significance may be attached to the fact that the introduction to the account of the Têmâ campaign deals with Nabonidus' rebuilding of Êḫulḫul, the noted temple of Sin at Ḫarrân.[513] Sidney Smith believes that the cuneiform record may be restored so as to furnish ground for the view that Nabonidus promulgated the worship of Sin in Têmâ after he had captured the city.[514] It is natural to suppose that the Babylonian king pursued such a course, but at present there is no unequivocal textual warrant for the inference. Neither is it possible to prove that Nabonidus was imbued with the spirit of deliberate religious propaganda in his choice of Têmâ as an object of conquest.

(2) Careful consideration of the question requires recognition of the fact that *Arabian interest in the moon god* was a distinct phase in the development of religion among the Semites. Information of a definite character comes from South Arabian inscriptions. According to these records the moon god was worshipped with much veneration by the Minaeans, the Sabaeans, the Katabanians, and the Hadramautians.[515] Different names were ascribed to the lunar deity, viz., *Wadd* by the Minaeans, *Haubas* by the Sabaeans, *Amm* by the Katabanians, *Ilmuqah* and *Sin* by the Hadramautians.[516] The sun god was also granted a prominent place by these peoples, but the persistence of nomadic forms of life kept homage to the moon god to the fore.[517] One may surmise that a similar religious condition prevailed in Northwest Arabia, where Têmâ was located, although a wealth of data is not available for this region.[518] It is unlikely, however, that recognition of the moon god at Têmâ in the sixth century B. C. was dependent upon the army and influence of a Babylonian king. If Nabonidus did

[513] *BHT* pp. 84, 88, col. II, lines 4–15.

[514] *BHT* p. 95, note for col. II, line 27.

[515] Cf. Weber, *Arabien vor dem Islam, Der alte Orient,* 3. Jahrgang, Heft 1, pp. 18ff; Hehn, *op. cit.*, pp. 141ff. Note especially Nielsen *Die altarabische Mondreligion und die mosaische Ueberlieferung*, pp. 1–122, and Nielsen, *Handbuch der altarabischen Altertumskunde*, I. Band, pp. 213–224.

[516] Weber, *op. cit.*, p. 20; Hehn, *op. cit.*, 142.

[517] Hehn, *op. cit.*, pp. 135, 144.

[518] See Hehn, *op. cit.*, p. 139, for a reference to the moon cult among the Nabataeans.

set up the image of Sin in Têmâ—and this was a most probable act on his part since he maintained his residence there for many years—it does not seem reasonable that he was sponsoring an entirely new religion for Arabia. No doubt his first thought was for the Babylonian community which his Arabian adventure forced to dwell at a great distance from the homeland. If he adorned Têmâ and made it 'like the palace of Babylon,' it is unthinkable that he should have failed to establish a sanctuary where his favorite deity could be worshipped. That some of the inhabitants of Arabia may have gained a new conception of the cult of the moon god from the Babylonians who lived among them is entirely possible, but that Nabonidus sought such a result is not indicated by the inscriptions.

(3) There are evidences that *priestly opposition to Nabonidus' religious program* was serious enough to affect his fortunes at the close of his reign. That some sort of disaffection began to reveal itself soon after he became king is suggested by passages in three cuneiform texts.[519] It is true that these three records represent Persian propaganda against Nabonidus and that their defamation of the Babylonian king cannot therefore be taken at face value. Nevertheless, some occasion for dissatisfaction must have existed. A text reveals that Nabonidus did not venerate Marduk as the supreme deity;[520] that honor he ascribed to Sin, the moon god.[521] Even in his interpretation of the lunar cult he appears to have deviated from the accepted ceremonies of his time. Furthermore, Nabonidus had brought the gods from various temples in the land to the city of Babylon, a move which seems not to have been received with favor.[522] On the other hand, the inscriptions of Nabonidus himself show that he was

[519] *Nabonidus Chronicle*, col. I, line 7 (*BHT* pp. 111, 114); *Cyrus Cylinder*, lines 9, 10 (*KA* p. 2f); *A Persian Verse Account of Nabonidus*, col. I, lines 1–19 (*BHT* pp. 83, 87); The last text quoted contains a more detailed accusation in col. V, lines 14–17 (*BHT* pp. 86, 90).

[520] *KA* p. 4f, line 17.

[521] The mother of Nabonidus calls Sin *šar ilâni*^{meš}, 'the king of the gods,' in the Eski-Ḫarrân text (*NKI* pp. 288–293, col. I, line 3; col. II, line 18, etc.). Nabonidus applies the same title to Sin in one of his long inscriptions (*NKI* p. 222f, col. II, line 26).

[522] *Nabonidus Chronicle*, col. III, lines 21, 22 (*BHT* pp. 113f, 118); *Cyrus Cylinder*, lines 33, 34 (*KA* p. 6f). *A Persian Verse Account of Nabonidus*, col. VI, lines 12, 13 (*BHT* pp. 86, 91) may be interpreted as agreeing with the *Nabonidus Chronicle* and the *Cyrus Cylinder* as to this phase of Nabonidus' sacrilege.

far from impious. The whole question is obscured with ambiguity and may hence be regarded as one of the enigmas of Nabonidus' career. Sidney Smith has made a careful survey of the texts dealing with the problem.[523] His conclusion is that Nabonidus claimed that his reforms in worship were really restorations of old ceremonies, but that the priestly orders resented them and so were willing to welcome Cyrus as a champion of the religious system in which they were interested. Consequently there was acclaim for the deliverer and vituperation for the dethroned king. It may be that Nabonidus was confronted with strong religious antipathy as early as the third year of his reign[524] and that he chose seclusion in the Westland as the best means of avoiding a serious crisis in his kingdom. At present there is no way of proving or disproving this theory. The mystery can be solved only by the discovery and decipherment of many more cuneiform inscriptions coming from the reign of Nabonidus. Probabilities may be estimated now, but records upon clay will furnish the ultimate decision.

6. The Sway of Personal Inclination

The question as to whether Nabonidus' interest in Têmâ arose from the influence of private choice rather than from the necessity of public policy requires consideration. Just how much freedom of action was possessed by a Babylonian king is not known with certainty. The history of the Neo-Babylonian empire indicates that its citizens were not inclined to condone inefficiency in administration or neglect of national needs on the part of their sovereign. Two kings had been put to death by violence[525] and Nabonidus himself had to deal with an antagonism which sprang from his personal program in the sphere of religion. This phase of the situation should not be overlooked in attempting to determine whether mere whim was responsible for Nabonidus' long stay at Têmâ. However, there was a circumstance which allowed him a certain measure of release from the responsibilities of government. He did not leave Babylonia with no provision for the

[523] *BHT* p. 62f.

[524] It is of course possible that Nabonidus had to deal with religious antipathy prior to his third year as king.

[525] Amêl-Marduk and Lâbâshi-Marduk. See Josephus, *Contra Apionem* I, 20.

direction of urgent home affairs during his absence. Belshazzar, his firstborn son, was entrusted with kingship in the land of Akkad. While this did not deprive Nabonidus of supreme sovereignty, it gave him opportunity to carry out his wishes in the Westland. Several motives based upon personal inclination may be suggested for Nabonidus' prolonged residence in Arabia.

(1) There is only an imaginary possibility that Nabonidus may have been actuated by *a preference for life among Aramaean peoples.* Têmâ was an important Aramaean center in the sixth century B. C.[526] Its inhabitants were not Arabs in the strict sense of the term, since evidence is not wanting that Aramaean speech and Aramaean culture predominated in the part of Arabia of which Têmâ was the focus.[527] That the tribes of Northern Arabia and even those of Central Arabia had received a strong infusion of the Aramaean race appears proven. The Aramaean background of Nabonidus seems to be indicated by the connection of his ancestry, so far as can now be determined, with the region of Ḫarrân. However, it is natural to inquire why Nabonidus should have undertaken the difficult expedition to Têmâ in order to settle in an Aramaean environment, when such a goal could have been attained much nearer at home. Furthermore, it would seem that his treatment of the inhabitants of Têmâ and its environs was too sanguinary for one imbued with friendship. These reasons may be regarded as refuting the view that Nabonidus' main object in going to Têmâ was to associate with people of his own stock.

(2) According to the former estimate of Nabonidus, *an impulse arising from antiquarian tastes* was the leading factor in his life.[528] He was pictured as a king who exhibited no concern for the political and military welfare of his empire. Digging down to old foundations and reading the inscriptions of his predecessors were regarded as his principal occupations. It is true that the ruins of Têmâ

[526] The Têmâ Stone is proof of this. See note 447.

[527] *ZA* N.F. III (XXXVII), Heft 1, 2, p. 97f.

[528] See King, *A History of Babylon*, p. 281; *CAH* III, p. 218; Hall, *The Ancient History of the Near East*, p. 550; Tiele, *Babylonisch-assyrische Geschichte* I, p. 459; Rogers, *History of Babylonia and Assyria* II, p. 552f. Goodspeed in *A History of the Babylonians and Assyrians*, p. 369f, rejects the view that Nabonidus was "a political weakling, a cultured dilettante, an archaeological virtuoso." He did engage in so-called antiquarian researches, but these were minor episodes in his career.

are very alluring to the modern archaeologist, but that there was anything at Têmâ in the sixth century B. C. capable of gratifying the antiquarian proclivities of a Babylonian king is doubtful. In reality Nabonidus is no longer presented to our view as a monarch who devoted most of his time to an investigation of the past. What is now known concerning his career shows that much more important matters absorbed his attention. Hence it is highly improbable that he was attracted to Têmâ by an interest in monumental remains.

(3) A final possibility is that Nabonidus in his choice of Têmâ as a residence yielded to *the appeal of a healthful climate.* All modern explorers agree in lauding the oasis of Têmâ, the name of which now appears as Teima upon maps. Its elevated location[529] and the non-miasmatic character of its atmosphere[530] are emphasized. It must therefore possess a special charm as compared with the fever-laden alluvial plain of the lower part of the Tigris-Euphrates valley. No doubt the same advantages belonged to Têmâ in the sixth century B. C. There are indications that Nabonidus was an elderly man when he became king and the *Nabonidus Chronicle* intimates that he suffered from illness just before he undertook the campaign against Têmâ.[531] For this reason the suggestion has been made that he chose to remain many years at Têmâ in order to avoid sickness. Several circumstances argue strongly against this view. If Nabonidus became ill in Syria, his recovery was complete enough for him to endure the hardships of a strenuous expedition. It seems unlikely that a king inclined to invalidism would embark upon a military venture into the desert of Arabia. In the next place, the climate of Têmâ could not have been more attractive than that of the 'orchards of Lebanon,' which were already a part of the Neo-Babylonian empire. Furthermore, there is not the slightest evidence in the numerous cuneiform inscriptions dated in the reign of Nabonidus that the general health of the king was other than normal. Another reason for rejecting the view that Nabonidus looked upon Têmâ merely as a place where he could keep well is the fact that he adorned the city to such an extent that it rivalled Babylon.[532] Hence, unless more positive proof is forthcoming,

[529] Doughty, *Travels in Arabia Deserta*, 1921, I, p. 285.
[530] *Ibid.*, I, p. 286f.
[531] *BHT* pp. 111, 115, col. I, line 14.
[532] *BHT* pp. 84, 89, col. II, lines 28, 29.

maintenance of bodily vigor cannot be decided upon as Nabonidus' real aim in choosing to exercise his power as king in a part of Arabia which none of his predecessors, so far as is known, had regarded as worthy of personal attention. It seems difficult to ascribe Nabonidus' interest in Têmâ to an inclination on his part which arose from individual preference.

7. *The Probable Aim of Nabonidus*

The preceding discussion indicates that it is not easy to determine the exact motive which actuated Nabonidus in his selection of Têmâ as his official residence during a large part of his reign. It may be that we must seek the reason, not in a single motive, but in a combination of them. However, a primary aim springing from personal preference and exhibiting no care for the empire's fate seems out of the question. The international situation was too tense and too much was at stake for a Babylonian king to be governed by mere caprice in a procedure involving the destiny of the nation. As to the control of Arabian trade routes, it should be noted that a Babylonian garrison at Têmâ under the command of a capable general could have accomplished all that was necessary for the welfare of Babylonian commercial interests in Arabia. The presence of the king was not needed for the achievement of this purpose. Abdication from the throne, either forced or voluntary, is also ruled out according to reliable cuneiform data. Consolidation and extension of the western part of his kingdom may be suggested as tangible results of the course which Nabonidus pursued. The attainment of such a goal can be regarded as commensurate with his conquest and domination of the most important city of Northwest Arabia. Subsidiary influences and secondary interests need not be dismissed entirely. It seems wholly possible that Nabonidus gave consideration to commercial matters and exalted his favorite deity after he had established his court in Têmâ; that he appreciated the benefits of the salubrious climate is undoubtedly true. It appears improbable, however, that these things constituted the main claim of Têmâ upon his attention. Unless we are to believe that Nabonidus was bereft of kingly sagacity, some overpowering political purpose, such as the establishment of real sovereignty over the Westland or the cementing of essential alliances, must have induced him to make Arabia the center from which his influence radiated.

XII

THE CONQUEST OF ARABIA BY CYRUS

No specific information is available as to when Nabonidus' sojourn in Arabia ended. Cuneiform texts intimate very strongly that he was absent from Babylonia as late as the twelfth year of his reign. His residence at Têmâ in the eleventh year of his reign is established with certainty,[533] and clay contract tablets dated in the following year indicate no change in Belshazzar's position at Babylon;[534] they tend rather to confirm it. Unfortunately no cuneiform documents have thus far been found which throw light upon the whereabouts of Nabonidus from the twelfth to the seventeenth year of his reign. There is a similar dearth of data concerning the activities of Belshazzar from the fourteenth to the seventeenth year of Nabonidus' reign. The records which are capable of dispelling our ignorance with respect to the last years of Nabonidus' reign remain to be discovered, since state and temple archives of Babylonia were complete for each year. Hence we may await the progress of cuneiform decipherment with eagerness, unless many of the inscriptions for the years mentioned have not been preserved.

In the absence of definite knowledge concerning the interim, all that can be stated with certainty is that Nabonidus resided in Têmâ as late as the eleventh year of his reign, and that he was in Babylonia in the seventeenth year of his reign. It is not impossible that he remained at Têmâ until events in the last year of his reign forced him to return to Babylon. A stay at Têmâ of eight years, from the third to the eleventh year of his reign, indicates that Nabonidus considered the city his permanent place of abode. Hence we may conclude that he was content to remain there as long as affairs went well with his kingdom. If his court continued at Têmâ until the seventeenth year of his reign, Arabia's position in the Neo-Babylonian empire must have had strategic importance. Under such circumstances Cyrus could not have overlooked the necessity of subduing Arabia in order to make his

[533] See p. 112.

[534] See p. 96f for the mention of Belshazzar in oaths sworn in the twelfth year of Nabonidus' reign.

conquest of Babylon more certain. It is interesting, therefore, that an examination of data derived from Greek and cuneiform sources suggests the probability that Cyrus vanquished Arabia before he proceeded against Babylon.

1. Berossus' Statement

In endeavoring to find traces of this event in recorded history it will be best to begin with Berossus and then work back to earlier sources. The statement of Berossus is as follows: *Οὔσης δὲ τῆς βασιλείας αὐτοῦ ἐν τῷ ἑπτακαιδεκάτῳ ἔτει, προεξεληλυθὼς Κῦρος ἐκ τῆς Περσίδος μετὰ δυνάμεως πολλῆς, καὶ καταστρεψάμενος τὴν λοιπὴν Ἀσίαν πᾶσαν, ὥρμησεν ἐπὶ τῆς βαβυλωνίας.*[535] Briefly this passage affirms that Cyrus hastened to Babylonia in the seventeenth year of Nabonidus' reign after 'all the rest of Asia' had been conquered. Cyrus advanced 'from Persia with a great force.' The chronological and historical significance of these assertions should be weighed carefully. They indicate that by the seventeenth year of Nabonidus' reign Cyrus had gained the ascendancy over all of Asia, as then known, with the exception of Babylonia. Since Arabia was a part of Asia,[536] the record of Berossus may be taken as an indication that Cyrus caused the Arabs to submit to his yoke before he sought to attack the main strength of the Neo-Babylonian empire.[537] Such a procedure is what one would expect if Arabia had become a strong integral part of the kingdom. It is hardly likely that Cyrus made an expedition into Arabia from the north with the idea of a later march straight across the desert to Babylonia. The phraseology used by Berossus does not lend itself to such a view, for he states definitely that Cyrus advanced from Persia. Babylon was the great prize which Cyrus desired and its fall enabled him to assume a title more glorious than that possessed by former Persian kings.

[535] Josephus, *Contra Apionem* I, 20.

[536] An examination of Herodotus' conception of the ancient world shows that the geographical term Asia as used by him included Arabia. See Herodotus IV, 39, where Asia west of Persia is described as embracing Arabia.

[537] See *BHT* p. 102f.

2. Xenophon's Statement

Xenophon, after having narrated the campaign of Cyrus against the Lydians, introduces his description of the fall of Babylon with the following brief statement: Προϊὼν δὲ τὴν ἐπὶ Βαβυλῶνος κατεστρέψατο μὲν Φρύγας τοὺς ἐν τῇ μεγάλῃ Φρυγίᾳ, κατεστρέψατο δὲ Καππαδόκας, ὑποχειρίους δ' ἐποιήσατο Ἀραβίους.[538] The gist of this Greek record is that Cyrus, while moving towards his main goal, *i.e.* the capture of Babylon, left no stone unturned in order to make his triumph inevitable. He subdued the Phrygians who dwelt in Great Phrygia and also the Cappadocians. The above text indicates that his next achievement was the subjugation of the Arabians. Xenophon then asserts that Cyrus obtained by means of these conquests a great deal of armor and a large number of horses. 'And he arrived before Babylon with a large body of cavalry, and a great army of bowmen and spearmen, and a multitude of slingers that was beyond count.'[539] This statement agrees with that of Berossus to the effect that Cyrus proceeded against Babylon with a huge army. Xenophon, however, specifies that part of the equipment of the invading host was secured from the vanquished Phrygians, Cappadocians, and Arabians. He indicates, furthermore, that Arabians as well as Phrygians, Lydians, and Cappadocians helped the Persians to encompass the walls of Babylon.[540] There is a strong suggestion in this that Cyrus pursued his preparatory campaigns for the purpose of recruiting as large a force as possible in order to assure victory in the final conflict. The scope of the Persian campaign against the Arabians is not mentioned. Apparently Xenophon knew nothing of Nabonidus' establishment of his court at Têmâ. It must be granted, nevertheless, that Xenophon's reference to Cyrus' conquest of the Arabians accords with what one would expect if Arabia had arisen to the status of an important Babylonian province during the reign of Nabonidus.

[538] *Cyropaedia* VII, 4, 16.
[539] *Ibid.*, VII, 4, 16.
[540] *Ibid.*, VII, 5, 13.

3. *Cyrus' Statement*

The *Cyrus Cylinder* furnishes interesting contemporaneous data. The passage which describes the homage accorded to Cyrus after the conquest of Babylon is as follows:

[28b]*Nap-ḫar šarri a-ši-ib parakkê*[meš] [29]*ša ka-li-iš*[541] *kib-ra-a-ta iš-tu tam-tim e-li-tim a-di tam-tim šap-li-tim a-ši-ib kul . . . . šarrâni*[meš] [mât]*A-mur-ri-i a-ši-ib kuš-ta-ri ka-li-šu-un* [30a]*bi-lat-su-nu ka-bi-it-tim ú-bi-lu-nim-ma qi-ir-ba Bâbili*[ki] *ú-na-aš-ši-qu še-pu-ú-a.*[542]

[28b]All kings dwelling in the royal palaces [29]of all the quarters (of the world), from the upper sea to the lower sea, those dwelling in . . . . , the kings of the Westland dwelling in tents, all of them [30a]brought heavy tribute to me and in Babylon kissed my feet.

The phrase 'kings of the Westland dwelling in tents' has significance because Têmâ is described as being in the midst of the Westland (*qi-rib A-mur-ri-i*).[543] It should be noted that the inscription makes a distinction between the kings of widespread parts of the world *dwelling in royal palaces* and the kings of the Westland *dwelling in tents.* There is considerable likelihood, therefore, that the Arabians of the land of Têmâ, many of whose native rulers were doubtless sheikhs *dwelling in tents*, are to be numbered among those who proffered tribute to Cyrus in Babylon. It is true that the *Cyrus Cylinder* mentions neither the land of Arabia nor the Arabian people. This cannot be used as proof that the above passage does not refer to Arabian tribal chieftans, for the cuneiform text which describes Nabonidus' expedition against Têmâ contains no allusion to 'Arabia' or 'Arabians.' One may infer with considerable assurance that the *Cyrus Cylinder* harmonizes with the view that the Persian conqueror of Babylon had imposed his sovereignty upon Arabia as a prelude to universal overlordship.

[541] The word *ka-li-iš* is an adverb, but it is difficult to translate it as such in the above context.

[542] *KA* p. 6f, lines 28b–30a; *BA* II, p. 212f.

[543] *BHT* pp. 84, 88, col. II, line 23. Ashurbanipal refers to the inhabitants of Arabia (*nišê*[meš] [mât]*A-ri-bi*) as dwelling in tents ([bît ṣêri]*kul-ta-ra-a-te*). See Streck, *Assurbanipal* II, p. 66, column VII, lines 117 and 121.

4. The Geographical Factor

The realm of possibility may now be investigated. Are there any indications that circumstances favored a Persian expedition into Arabia against the Babylonian sphere of influence which had been developed there? An affirmative answer to this question is not difficult to find. In the first place it must be noted that a campaign of conquest in the land of Têmâ presented no greater difficulties to Cyrus than to Nabonidus. The account of Nabonidus' march to Têmâ emphasizes the farness of the journey and the uniqueness of the objective. However, Nabonidus succeeded in traversing the desert terrain which it was necessary to cross in order to reach Têmâ in a journey from Syria. The record states that he accomplished this feat with the help of the military power of Akkad, *i.e.* Babylonia.[544] In other words, his invading force was not an ordinary caravan; it was a real army. If a large contingent of Babylonian troops could proceed to Têmâ in 552 B. C., the launching of a Persian attack upon the same part of Arabia was equally feasible during the closing years of Nabonidus' reign. The main climatic conditions of Arabia could not have varied much in ten or twelve years. At any rate one cannot imagine that the ambitious Cyrus would have hesitated to strike at the heart of Arabia if he felt that such a course was demanded by his strategic plans. In reality the example of Nabonidus' daring may have been an incentive to him. No argument against Cyrus' conquest of Arabia can be found in the difficulty of the enterprise.

5. The Chronological Factor

The query presents itself as to whether Cyrus was not so occupied with other projects that he could not find time for a campaign in Arabia. The annals of his reign, as they are known at present, furnish no basis for the view that Cyrus was too busy to pay any attention to Arabia. He established his power over the Lydians in 546 B. C., and in 540 B. C. he began his attack upon Babylon.[545] No definite major operation is ascribed to the interim of six years. The statement of Berossus that Cyrus conquered all the rest of Asia before he

[544] *BHT* pp. 84, 88, col. II, line 22.
[545] *CAH* III, pp. 222f, 305, 520f.

advanced against Babylon and that of Xenophon that he subdued the Phrygians, the Cappadocians, and the Arabians prior to his attack upon the Babylonian capital may be regarded as referring to events which took place between 546 B. C. and 540 B. C.[546] There was ample opportunity in this period for an Arabian expedition of suitable proportions. No chronological difficulty opposes the theory that Cyrus used military force to deprive the Babylonians of their dependency in Arabia. It is not necessary to assume that Cyrus conducted the expedition in person. Cambyses, the heir to the throne, was old enough in 539 B. C. to share the responsibilities of government,[547] and it is not impossible that he may have been entrusted with some of the military projects of his father prior to that date. As to this there can be no certainty, however, and hence it is best not to regard it as more than a suggested hypothesis. If the king of Babylon was still at Têmâ, it is conceivable that the king of Persia himself commanded whatever expedition was made against the Arabian city.[548]

Although the sources at our disposal furnish meager data, the evidence which is available favors the view that Cyrus had wrested Arabia from Babylonian control before he marched against Babylon. The details of this conquest of Arabia are not at hand. Reliance must be placed upon future discoveries to reveal the true course of events.

[546] Cyrus had the Bactrians, the Sacae, and the Egyptians as well as the Babylonians upon his hands. See Herodotus I, 153.

[547] See p. 95 and note 311.

[548] The possibility that a Persian general conducted a military campaign in Arabia at the behest of Cyrus should be kept in mind. Herodotus I, 153, indicates that Cyrus placed one of his officers in charge of military operations against the Ionians.

XIII

EVENTS CONNECTED WITH THE FALL OF BABYLON

In the introductory section of this chapter it is not necessary to enumerate all the catastrophes which overtook the city of Babylon, for it fell more than once into the hands of its foes. However, there is advantage in noting that Babylonia's great metropolis succumbed five times to foreign invasion during a period of about two centuries, extending from the latter part of Assyrian overlordship to the fourth Persian king. When Sennacherib captured it in 689 B. C., he devastated much of its area. Ashurbanipal caused the city to surrender in 648 B. C. Cyrus added it to his kingdom in 539 B. C. Darius I subdued the rebellious capital in 521 B. C. Xerxes I turned much of it into ruins in 483 B. C. All these events are described in any good history of Babylonia. Military conquest affected the fortunes of Babylon at many critical stages in its history. It is all the more remarkable, therefore, that its capitulation to Cyrus in 539 B. C. should be designated 'The Fall of Babylon,' as if no other like event had occurred in the city's history. Even the submission of Babylon to Alexander in 331 B. C. pales in importance when compared with the disaster which brought the Neo-Babylonian empire to a close.

A reasonable explanation of this phenomenon commends itself to the inquirer. Cyrus' capture of Babylon brought about far-reaching consequences. Its subjugation by Sennacherib and Ashurbanipal had not removed the balance of power from Semitic control, but the triumph of Persia in 539 B. C. introduced a new predominating influence in ancient Oriental developments. That date marks the turning-point in favor of Aryan leadership, a directing force which has maintained itself at the forefront of civilization down to the present day. The victories of Cyrus culminating in Babylon's inclusion in the Persian empire laid the foundation for later historical developments.[549] It is probable that Greek and Roman conquests in the East would have resulted even if domination by Persia had not prepared the way, but the fact remains that Cyrus assumed the rôle

[549] The prominence of the date in Biblical history has also accentuated its importance.

of arbiter in Oriental affairs two centuries before the time of Alexander. For this reason events connected with the fall of Babylon in 539 B. C. merit careful study.

1. Data Furnished by the Nabonidus Chronicle

Babylonian literature, as recovered thus far, provides no minute record of the events connected with the capture of Babylon by Cyrus. The *Nabonidus Chronicle* contains the most lengthy cuneiform account of the occurrences which preceded and accompanied the fall of the city. However, the statements in this narrative are so brief that most details are left to the imagination. It is evident that the chronicler did not endeavor to describe all that happened in connection with Cyrus' campaign against Babylonia. Each prominent incident in the unfolding of the drama of a dynasty's collapse is alluded to very briefly. The cuneiform scribe was handicapped by his effort to place the annals of Nabonidus' reign and the story of the victorious Persian invasion upon a single clay tablet. It is very likely that this procedure resulted in the omission of much that would be of extreme interest to the modern historian. That the *Nabonidus Chronicle* is silent concerning many things which we should like to know is regrettable; that it reveals many facts not stated in other sources causes it to be recognized as a valuable cuneiform document. The sections of the *Nabonidus Chronicle* dealing with the fall of Babylon will now be considered.[550]

(1) New Year's Festival Observed

All authorities agree that the passage about to be quoted represents the beginning of the record of the seventeenth year of Nabonidus' reign. It is highly probable that line 5 began with the words *Šattu 17*^{kam}, 'In the seventeenth year.' The text proceeds thus:

[5]. . . . *^{d}Nabû ultu Bar-sip^{ki} ana maḫrie(-e)* . . . . [6]. . . . *ab šarru a-na Ê-tur-kalam-ma êrub ina* . . . . [7]. . . . *ut-tim bal-tum karâni pal-ki-tum libbi*

[550] Cyrus seems to have made his first move against Babylonia in the ninth year of Nabonidus' reign. It was in this year that Cyrus crossed the Tigris below Arbela and slew a king. See *BHT* pp. 101, 112, 116, col. 88, line 15f. Cf. *Cyropaedia* VII, 2, 4–8; *CAH* III, p. 223. In this connection the fact that Nabonidus in the ninth year of his reign, according to Herodotus I, 77, made an alliance with the Lydians and the Egyptians against Cyrus should be kept in mind.

um-[ma-ni] .... ^{8}.... ^{d}*Bêl ittaṣâ(-a) isinnu a-ki-tu kî šal-mu êpušu(-šu) ina* ^{araḫ}.... ^{9}....^{meš} *ša Maradda(-da)*^{ki} ^{d}*Za-bà-bà u ilâni*^{meš} *ša Kiš*^{ki} ^{d}*Nin-lil* .... ^{10}*Ḫar-sag-kalam-ma ana Bâbili*^{ki} *êrubûni*^{meš}*(-ni) adi qît* ^{araḫ}*Ulûli ilâni*^{meš} *ša* ^{mât}*Akkadî* .... ^{11}*ša eli irṣiti u šapal irṣiti ana Bâbili*^{ki} *êru-bûni*^{meš}*(-ni) ilâni*^{meš} *ša Bar-sip*^{ki} *Kuti* .... ^{12a}*u Sip-par*^{ki} *lâ êrubûni*^{meš}*(-ni).*[551]

^{5}[In the seventeenth year] Nabû came from Borsippa to meet .... ^{6}.... The king entered Êturkalamma .... ^{7}.... The abundance of wine was ample among the [troops] .... ^{8}.... Bêl went forth. They kept the New Year's festival as is right. In the month .... ^{9}.... [the gods] of Maradda, Zababa (Ilbaba) and the gods of Kish, Ninlil, [and the gods of] ^{10}Ḫarsagkalamma entered Babylon. Until the end of Elul the gods of Akkad ...., ^{11}who were above the earth and below the earth, entered Babylon. The gods of Borsippa, Kutha .... ^{12a}and Sippar did not enter [Babylon].

The above passage contains the only intimation in extant cuneiform literature of Nabonidus' presence in Babylon after his stay at Têmâ in Arabia. The *Nabonidus Chronicle* asserts that the New Year's festival was neglected in the seventh, ninth, tenth, and eleventh years on account of Nabonidus' absence from Babylon. His return is indicated in the record of the seventeenth year. Because of his presence in the capital the proper observance of the New Year's festival could take place. Jubilation among the troops with a plentiful supply of wine was one of the features of the celebration. The religious character of the festival is shown by the participation of numerous city cults which were represented by their respective deities.

(2) Opis Attacked by Cyrus

In the march of Cyrus' army against Babylon the only real battle of the campaign was fought at Opis:

^{12b}*Ina* ^{araḫ}*Tišrîti* ^{m}*Ku-raš ṣal-tum ina Upie*^{ki} *ina muḫ-⌈ḫi⌉* $^{13\,nâr}$*I-dig-lat ana libbi ummani(-ni)* ^{mât}*Akkadî*^{ki} *kî êpušu(-šu)* [*erasure*] *nišê*^{meš} ^{mât}*Akkadî*^{ki} ^{14a}*iqqur itti napiḫti nišê*^{meš} *idûk.*[552]

^{12b,13}In the month Tishri,[553] when Cyrus fought at Opis on the Tigris river

[551] *TSBA* VII, pp. 162–164; *KB* III, 2, p. 132f; *BA* II, p. 220f; *BHT* p. 113, pl. XIII.

[552] *TSBA* VII, p. 164f; *KB* III, 2, p. 132f; *BA* II, 222f; *BHT loc. cit.*

[553] That Opis was conquered as the result of a strenuous military operation is indicated by the fact that the battle raged during a period of days. The intimation of the cuneiform statement is that a portion of the month of Tishri was required for this part of Cyrus' campaign. Hagen, *BA* II, p. 223, reads 'Tammuz' instead of 'Tishri.'

against the troops of Akkad, the people of Akkad [14a]he destroyed by means of a conflagration; he put the people to death.

(3) *Sippar Captured by Cyrus*

The account of the capture of Sippar is in the form of a mere statement by the chronicler:

[14b]*Ûmu 14*$^{[kam]}$*Sippar*^{ki} *ba-la ṣal-tum ṣa-bit* [15a] ^{md}*Nabû-nâ'id iḫliq*(*ḪA-A*).[554]

[14b]On the fourteenth day Sippar was captured without fighting. [15a]Nabonidus fled.

(4) *Gobryas in Babylon*

Babylon fell without a drastic struggle into the hands of Gobryas, the main general of Cyrus:

[15b]*Ûmu 16*$^{[kam]}$ ^{m}*Ug*(?)*-ba-ru* ^{amêl}*paḫât* ^{mât}*Gu-ti-um u ummanâte*^{meš} ^{m}*Ku-raš ba-la ṣal-tum* [16]*ana Bâbili*^{ki} *êrubûni arki* ^{d}*Nabû-nâ'id kî šib-sa ina Bâbili*^{ki} *ṣa-bit adi qît arḫi* ^{mašak}*tuk-ku*^{me} [17]*ša* ^{mât}*Gu-ti-um bâbâni*^{meš} *ša Ê-sag-gil isḫurûni be-la ša manma ina Ê-sag-gil u Êkurâti*^{meš} [18a]*ul iš-ša-kin ù si-ma-nu ul êtiq*(*-iq*).[555]

[15b]On the sixteenth day Ugbaru (Gobryas),[556] the governor of Gutium, and the troops of Cyrus without fighting [16]entered Babylon. Afterwards when Nabonidus returned he was taken captive in Babylon. Until the end of the month the shields [17, 18a]of Gutium surrounded the gates of Êsagila. No one's weapon was placed in Êsagila or the sanctuaries, and no appointed time was disregarded.

The passage referring to Nabonidus has been interpreted in different ways. Some draw the conclusion that Nabonidus was captured because he 'delayed' or 'remained' in Babylon. Sidney Smith prefers the following translation: 'Afterwards Nabonidus, when he returned to Babylon, was taken prisoner.'[557] The above translation by the

---

Smith, *BHT*, p. 121, states that the reading 'Tishri' is certain. See *BHT*, pl. XIII, line 12, where the signs for *Ina* ^{arab}*Tišrîti* may be clearly seen in the new copy made by Smith.

[554] *TSBA* VII, p. 165; *KB* III, 2, p. 134f; *BA* II, p. 222f; *BHT loc. cit.*

[555] *TSBA* VII, p. 165f; *KB* III, 2, p. 134f; *BA* II, p. 222f; *BHT loc. cit.*

[556] For Sidney Smith's view of Ugbaru and Gubaru see *BHT* p. 121f.

[557] See *BHT* p. 117, col. III, line 16. See *ibid.*, p. 121, note on *kî šibsa* line 16. If tablets dated at the close of Nabonidus' reign and at the beginning of Cyrus' reign are to be relied upon, some doubt must be entertained as to when the reign of Nabonidus

writer varies very little from this in sense. According to Berossus Nabonidus was finally exiled to Carmania. The reference to the fact that the temple Êsagila and the other sanctuaries of the city were kept inviolate indicates that the invaders maintained a punctilious regard for the religious scruples of the Babylonians. There was no tendency to run counter to any of the pious customs of those who were called upon to acclaim the new régime. Every impulse which was sacred in the eyes of the people was allowed its due expression.

---

closed officially. The last completely dated tablet of the reign of Nabonidus belongs to the tenth day of the eighth month of his seventeenth year (*StrNbn* 1054: 8, 9). An incompletely dated tablet belongs to the ninth month of the same year (*StrNbn* 1055: 3, 4; *BE* VIII, 1, p. 3f). The earliest tablet dated in the reign of Cyrus belongs to the seventh month of his accession year, the day of the month being illegible (*StrCyr* 1: 14, 15). The next Cyrus tablet belongs to the twenty-fourth day of the eighth month of his accession year (*StrCyr* 2: 5, 6). The situation can be explained best by listing from available cuneiform sources the important dates of the Babylonian year, the first part of which is known as the seventeenth year of Nabonidus and the last part of which is known as the accession year of Cyrus. The list is as follows:

	Month	*Day*
New Year's festival observed	1	—
Opis attacked by Cyrus	7	—
Sippar captured by Cyrus	7	14
Babylon taken by Gobryas	7	16
First Cyrus tablet	7	—
Babylon entered by Cyrus	8	3
Next to last Nabonidus tablet	8	10
Death of a prominent person	8	11
Second Cyrus tablet	8	24
Last Nabonidus tablet	9	—
Beginning of period of mourning	12	28

The above suggests that there may have been a state of considerable political confusion in connection with the fall of Babylon, since there was a period of about two months when there seems to have been a difference of opinion as to who the real ruler was. The exact length of the period cannot be determined because the day of the month is missing on the first Cyrus tablet, and hence it is not known to which part of the seventh month it belongs. However, it seems more likely that the earliest tablet mentioning Cyrus as king was written after Gobryas' occupation of Babylon. During the period of confusion some scribes continued to recognize Nabonidus as king, while others accepted Cyrus as king. This may mean that certain Babylonians remained loyal to Nabonidus as long as possible, while others accepted Cyrus as king at the earliest opportunity. See p. 73f for a discussion of the political disorder which seems to have existed at the beginning of Nabonidus' reign.

(5) *Cyrus in Babylon*

Cyrus entered Babylon in peace. He reorganized the city politically and restored the religious order of the land:

[18b] ^{araḫ}*Araḫsamnu ûmu 3*^{kam} ^{m}*Ku-raš ana Bâbili*^{ki} *êrub* [19]*ḫa-ri-ni-e ina pâni-šu šêṭu*^{meš} *šú-lum ana âli ša-kin* ^{m}*Ku-raš šú-lum ana Bâbili*^{ki} [20]*gab-bi-šu qi-bi* ^{m}*Gu-ba-ru* ^{amêl}*paḫâtu-šu* ^{amêl}*paḫâti*^{meš} *ina Bâbili*^{ki} *ip-te-qid* [21]*ultu* ^{araḫ}*Kislimi adi* ^{araḫ}*Addari ilâni*^{meš} *ša* ^{mât}*Akkadî*^{ki} *ša* ^{md}*Nabû-nâ'id ana Bâbili*^{ki} *ú-še-ri-du* . . . . [22a]*a-na ma-ḫa-zi-šu-nu itûrû*^{meš}.[558]

[18b]In the month Marchesvan, the third day, Cyrus entered Babylon. [19, 20]*Ḫarinê*[559] were carried before him. Peace was established in the city; Cyrus decreed peace for all in Babylon. Gobryas, his governor, placed governors in charge of Babylon. [21]From the month Kislev to the month Adar, the gods whom Nabonidus had brought up to Babylon . . . . [22a]they returned to their cities.

It should be noted that the entry of Cyrus into Babylon did not take place until seventeen days after the military occupation of the city had been achieved by Gobryas. There had been sufficient time for adjustment to the new situation. If there was a faction in the city which failed to sympathize with Cyrus' aims it was effectually quelled. The Persian king was welcomed by the Babylonians. He reciprocated by proclaiming peace to all in the city. Systematic political control was established under the direction of Gobryas, and the religious policy of Nabonidus was reversed by returning to their proper cities those gods which had been brought to Babylon.[560]

(6) *Death and Lamentation*

The joyful acclamation of Cyrus by the Babylonians was followed quickly by the death of a prominent personage and a period of mourning:

[22b] ^{araḫ}*Araḫsamnu muši ûmu 11*^{kam} ^{m}*Ug-ba-ru BAD*[561] *ina* $^{\text{[araḫ]}}$. . . . [23] . . .

[558] *TSBA* VII, p. 166f; *KB* III, 2, p. 134f; *BA* II, p. 222f; *BHT loc. cit.*

[559] The meaning of *ḫarinê* is uncertain. See suggestions in *CD* p. 339.

[560] See note 522 for parallel references.

[561] The reading (*BAD* = *imût*) in *BHT* p. 114 is textually correct, and hence there is warrant for the conclusion that Ugbaru died. If so, then, on the assumption that Gubaru and Ugbaru refer to the same person, we must assume that there was another Gubaru (Gobryas), who was governor of Babylon and the District beyond the River

šarri BAD-at ultu [*ûmi*] *28*[*[kam]*] *ša* [*arah*]*Addari adi ûmi 3*[*kam*] *ša* [*arah*]*Nisanni biki-tum ina Akkadî*[*[ki]*] .... [24a]*nišê*[*meš*] *gab-bi qaqqad-su-nu ilbinû*(*GAB*[*meš*]).[562]

[22b]In the month Marchesvan, on the night of the eleventh, Ugbaru (Gobryas) died. In the month .... [23]. ... of the king died. From the twenty-eighth day of the month Adar to the third day of the month Nisan there was weeping in the land of Akkad .... [24a]All the people prostrated their heads.

The original text indicates the 28th day in line 23 instead of the 27th. Several fragmentary lines follow, with an indefinite reference to Cambyses, the son of Cyrus. It seems that Cambyses participated in a New Year's temple ceremony which took place on the fourth day of the month Nisan.

There has been considerable difference of opinion as to the reading of the opening part of line 23. Pinches was the first to publish the text in 1882. He read the passage *ù šarru IM-at*, 'and the king died.'[563] Winckler in 1889 read *DAM šarri BE-at*, 'the wife of the king died.'[564] Schrader in 1890 transliterated and translated the passage as follows: *aššat šarri mîta-at*, 'the wife of the king died.'[565] Hagen in 1894 read *u(?) mâr šarri ušmât(-at)*, 'and he killed the son of the king.'[566] This uncertainty exists because the sign before *LUGAL* = *šarru*, 'king,' is badly preserved upon the tablet. Hagen in making his new

during the early part of Persian control of Babylonia. If, as Smith suggests (*BHT* p. 121), Gubaru and Ugbaru were different persons, there is less difficulty in interpreting the text, but there must be more light upon the historical situation before final conclusions can be reached.

[562] *TSBA* VII, p. 167; *KB* III, 2, p. 134f; *BA* II, p. 222f; *BHT* p. 114. For several suitable meanings of *GAB* (line 24a), including *labânu*, 'throw down,' see *Bar* 180. Note the idiom *laban appi*, 'prostration of the face.' Thus *qaqqad-su-nu* could be construed with the verb *labânu*. This is Hagen's view, *BA* II, p. 222. Schrader in *KB* III, 2, p. 134f, reads *nišê gab-bi qaqqad-su-nu upaṭṭiru*, 'Alle Leute spalteten ihren Scheitel.' Smith in *BHT* p. 114 reads *nišê(pl) gab-bi qaqqad-su-nu ipaṭṭaru(pl)*, 'All the people struck their heads.' If *GAB* in this context stands for the verb *paṭâru*, Smith's rendering is more likely than Schrader's. It seems that the reading *nišê*[*meš*] *gab-bi qaqqad-su-nu ilbinû*, 'All the people prostrated their heads,' is not without some appropriateness.

[563] *TSBA* VII, p. 167. For *BE* = *mâtu*, 'die,' see *B* 1517; *Bar* 70.

[564] *Untersuchungen zur altorientalischen Geschichte*, p. 154f.

[565] *KB* III, 2, p. 134.

[566] *BA* II, p. 222. *BE-at* can stand for *ušmât*, the masculine form of the causative stem, third person, singular, or *mîtat*, the feminine permansive form, third person, singular.

copy of the text in 1894[567] read *u TUR* = *u mâru* instead of the *ù* of Pinches and the *DAM* = *aššatu* of Winckler. The most recent copy and interpretation of the text were published by Sidney Smith in 1924.[568] He represents line 23 as beginning with cuneiform wedges which may be regarded as part of a mutilated *DAM*.[569] His comment is as follows: "The traces favor Pinches' reading *DAM*. Hagen's reading is impossible, though Pinches accepted it; see Craig Robinson, *The Fall of Babylon*, p. 14 (a paper read before the Victoria Institute)."[570] Smith translates: '(the wife) of the king died,'[571] thus favoring the interpretation of Winckler and Schrader. The writer would state, after an examination of the tablet itself in the British Museum, that the traces which remain of the original cuneiform sign or signs at the beginning of line 23 are not sufficiently legible for decisive conclusion as to what the scribe actually wrote. The discovery of an unmutilated duplicate of the text can alone settle the matter.

It should be noted, however, that several circumstances favor the view that the text records the death of the wife of the king. The fifth chapter[572] of Daniel and Xenophon[573] agree that the death of Belshazzar occurred in connection with the actual capture of Babylon. According to the cuneiform account Babylon fell into the hands of

[567] *BA* II, opposite p. 248. On p. 247, *ibid.*, Hagen says: "Ich glaube in der That *mâr šarri* sicher erkennen zu können." Delitzsch, *ibid.*, *loc. cit.*, in commenting upon the original text which he examined, says: "Am Anfang von Z. 23 glaube auch ich *TUR* noch deutlich zu erkennen, vorher aber stand wohl noch ein ganz schmales Zeichen wie *ši* oder *ša*. Das Wahrscheinlichste ist mir *ša* und ich möchte darum, natürlich unter Vorbehalt, vorschlagen zu lesen: *ina muḫ-ḫi ŠA*, d.i., *iššakin* (er ging drauflos, oder viell. besser: er siegte ob) tödtet den Sohn des Königs." Pinches, *The Old Testament in the Light of the Historical Records of Assyria and Babylonia*, p. 417, contributes the following comment: "An earlier explanation was that the doubtful group (of cuneiform signs) stood for 'the wife' of the king, but in this case it would be difficult to explain how it is that the verbal form (which is ideographically written, and may be read either *imât*, 'he dies,' *tamât*, 'she dies,' or *metât*, 'she died') should differ from that used in the case of the king's mother, where *imtût*, the historical tense of the secondary form of the *qal*, is the form used. The use of *imât* for *imût*, 'he died,' would be paralleled by the use of *îrab* for *îrub*, 'he entered,' in other parts of the inscription."

[568] *BHT* pls. XI–XIV. See ibid., pp. 98–123.

[569] *Ibid.*, pl. XIII, line 23.

[570] *Ibid.*, p. 122, note on line 23.

[571] *Ibid.*, p. 118.

[572] Daniel 5: 30.

[573] *Cyropaedia* VII, 5, 30.

Gobryas without general resistance on the sixteenth day of the month Tishri. It was after this event that Nabonidus was captured.[574] Cyrus entered the city a little over two weeks later. If there is any harmony at all between the cuneiform record, the account of Xenophon, and the statement found in the fifth chapter of Daniel, Belshazzar must have been slain at the time Gobryas took possession of Babylon. This being the case, it is not hard to believe that 'the wife of the king,' Belshazzar's mother, died after the entrance of Cyrus into Babylon. Grief on account of the death of her son and the passing of Babylon into foreign hands may have hastened the death of Nabonidus' queen. Like him she was probably advanced in years.[575] If, as has been shown,[576] the wife of Nabonidus was Nitocris and if the probability that she was a daughter of Nebuchadrezzar[577] is taken into account, the lamentation which took place gains new significance. These are considerations which should not be overlooked in an endeavor to determine the original meaning of the *Nabonidus Chronicle*.

2. Data Furnished by the Cyrus Cylinder

Another cuneiform document dealing in a general way with the close of Nabonidus' reign and the establishment of Persian rule in Babylonia is known as the *Cyrus Cylinder*. This is not a circumstantial narrative of events. The text is confined to an exaltation of Cyrus' rôle as champion of the rights of the Babylonian people. The first part of the record is in a very fragmentary condition.[578] It is possible to determine, however, from the portions of lines which remain that the aim of the chronicler was to make a strong case in favor of Persian intervention in the affairs of Babylonia. The inhabitants of the land are represented as suffering under the tyranny of an impious oppressor, so much so that Marduk, their supreme god, is moved to pity. This induces the deity to select a leader who will save the people from the consequences of their deplorable condition.

[574] There is no reference to the death of Nabonidus. Berossus states that Cyrus gave Nabonidus Carmania as a place in which he could spend the rest of his life. See Josephus, *Contra Apionem* I, 20.

[575] See p. 32f.

[576] See pp. 38ff.

[577] See pp. 51–63.

[578] *KA* p. 2f, line 1–10.

(*1*) *Cyrus Chosen as Universal Ruler*

^{11b}*Kul-lat ma-ta-a-ta ka-li-ši-na i-ḫi-iṭ ib-ri-e-šu* ^{12}*iš-te-'-e-ma ma-al-ki i-ša-ru bi-bil lib-bi šá it-ta-ma-aḫ qa-tu-uš-šu* ^{m}*Ku-ra-aš šar* ^{âl}*An-ša-an it-ta-bi ni-bi-it-su a-na ma-li-ku-tim kul-la-ta nap-ḫar iz-zak-ra šú-*[*ma-šu*] ^{13} ^{mât}*Ku-ti-i gi-mir Um-man-man-da ú-ka-an-ni-šá a-na še-pi-šú nišê*^{meš} *ṣal-mat qaqqadu(-du) šá ú-šá-ak-ši-du qa-ta-a-šu* ^{14}*i-na ki-it-tim ù mi-ša-ru iš-te-ni-'-e-ši-na-a-tim* ^{d}*Marduk bêlu rabû ta-ru-ú nišê*^{meš}*-šu ip-še-e-ti šá dam-qa-a-ta ù lib-ba-šú i-šá-ra ḫa-di-iš ip-pa-*[*al*]*-li-is* ^{15}*a-na âli-šú Bâb-ilâni*$^{\text{meš ki}}$ *a-la-ak-šú iq-bi ú-ša-aṣ-bi-it-su-ma ḫar-ra-nu Bâbili*^{ki} *ki-ma ib-ri ù tap-pi-e it-tal-la-ka i-da-a-šú.*[579]

^{11b}The totality of all lands he (Marduk) surveyed (and) inspected. ^{12}He sought a righteous prince according to his heart's desire who would grasp his hands. Cyrus, the king of Anshan, whose name he uttered, he proclaimed for lordship over everything. ^{13}The land of Kutha, the totality of the Umman-Manda he subdued to his feet. The black-headed people, whom he allowed to approach his hands, ^{14}he was mindful of in truth and righteousness. Marduk, the great lord, the protector of his people, looked joyfully upon his pious deeds and his righteous heart. ^{15}He decreed his march upon his city, Babylon, and caused him to take the road to Babylon. Like a friend and companion he went by his side.

(*2*) *Babylon's Submission to Cyrus*

^{16}*Um-ma-ni-šú rap-šá-a-tim šá ki-ma me-e nâri lâ ú-ta-ad-du-ú ni-ba-šú-un kakkê*^{meš}*-šú-nu ṣa-an-du-ma i-šá-ad-di-ḫa i-da-a-šú* ^{17}*ba-lu qab-li ù ta-ḫa-zi ú-še-ri-ba-aš qi-rib Bâbili*^{ki} *âla-šú Bâb-ilâni*$^{\text{meš ki}}$ *i-ṭi-ir i-na šap-šá-qi* ^{md}*Nabû-nâ'id šarru lâ pa-li-ḫi-šú ú-ma-al-la-a qa-tu-uš-šu* ^{18}*nišê*^{meš} *Bâbili*^{ki} *ka-li-šú-nu nap-ḫar* ^{mât}*Šú-me-ri u Akkadî*^{ki} *ru-bi-e ù šak-kan-nak-ka šá-pal-šú ik-mi-sa ú-na-aš-ši-qu še-pu-uš-šú iḫ-du-ú a-na šarru-ú-ti-šu im-mi-ru pa-nu-uš-šu-un* ^{19}*be-lu šá i-na tu-kul-ti-šá ú-bal-li-ṭu mi-tu-ta-an i-na bu-ta-qu ù pa-ki-e ig-mi-lu kul-la-ta-an ṭa-bi-iš ik-ta-ar-ra-bu-šú iš-tam-ma-ru zi-ki-ir-šú.*[580]

^{16}His widespread troops, whose number like the waters of a river is not known, put on their weapons and advanced at his side. ^{17}Without encounter and battle he caused him to enter into the midst of Babylon, his city. He saved Babylon from need. Nabonidus, the king who did not venerate him (Marduk) he (Marduk) delivered into his hands (*i.e.* the hands of Cyrus).

[579] *KA* pp. 2–5.
[580] *KA* p. 4f.

[18]All the people of Babylon, the totality of the land of Sumer and Akkad, the princes and governors prostrated themselves unto him (and) kissed his feet. They rejoiced in his sovereignty (and) their countenances shone. [19]The lord (*i.e.* Cyrus), who through his might brought the dead to life (and) through destruction and *pa-ki-e* protected all, they served gladly (and) revered his name.

The two sections which have been quoted in transliteration and translation represent that part of the text of the *Cyrus Cylinder* which describes Marduk's appointment of Cyrus as universal sovereign with the resultant yielding of Babylon to his rule. Affirmations are made in the third person so as to give due recognition to the influence and power of Marduk. The rest of the inscription is in the first person with Cyrus as spokesman. He begins with the usual formula, viz., 'I (am) Cyrus, the king of totality, the great king, the mighty king, the king of Babylon, the king of Sumer and Akkad, the king of the four quarters (of the world),' etc. This is followed by a passage recounting some of the benefits which accrued from Cyrus' assumption of authority:

(3) *Cyrus' Interest in Babylon's Welfare*

[22b]*E-nu-ma a-*[*na qi*]*-rib Bâbili*^{ki} *e-ru-bu sa-li-mi-iš* [23]*i-na ul-ṣi ù ri-šá-a-tim i-na êkal ma-al-ki ar-ma-a šú-bat be-lu-tim* ^{d}*Marduk bêlu rabû lib-bi ri-it-pa-šú ša mârê*$^{[meš]}$ *Bâbili*^{ki} *ù . . . . an-ni-ma ū-mi-šam a-še-'-a pa-la-aḫ-šu* [24]*um-ma-ni-ia rap-šá-a-tim i-na qi-rib Bâbili*^{ki} *i-šá-ad-di-ḫa šu-ul-ma-niš nap-ḫar* ^{mât}[*Šú-me-ri*] *ù Akkadî*^{ki} *mu-gal-*[*li*]*-tim ul ú-šar-ši* [25]*qi-rib Bâbili*^{ki} *ù kul-lat ma-ḫa-zi-šu i-na šá-li-im-tim aš-te-'-e mârê*^{meš} *Bâbi*[*li*^{ki}] *. . . .*^{ki} *ma-la lib . . . . ma ab-ša-a-ni lâ si-ma-ti-šu-nu šú-bat-su-*[*un*] [26]*an-ḫu-ut-su-un ú-pa-aš-ši-ḫa ú-šá-ap-ṭi-ir sa-ar-ba-šú-nu a-na ip-še-e-ti-*[*ia*] ^{d}*Marduk bêlu rabû-*(*ú*) *iḫ-di-e-ma* [27]*a-na ia-a-ti* ^{m}*Ku-ra-aš šarru pa-li-iḫ-šú ù* ^{m}*Ka-am-bu-zi-ia mâri ṣi-it lib-bi-*[*ia ù a*]*-na nap-ḫar um-ma-ni-ia* [28]*da-am-qi-iš ik-ru-ub-ma i-na ša-lim-tim ma-ḫar-šá ṭa-bi-iš ni-it-ta-*[*'-id i-lu-ti-šú*] *ṣir-ti.*[581]

[22b]When I had entered into the midst of Babylon in peace, [23]I took the seat of lordship in the palace of princes amidst jubilation and rejoicing. Marduk, the great lord, the receptive heart of the inhabitants of Babylon . . . . , while I daily attended to his worship. [24]My numerous troops advanced peacefully into the midst of Babylon. I did not permit an enemy

[581] *KA* pp. 4–7.

in all the land of Sumer and Akkad. [25]The inner part of Babylon and all its cities I cared for in peace; the inhabitants of Babylon . . . . [I freed] from a yoke which was not fitting. (As to) their dwellings, [26]I repaired their dilapidation; I removed their ruins.[582] Marduk, the great lord, rejoiced on account of my deeds. [27]Unto me, Cyrus, the king who venerates him, and Cambyses, the son (and) offspring of my heart, and unto the totality of my troops [28]he was graciously favorable; in peace before it[583] we gladly praise his lofty divinity.

The above passage is followed by a reference to the wide tribute and homage which was accorded to Cyrus. The few lines containing this statement have already been translated.[584]

(4) *Cyrus' Restoration of the Gods to their Sanctuaries*

[30b]*Iš-tu . . . . a-di* ^{âl}*Aššur*^{ki} *ù Šušan*^{ki} [31]*A-ga-de*^{ki} ^{mât}*Eš-nu-nak* ^{âl}*Za-am-ba-an* ^{âl}*Me-tur-nu Dêri*^{ki} *a-di pa-aṭ* ^{mât}*Ku-ti-i ma-ḫa-za [ša e-bir]-ti* ^{nâr}*Diqlat šá iš-tu ap-na-ma na-du-ú šú-bat-su-un* [32]*ilâni*^{meš} *a-ši-ib lib-bi-šu-nu a-na aš-ri-šú-nu ú-tir-ma ú-šar-ma-a šú-bat da-er-a-ta kul-lat nišê*^{meš}*-šu-nu ú-pa-aḫ-ḫi-ra-am-ma ú-te-ir da-ad-mi-šu-un* [33]*ù ilâni*^{meš} ^{mât}*Šú-me-ri ù Akkadî*^{ki} *šá* ^{md}*Nabû-nâ'id a-na ug-ga-tim bêl ilâni*^{meš} *ú-še-ri-bi a-na qi-rib Bâbili*^{ki} *i-na qi-bi-ti* ^{d}*Marduk bêlu rabû i-na šá-li-im-tim* [34]*i-na maš-ta-ki-šú-nu ú-še-ši-ib šú-ba-at ṭu-ub lib-bi.*[585]

[30b]From . . . . unto Ashur and Susa, [31]Agade, Eshnunak, Zamban, Me-Turnu (and) Dêr including the district of Kutha, the cities beyond the Tigris, whose settlements were established of old, [32]I returned unto their (proper) place the gods who dwelt in them and established (them in) an eternal habitation. All their peoples I assembled and restored (to) their dwellings. [33]And the gods of the land of Sumer and Akkad, whom Nabonidus to the rage of the lord of the gods brought into Babylon, at the command of Marduk, the great lord, unmolested [34]I caused to reside in their dwellings, an abiding-place of joy to the heart.[586]

The rest of the inscription consists of an unmutilated section a line and a half long and ten almost entirely illegible lines. The

[582] See *KA* p. 4, note *e*, where Weissbach holds that *sarba* stands for *zarba*, from *zarâbu*, 'fallen.'

[583] It is evident that the *ša* of *ma-ḫar-ša* refers to *ilûtu*, the gender of which is feminine. See *Hwb* p. 59.

[584] See p. 164.

[585] *KA* p. 6f.

[586] See note 522 for other references to Nabonidus' impiety.

part that can be read records a prayer by Cyrus for himself and Cambyses.[587]

3. Data from Greek Sources

Herodotus, Xenophon, and Berossus describe certain incidents which they represent as having occurred in connection with the capture of Babylon by Cyrus. A brief summary of their statements will suffice.

(1) Herodotus[588] asserts that the Babylonians advanced to meet the invading army of Cyrus and that a battle was fought in which the Babylonians were defeated. The latter retreated to their city and shut themselves in, having confidence in a great store of provisions which had been gathered. Herodotus emphasizes the warlike rather than the peaceful character of Cyrus' attitude towards the Babylonians. A tedious siege followed the investment of their capital. At length Cyrus diverted the waters of the Euphrates to such an extent that the stream was shallow enough to allow his troops access to the city. The end came at a time when a festival was being celebrated with much revelry.

(2) Xenophon[589] begins his account of the fall of Babylon by describing the maneuvers of Cyrus' army when it first encompassed the city. So extensive was the circumference of the walls that the troops presented a weak line in their attempt to surround them. On this account Cyrus withdrew his soldiers to their tents in the face of missiles from the Babylonians. The Persian king was convinced that he could not take the city by assault and hence he had a large trench dug for the purpose of deflecting part of the stream which flowed through Babylon. At the same time he built numerous watch-towers, using the trunks of palm trees for foundations. All the while the Babylonians derided these operations because they felt assured that they were capable of withstanding a siege of more than twenty years. When all preparations had been made Cyrus waited until the time of a festival which the Babylonians were in the habit of observing with drinking and revelry throughout the night. Then he lowered the river by causing much of its water to flow aside and thus the city was

[587] *KA* p. 6f, line 35f.
[588] Herodotus I, 190, 191.
[589] *Cyropaedia* VII, 5, 1–36.

entered. The attack was conducted by Gobryas, who made his way to the palace where 'the impious king' was slain. All the citadels of the city were captured and every Babylonian was forced to give up his arms. Xenophon comments upon the fact that Babylon was extremely hostile to Cyrus.[590] There is intimation that Cyrus used all possible means to establish his complete authority over the Babylonians.

(3) Berossus[591] states that when Cyrus approached Babylon Nabonidus met him in force. In the ensuing battle Nabonidus was defeated. He thereupon fled with a small company and found refuge in Borsippa. After Cyrus had captured Babylon he ordered its walls razed.[592] Thinking to besiege Nabonidus he advanced against Borsippa, but Nabonidus surrendered without attempting to defend himself. Due to the mercy of Cyrus, Nabonidus suffered only deportation to Carmania, where he spent the rest of his life.

4. Comparison of Data

Grouped according to sources the above data concerning the fall of Babylon may be regarded as exemplifying diversified views of the actual course of events. Three distinct strands of evidence are recognizable, viz., Persian, Greek, and Graeco-Babylonian. An attempt will be made to see whether these three groups of historical data can be harmonized.

(*1*) *Persian Data*

The *Nabonidus Chronicle* and the *Cyrus Cylinder*, although written in cuneiform, represent the Persian interpretation of what took place in connection with the fall of Babylon. Both these documents were recorded for the purpose of glorifying Cyrus and villifying Nabonidus. A third cuneiform document, *A Persian Verse Account of Nabonidus*,[593] strives to attain the same object, but, on account of defacement of some of its lines and difficulty in divining the meaning of many passages, it cannot be rated as throwing additional light

[590] *Ibid.*, VII, 5, 58.
[591] Josephus, *Contra Apionem* I, 20.
[592] The record of Berossus also emphasizes the hostility of Cyrus towards Babylon.
[593] *BHT* pp. 27–97. Note especially *ibid.*, p. 31f.

upon the capture of Babylon by Cyrus. That it endeavors to represent Nabonidus in an exceedingly unfavorable light is true and for this reason it must be classed with the *Nabonidus Chronicle* and the *Cyrus Cylinder*. These three texts furnish cumulative proof that there was a determined effort by means of Persian propaganda to undermine the influence of Nabonidus. He is depicted as the arch-heretic and defier of the wishes of the people. Cyrus, on the other hand, is portrayed as a divinely-chosen deliverer of the Babylonians and a restorer of the worship of the gods to its former prestige. That Nabonidus may have aroused some enmity towards himself among his subjects is entirely possible; that the Persians fostered exaggerated accounts of this disaffection for political ends is also conceivable. It does not seem that the situation could have been as bad as pictured. If it had been, the Babylonians would have known how to end the dynasty without looking to Cyrus for aid.[594] To admit the presence of a certain type of overstatement in the *Nabonidus Chronicle* does not invalidate the circumstantial data contained in it. This is shown by the fact that its assertions concerning Nabonidus' stay at Têmâ are corroborated by other cuneiform records.[595] The same is true of *A Persian Verse Account of Nabonidus*, which gives a detailed narrative of Nabonidus' campaign against Têmâ.[596] There is little in the *Cyrus Cylinder* which can be judged in the light of historical facts furnished by other documents now available. In spite of this some of its important assertions may possess historicity. Ultimately there must be comparison with fresh sources of information before literary records can be discarded as worthless. Belshazzar is not mentioned by name in any one of these three cuneiform texts. Nothing is more certain, however, than that the title *mâr šarri*, 'the son of the king,' of the *Nabonidus Chronicle* and the expression *reš-tu-ú bu-kur-šu*, 'his eldest, firstborn son,' of *A Persian Verse Account of Nabonidus* refer to Belshazzar, the son of Nabonidus. There are other cuneiform inscriptions which attach similar descriptive phrases to the name Bel-

[594] Both Amêl-Marduk and Lâbâshi-Marduk lost their lives as the result of conspiracy. See *CB* p. 30; Josephus, *Contra Apionem* I, 20; Cory, *Ancient Fragments*, etc., pp. 41, 45.

[595] See pp. 111–124.

[596] See p. 106f.

shazzar, and hence no doubt need be entertained as to their meaning when used alone in texts dated in the reign of Nabonidus.[597] As has been pointed out before, no allusions to Belshazzar occur in available Babylonian tablets after the fourteenth year of Nabonidus' reign.[598] The *argumentum e silentio* is an unsound one, and so it is wrong to conclude that Belshazzar's influence in the kingdom had come to naught several years before the fall of Babylon in 539 B. C. One may take it for granted that the latter part of his career will receive much illumination when many more texts of the period have been recovered and translated. For the same reason the non-mention of Belshazzar in the above-quoted cuneiform passages dealing with the actual fall of Babylon cannot be made the basis of definite inference.[599] The main purpose of these literary productions, inspired as they were by Persian political intrigue, was to calumniate Nabonidus. In seeking this aim there may have been scribal indifference to the rôle played by Belshazzar. The real explanation depends upon what discoveries will be made in the future.

2. Greek Data

Greek tradition as to what occurred in connection with the fall of Babylon has been preserved by Herodotus and Xenophon. The former begins by referring to a battle in which the Babylonians were defeated; the latter's initial account describes a slight skirmish at the walls of Babylon. As to further developments the two writers are in practical agreement. A long siege was in prospect because the Babylonians had laid up an immense store of provisions. This led to the lowering of the stream flowing through the city. The successful attack was made at a time when the Babylonians were absorbed in a festival. Both Herodotus and Xenophon indicate that there was hostility rather than amity between the Babylonians and Cyrus.[600]

[597] Nabonidus seems to have had a son called Nebuchadrezzar, but there is no evidence that Belshazzar had a real rival as *mâr šarri*. See note 325 and note 440.

[598] See p. 85.

[599] The value of the *Nabonidus Chronicle* as evidence is weakened by the fragmentary character of the inscription. See p. 191f. The *Cyrus Cylinder* does not attempt to give a circumstantial account of occurrences.

[600] Herodotus I, 190, indicates that the Babylonians shared the opinion of other nations that Cyrus 'was aggressive.' *Cyropaedia* VII, 5, 58, asserts that Cyrus knew that Babylon 'was as hostile to him as a city could be to a man.'

Herodotus calls the last Neo-Babylonian king Labynetus, the son of a king by that name.[601] Xenophon does not preserve the name of the king who was killed at the time Babylon was captured.[602] The name Belshazzar was unknown to both Herodotus and Xenophon. Can the facts of this Greek tradition as contained in the records of Herodotus and Xenophon be harmonized with what cuneiform inscriptions tell concerning the fall of Babylon? According to the latter, Cyrus defeated the Babylonians at Opis. This may be the battle to which Herodotus refers and concerning which Xenophon is silent. As to the taking of Sippar without a battle, non-Babylonian historians may not have been interested in chronicling so tame an event. Babylon was the preëminent Eastern city to the Greeks, and their writers seem to have been more interested in what took place at its capture than in the preliminary victories of Cyrus in Babylonia. The *Nabonidus Chronicle* mentions nothing concerning a siege of Babylon or the lowering of the river to gain access to the city. If these events were historical, it would appear that there ought to be evidences of them in cuneiform literature. However, the text of the *Nabonidus Chronicle* is extremely terse, and there is no assurance that it contains a complete statement of all that occurred in connection with Cyrus' conquest of Babylon. Nevertheless, it is in this connection that the greatest divergence exists. The *Nabonidus Chronicle* states that Gobryas and the troops of Cyrus entered Babylon *bala ṣaltum,*[603] 'without fighting.' In the record concerning Cyrus' battle with the Babylonians at Opis the idiom used to denote armed conflict is *ṣaltum epêšu,*[604] 'exercise hostility,' 'fight.' In the passage describing the taking of Sippar the expression employed is *bala ṣaltum ṣabit,*[605] 'was captured without fighting.' The import of the word *ṣaltum* is indicated by the slaughter which occurred at Opis. Therefore the statement that Babylon was entered 'without fighting' may mean that no general sanguinary battle transpired. Herodotus presents this view of the seizure of Babylon, but Xenophon's narrative gives the impression that there

[601] Herodotus I, 188.
[602] *Cyropaedia* VII, 5, 29, 30.
[603] See p. 170, line 15b of cuneiform passage quoted.
[604] See p. 169, lines 12b, 13, of cuneiform passage quoted.
[605] See p. 170, line 14b of cuneiform passage quoted.

was considerable bloodshed. The *Cyrus Cylinder* characterizes Cyrus' entry into Babylon with the following words: *Ba-lu qab-li ù ta-ḫa-zi ú-še-ri-ba-aš qi-rib Bâbili*[ki],[606] 'Without encounter and battle he (Marduk) caused him (Cyrus) to enter into the midst of Babylon.' A further statement of the same text is: *Um-ma-ni-ia rap-šá-a-tim i-na qi-rib Bâbili*[ki] *i-šá-ad-di-ḫa šu-ul-ma-niš*,[607] 'My numerous troops advanced peacefully into the midst of Babylon.' These affirmations accord with the language used by the *Nabonidus Chronicle* in depicting Cyrus' reception when he entered Babylon. Whether they can be applied without qualification to the actual capture of Babylon by Gobryas may be regarded as debatable. A reasonable interpretation of events is that the main test of military strength took place at Opis, that Sippar and Babylon yielded with no show of determined resistance, and that Cyrus was able to enter Babylon in royal procession after it had been brought under thorough control by his troops.[608] The battle at Opis proves that the Babylonians at first resisted Cyrus with great animosity, and the *Cyrus Cylinder* indicates that the Persian king demanded complete submission.[609] These considerations show that the enmity which Herodotus and Xenophon predicate as having existed between Cyrus and the Babylonians can claim some corroboration from cuneiform sources. Hence the picture of Cyrus as an entirely peaceful overthrower of the Neo-Babylonian dynasty cannot be accepted without modification.

3. Graeco-Babylonian Data

Berossus presents the Graeco-Babylonian version of the fall of Babylon. His account of an initial disastrous battle at a distance from Babylon agrees with what is stated in the *Nabonidus Chronicle* and with the narrative of Herodotus. New information furnished by Berossus is that Nabonidus was present in person at this battle and that he fled to Borsippa, where he surrendered after the fall of Babylon.

[606] See p. 176, line 17 of cuneiform passage quoted.

[607] See p. 177, line 24 of cuneiform passage quoted.

[608] The statements in Jeremiah 50, 51 are more in accord with what the *Nabonidus Chronicle* records concerning the conflict at Opis than with the description of Babylon's comparatively peaceful submission.

[609] Cyrus did not permit 'an enemy in all the land of Sumer and Akkad.' See p. 177, line 24 of translation.

This course of events may be accepted as partially possible, for there is nothing in the other sources capable of entirely disproving it. The *Nabonidus Chronicle* states that Nabonidus fled in connection with the capture of Sippar which occurred soon after the battle at Opis. That Nabonidus was within reach of his troops during the conflict at Opis is not improbable. His flight to Borsippa, which was not far from Babylon, is more difficult to understand.[610] An interesting point should not be overlooked. Berossus' indication that Nabonidus was not in Babylon when it was captured is in harmony with the assertion of the *Nabonidus Chronicle* that Nabonidus was taken prisoner when he returned to Babylon after Gobryas and the troops of Cyrus had entered it. That Belshazzar, who acted as the co-regent of Nabonidus, was with the army in Babylon is altogether likely. The further statement of Berossus that Nabonidus was exiled to Carmania cannot be refuted or corroborated. Its degree of historicity will be determined by future documentary finds. A final observation must be made. Berossus does not mention Belshazzar and seems not to have known anything of the existence of this energetic and influential son of Nabonidus.

[610] The *Nabonidus Chronicle* (p. 170) states that Nabonidus fled after the capture of Sippar. Can it be that Berossus has this event in mind? In cuneiform Sippar was written *Sip-par*[ki] and Borsippa was written *Bar-sip*[ki]. It is easy to see how the one might be confused with the other.

XIV

THE MEANING OF NON-CUNEIFORM ALLUSIONS TO BELSHAZZAR

Cuneiform allusions to Belshazzar have thrown so much light upon the rôle which he played that his place in history stands clearly revealed. There are many texts which indicate that Belshazzar almost equalled Nabonidus in position and prestige. Dual rulership during most of the last Neo-Babylonian reign is an established fact. Nabonidus exercised supreme authority from his court at Têmâ in Arabia, while Belshazzar acted as co-regent in the homeland with Babylon as his center of influence. It is evident that Belshazzar was not a feeble viceroy; he was entrusted with 'the kingship.' That Nabonidus gave orders to Belshazzar concerning certain matters does not disprove the conclusion that the latter possessed regal dignity and jurisdiction. Hence there were two potentates in the empire, one who maintained his seat of power in distant Arabia and one who directed affairs in Babylonia.

This situation was capable of creating confusion in the minds of later historians. Writers not supplied with authentic documentary information or reliable oral tradition might apprehend events distorted by the haze of intervening years. Various one-sided views, representing half-truths, could result. Such historical vestiges are in reality embedded in literary records which have long been at our disposal. Before the assembling of pertinent data from Babylonian tablets belonging to the reign of Nabonidus these incomplete reflections of what took place in the sixth century B. C. were difficult to interpret. This handicap no longer exists, for it now seems possible to unravel the meaning of statements which puzzled many who attempted their exposition.

1. *Indirect Allusions to Belshazzar*

The name Belshazzar is not mentioned by ancient Greek writers. Megasthenes and Berossus do not refer to the son of Nabonidus even indirectly. Statements made by Herodotus and Xenophon may be interpreted as alluding to Belshazzar, but his name does not occur in their writings.

(1) *Herodotus' Obscure Reference to Belshazzar*

Herodotus' record concerning the one whom he regards as the last Neo-Babylonian king is very brief. It is the simple affirmation that the king of Babylon at the time the city fell was Labynetus, the son of an older Labynetus and Queen Nitocris.[611] In a previous section of his work he places the first Labynetus in the reign of Nebuchadrezzar.[612] Can the statement of Herodotus be looked upon as incorporating a tradition of the actual situation in the time of Nabonidus? It has been shown in an earlier part of this monograph that this question may be answered affirmatively.[613] Keeping in mind the fact that there were two persons with kingly authority during the last Neo-Babylonian reign, a father and his son, with the father absent from Babylon most of the time, we can understand how it would be possible for a later historian to confuse the two. Such a writer could easily present a modified interpretation of the situation. What shall be our conclusion, then, as to the real characters impersonated by Labynetus I and Labynetus II? It is entirely within the range of possibility that Herodotus was dealing with Nabonidus and Belshazzar. That Labynetus I was Nabonidus has been proven with definite conclusiveness.[614] Hence there can be little doubt that Labynetus II was Belshazzar. That Herodotus gives the same name to both suggests that he had some inkling of their association as co-regents.

(2) *Xenophon's Obscure Reference to Belshazzar*

Xenophon in his *Cyropaedia* has preserved an extensive account of the events leading up to and including the fall of Babylon.[615] His story centers about the actions of Cyrus and Gobryas, and some have regarded it as mere romance. Xenophon describes Gobryas as a man of years coming to Cyrus and proffering his help in the capture of Babylon. The motive for the hostility of Gobryas towards Babylon was the fact that he had been mistreated by the Babylonian king. The king's father, represented as the predecessor on the throne, had

[611] Herodotus I, 188.
[612] Herodotus I, 74.
[613] See pp. 33ff.
[614] See pp. 36–42.
[615] *Cyropaedia* IV, 6; VII, 5.

offered his daughter in marriage to the son of Gobryas. In response Gobryas sent his son to the Babylonian court. The prince, who according to the narrative afterwards became king, invited the son of Gobryas to a hunt and assassinated him. Gobryas had planned to give his daughter in marriage to the young prince, but this alliance was now impossible. Both Gobryas and his daughter sought to avenge themselves after the Babylonian prince became king. Thus is explained the animus back of Gobryas' offer to help Cyrus. At the actual capture of Babylon it was Gobryas who with his attendants gained entrance to the palace and slew the young Babylonian king. Xenophon gives no names to these two Babylonian kings, but it seems possible that his story was constructed around the characters of Nabonidus and Belshazzar.[616] It is evident that Xenophon knew nothing of the extended stay of Nabonidus in Arabia. Nor was he aware that Belshazzar was co-regent with his father. With limited data at his disposal, he would naturally look upon the father of Belshazzar as no longer living when the latter was exercising the powers of a ruler in Babylonia. There may be some fanciful elements in Xenophon's record, but, if due allowance is made for his restricted knowledge and his excessive imagination, a modicum of truth is gained. The absent Nabonidus figures as the former king; Belshazzar, his son and associate on the throne, appears as his successor.

It is clear that Herodotus and Xenophon had different sources of information with regard to the last Neo-Babylonian reign.[617] The former preserved the name of Nabonidus, although in a slightly garbled form, but was entirely ignorant of the name of Belshazzar. The latter's narrative is devoid of any reference to Nabonidus and Belshazzar by positive citation, but the name and rôle of Gobryas, the *Gubarru*[618] of cuneiform inscriptions, are recorded.

[616] See *Klio* II, pp. 341–345, for Lehmann's discussion of *Gobryas und Belsazar bei Xenophon*.

[617] Lehmann in *Klio* II, p. 345, says: "Mir kommt es nur darauf an nachzuweisen, dass Xenophon ausser Herodot einer älteren Quelle vorgelegen hat, die er mit Bewusstsein und Bedacht in seinen Roman verwertet hat." See *Klio* XVIII, p. 226.

[618] For an exhaustive study of *Gobryas* see Schwenzner in *Klio* XVIII, pp. 41–58; 226–252. The name *Gubarru* occurs also as *Gubaru*, and possibly as *Ugbaru*.

2. Direct Allusions to Belshazzar

The preceding discussion has indicated that there are no direct allusions to Belshazzar in ancient Greek histories. Specific references to Belshazzar are found in the writings of Josephus and in the books of Baruch and Daniel. They will be reviewed in this order.

(1) Belshazzar's Rôle According to the History of Josephus

Josephus states that Labosordachus (Lâbâshi-Marduk) was succeeded by Baltasar (Belshazzar), who was called Naboandelus (Nabonidus) by the Babylonians.[619] He affirms further that Babylon was captured after Baltasar had reigned seventeen years, and that this was the end of the posterity of Nabuchodonosor (Nebuchadrezzar).[620] The most remarkable assertion is that Baltasar was called Naboandelus by the Babylonians. Even if we cannot ascertain with exactness what was in the mind of Josephus when he declared that Baltasar was called Naboandelus—whether he was endeavoring to harmonize canonical and secular history by a theory of his own or was preserving a tradition upon which he had chanced in his investigations[621]—nevertheless the fact remains that his statement is an example of the kind of confusion which could arise in later times with reference to a dual rulership such as that of Nabonidus and Belshazzar.[622] The seventeen-year period of power ascribed by Josephus to Belshazzar, *i.e.* a length of rule equal to that of Nabonidus, is practically supported by the cuneiform chronicles which have thus far been recovered. Babylonian tablets indicate that Belshazzar was associated with Nabonidus in the kingdom during a large part of the latter's reign, and the implication of all available documentary evidence is that this dual rulership lasted until the capture of Babylon by Cyrus in 539 B. C.

[619] Josephus, *Antiq. Jud.* X, 11, 2.

[620] *Ibid.*, X, 11, 4.

[621] The latter is more likely to have been the case because of his use of the name Naboandelus, although his Baltasar deviates very little from the Balthasar of Baruch 1:11, 12. Josephus exercises interpretative freedom because he refers to the queen, who advised that Daniel should be summoned, as the grandmother of Belshazzar. He also states that Belshazzar rewarded Daniel with 'the third part of his kingdom' (τὸ τρίτον τῆς αὐτοῦ ἀρχῆς μέρος). See Josephus, *Antiq. Jud.* X, 11, 3.

[622] See p. 9f for the strange statements of Syncellus: *Nabonadii, qui et Astyages; Nabonadius, qui et Astyages, Darius, Assuerus, et Artaxerxes.* Syncellus seems to preserve a vague reminiscence of a dual rulership during the reign of Nabonidus.

The origin of Josephus' assertion that Belshazzar was the end of the posterity of Nebuchadrezzar is difficult to trace. We know that Josephus had sources of information other than the sacred writings of the Jews. Some of these he quotes quite fully. It may be that he means to imply nothing more than that the Neo-Babylonian dynasty came to an end with the fall of Babylon, a result known to classical writers long before his time. In spite of this ambiguity the expression 'posterity of Nebuchadrezzar' is in harmony with the view that Nabonidus married a daughter of Nebuchadrezzar and that Belshazzar was the firstborn son of this union.

(2) Belshazzar's Rôle according to the Book of Baruch

The book of Baruch should be quoted next. It contains the following unusual passage as part of a letter which the context indicates was sent by Baruch from the Jews in Babylon to those that remained in Palestine: 'And pray ye for the life of Nabuchodonosor, the king of Babylon, and for the life of Balthasar, his son, that their days may be upon earth as the days of heaven; and that the Lord may give us strength and enlighten our eyes, that we may live under the shadow of Nabuchodonosor, the king of Babylon, and under the shadow of Balthasar, his son, and may serve them many days, and may find favor in their sight.'[623] With a tone that is distinctly Babylonian,[624] this passage produces an impression of exceptional literary uniqueness. The statements representing Nabuchodonosor (Nebuchadrezzar) and Balthasar (Belshazzar) as living at the same time are anachronous. However, they may preserve a tradition of a reign in the Neo-Babylonian empire when a king and his son, Nabonidus and Belshazzar, were ruling together, mingled with a tradition that the son was descended from Nebuchadrezzar.

[623] Baruch 1: 11, 12.

[624] Note in 1: 11 the idiom 'pray ye for the life of,' which is paralleled in the salutations of Neo-Babylonian letters by the idiom *ana balâṭ napšâti ṣalû* 'to pray for the life of;' *NLE* 8: 4, 5, etc. Note also in Baruch 1: 12 the idiom 'under the shadow of,' with the meaning 'under the protection of.' In Neo-Babylonian letters this is represented by *ina ṣilli ilâni*^{meš}, 'in the shadow of the gods;' *NLE* 9: 6, 7; 88: 6. Comparison should be made with Hebrew צל.

(3) *Belshazzar's Rôle according to the Book of Daniel*

We come last of all to the fifth chapter of Daniel. Numerous cuneiform inscriptions, differing widely in character, depict, as only contemporaneous documents can, the actual political situation which existed during the last Neo-Babylonian reign and indicate what happened when the dynasty fell. To what extent does the main historical framework of the fifth chapter of Daniel accord with these cuneiform sources? An attempt will be made to answer this question with an impartial facing of all difficulties connected with the comparison of ancient documents.

(*a*) A preliminary statement of *the crux of the problem* is necessary. The *Nabonidus Chronicle* furnishes no positive information concerning Belshazzar beyond the eleventh year of Nabonidus' reign. Available contract tablets of the time of Nabonidus contain no reference to Belshazzar beyond the fourteenth regnal year.[625] Hence no definite knowledge of Belshazzar's career during the last few years of Nabonidus' reign can be gained from cuneiform documents now at our disposal. How shall this silence be interpreted? It should be noted, in the first place, that the lower part of the obverse side and the upper part of the reverse side of the tablet inscribed with the *Nabonidus Chronicle* are in a state of complete mutilation.[626] It is difficult to determine how much of the tablet has been shattered. The statement concerning the eleventh year of Nabonidus' reign occurs just before this break. Regrettable defacement obscures other parts of the record. The impossibility of basing final conclusions concerning Belshazzar upon such a fragmentary inscription will be recognized. Imagination as to what the missing lines contained cannot be accepted as evidence. This is particularly true of the line which some have restored so as to obtain a reference to the death of Belshazzar after the entry of Cyrus into Babylon.[627] A second qualification of the text should not be overlooked. It seems to have been written at the behest of Persian interests which demanded the villification of Nabonidus.[628] The com-

[625] See p. 85.

[626] See *BA* II, p. 248, for plates containing autographed copies of both sides of the *Nabonidus Chronicle.*

[627] See *ibid.*, p. 222, col. III, line 23. Cf. discussion on p. 173f of this monograph.

[628] See pp. 180ff.

plete rôle of Belshazzar may not have been recorded in such a document. As to the testimony of contract tablets ranging in date from the fourteenth to the seventeenth year of Nabonidus' reign, it must be remembered that those now published and deciphered do not comprise the total documentary output of Babylonia for the period mentioned. The likelihood that they represent a mere fraction of the cuneiform records of the time should be kept in mind. Definite inferences based upon their non-mention of Belshazzar would not be valid. All these considerations, however, do not alter the fact that it is necessary for us to deal with cuneiform silence concerning Belshazzar during the closing years of Nabonidus' reign. Berossus, whose record may go back to a Babylonian origin, gives no place to Belshazzar in his narrative.[629] On the other hand, Herodotus and Xenophon, if their statements have been interpreted correctly, testify in favor of the presence of Belshazzar in Babylon when it fell, although he is not mentioned by name.[630] A conclusion may now be stated. No document of Babylonian origin affirms that Belshazzar was present at the fall of Babylon. Nevertheless, no positive cuneiform evidence against his participation in the events of 539 B. C. has been found. Not a single intimation that he was deprived of power or that he was removed by death before the taking of Babylon by Gobryas is at hand. Balancing this with the apparent implications derived from Herodotus and Xenophon, we have some basis for the deduction that Belshazzar acted as co-regent until the end of the Neo-Babylonian empire. Future discoveries must determine how unequivocal this conclusion ought to be.

(*b*) *The opening words* of the fifth chapter of Daniel, viz. 'Belshazzar the king,' attract singular attention. It is an incontrovertible fact that there was a Babylonian prince by the name of Belshazzar; that he acted as co-regent in Babylonia during the absence of his father in Arabia is equally indisputable.[631] Emphasis should be placed upon the full meaning of these two assertions. The name Belshazzar (בלשׁאצר, var. בלאשׁצר) is the Aramaic equivalent of Babylonian

[629] See Josephus, *Contra Apionem* I, 20.

[630] Herodotus I, 188; *Cyropaedia* VII, 5, 29f.

[631] See pp. 105–137.

Bêl-šar-uṣur[632] = *Bêl-shar-u-tzur*. It is quite possible, however, that *Bêl-šar-uṣur* may in practice have been pronounced something like *Bêl-shar-tzur, i.e.* with a suppression of the initial vowel of the final element (the imperative of the verb *naṣâru*) of the name. The approximation of *Bêl-shar-tzur* to Belshazzar is very apparent. Baruch's Balthasar[633] and Josephus' Baltasar[634] cannot be compared so convincingly with the Babylonian form of the name. Hence the fifth chapter of Daniel is linked with original cuneiform documents by the name Belshazzar. With reference to the second assertion, a cuneiform text states that Nabonidus empowered Belshazzar with 'the kingship' in the third year of his reign.[635] All accessible cuneiform documents capable of throwing light upon the situation indicate that Belshazzar occupied this high position until the fourteenth year of Nabonidus' reign and the probability is that he functioned as co-regent until the end of the reign. There is no room for doubt that Belshazzar ruled in the kingdom next to Nabonidus. The writer of the fifth chapter of Daniel comports with cuneiform data in picturing the chief character of his narrative as having enjoyed kingly dignity.

(*c*) The fact that *Nebuchadrezzar is referred to as the father of Belshazzar* is one of the main features of the fifth chapter of Daniel.[636] This should be interpreted with the following facts in mind. Babylonian texts and Greek data indicate that Nabonidus' ancestry and early life fitted him for marriage with a daughter of Nebuchadrezzar.[637] Such connection with the reigning dynasty may be regarded as explaining Nabonidus' accession to the throne in the most satis-

632 The meaning of the name is 'O Bêl, protect the king!' For the form בלסראצר see Lidzbarski, *Ephemeris für semitische Epigraphik*, III, p. 117, and Lidzbarski, *Altaramäische Urkunden aus Assur*, p. 15f. The former work refers to the occurrence of the name upon a stone statue, thought to have been found in Egypt; the latter refers to the occurrence of the name on two clay tablets bearing Aramaic records.

633 Baruch 1: 11, 12.

634 Josephus, *Antiq. Jud.* X, 11, 2f. Note the βαλτασάρ of LXX, Daniel 5.

635 *BHT* pp. 84, 88, col. II, line 20. See p. 106f of this monograph.

636 Daniel 5: 2, 11, 13, 18, 22. The form of the name used is *Nebuchadnezzar* and not *Nebuchadrezzar*. This is not a serious deviation from the cuneiform pronunciation. For Semitic interchange of *r* and *n* see Brockelmann, *Grundriss der vergleichenden Grammatik der semitischen Sprachen* I, pp. 224, 225, 226, 228, 229, 230, 231. It must be admitted, however, that if the form *Nebuchadrezzar* were present in the fifth chapter of Daniel it would represent the original cuneiform more accurately.

637 See pp. 16–33.

factory way.[638] There are intimations in cuneiform inscriptions that Nabonidus considered himself in thorough accord with the house of Nebuchadrezzar.[639] The queen who steps upon the stage in Daniel 5:10 is conversant with things that occurred in the court of Nebuchadrezzar. Her tone of address shows that she was not the wife of Belshazzar, for her solicitude appears to have been that of a mother. It has been shown that the consort of Nabonidus was the queen whom Herodotus calls Nitocris.[640] The possibility and to some extent the probability that Nitocris was a daughter of Nebuchadrezzar has been dealt with at length in a previous chapter.[641] If the inferences which have been drawn are valid, Belshazzar was a grandson of Nebuchadrezzar. Should this prove to have been the relationship which existed between the two, one need not be surprised that the fifth chapter of Daniel calls Nebuchadrezzar the father instead of the grandfather of Belshazzar, as this is entirely in harmony with Semitic usage under such circumstances.[642] Of course it is impossible to know with exactness what was in the mind of the ancient author, but his reference to Nebuchadrezzar as the father of Belshazzar cannot be regarded as scientifically-established error.

(*d*) *That a festival could have taken place in Babylon* when it was being besieged is not unlikely. The walls of the city were regarded as impregnable by the Babylonians. Furthermore, the beleaguered inhabitants were supplied with a vast store of provisions according to Herodotus and Xenophon.[643] There is little need to question the

[638] See pp. 60ff.

[639] See p. 73.

[640] See pp. 42ff.

[641] See pp. 51ff.

[642] The Hebrew and Aramaic word for father is used in the sense of ancestor. See I Kings 15: 11; II Kings 14: 3; 18: 3; Isaiah 51: 2. In Genesis 28: 13 Abraham is called the father of Jacob. In II Samuel 9: 7 Saul is called the father of Mephibosheth, who was in reality the grandson of Saul. In Tobit 1: 15 Sennacherib is referred to as the son of Shalmaneser, omitting Sargon, the king who came between them. It was customary for Babylonian kings to refer to any one of their predecessors as their father. Thus Nebuchadrezzar called Narâm-Sin his *a-ba-a-am la-bé-ri*, 'ancient father.' See *NKI* p. 78, col. III, line 27. Note *šarrâni ab-bi-e-a*, 'the kings, my fathers,' *ibid.*, p. 74, col. II, line 46. Cf. *ibid.*, p. 110, col. II, line 77. In using the term 'father' for 'ancestor,' particularly of a royal predecessor, the fifth chapter of Daniel is in harmony not only with Hebrew and Aramaic, but also with Neo-Babylonian custom. See *Hwb* p. 3 for *abu*, 'Ahn,' 'Vorfahre.'

[643] Herodotus I, 190; *Cyropaedia* VII, 5, 13.

strongly-protected state of the city. Similarly, its abundant reserves of the necessities of life seem credible, for the certainty of Cyrus' attack must have been realized long before his arrival. Hence a spirit of revelry connected with the observance of a festal occasion could have expressed itself in the Babylonian metropolis, even though the army of Cyrus had completely invested it. At the beginning of the cuneiform chronicle of events leading up to the fall of Babylon mention is made of the fact that there was plenty of wine among the Babylonian troops at the New Year's festival.[644] This is suggestive, but Babylon did not surrender to Gobryas until about six months later and the cuneiform record is silent as to what was taking place in Babylon when it actually fell.[645] However, both Herodotus and Xenophon lay stress upon the celebration of a convivial fête at the time when the soldiers of Cyrus gained access to the city.[646] The parallel Biblical account is presented in dramatic manner.[647]

(*e*) *Why is Nabonidus not mentioned* in the Scriptural narrative of the fall of Babylon? It must be remembered that the fifth chapter of Daniel was not written as a complete record of occurrences which took place in connection with Babylon's capture. Only a few events of the fatal night are depicted. There is no reference to preliminary happenings or subsequent incidents. The sacred chronicler cannot be adjudged guilty of error because he fails to name Nabonidus in his portrayal of the last act of the drama of Neo-Babylonian collapse. There is a possibility that Nabonidus was not in Babylon when it was captured; the *Nabonidus Chronicle* and the account of Berossus appear to agree on this point.[648] Hence the fifth chapter of Daniel may be regarded as comporting with fact in not giving any place to

[644] See p. 168, line 7 of transliterated and translated text.

[645] It should be noted, however, that the spirit of revelry could have lasted for months, even down to the eve of Babylon's capture. See *BHT* p. 103.

[646] Herodotus I, 191; *Cyropaedia* VII, 5, 15 and 25. It is evident that Gobryas was able to give information to the Persians concerning the celebration of the festival.

[647] Daniel 5: 1–4.

[648] See p. 170, line 16 of transliterated and translated text. Cf. p. 180 for Berossus' story. Baumgartner in *Zeitschrift für die alttestamentliche Wissenschaft*, XLIV, p. 50, note 2, opposes the transliteration *šib-sa* as propounded by Sidney Smith, *BHT* p. 121, note on line 16. However, Smith shows good reasons why the reading should be *ME-sa* (*šib-sa*) rather than *LAL-sa*, and hence the translation 'Afterwards Nabonidus, when he returned to Babylon, was taken prisoner,' appears to have textual warrant.

Nabonidus in the narrative, for he seems to have had no share in the events which transpired when Gobryas entered the city.[649]

(*f*) Although Nabonidus was not present in the imperial capital when it yielded to the troops of Cyrus, he was still *regarded as the king of Babylon*.[650] In fact there were those of his subjects who looked upon him as their sovereign until the second month after Babylon fell. Even if it cannot be substantiated by present data derived from cuneiform sources, there is no reason for doubting, while awaiting further evidence, that Belshazzar was acting as co-regent when Babylon was captured. On this assumption there were two sovereigns in the kingdom at that time. Nabonidus was the titular head of the nation, but Belshazzar who had been delegated with royal authority by his father, was the second ruler. The fifth chapter of Daniel is in remarkable harmony with such a state of affairs. It describes a situation in which a man meriting royal favor could be rewarded by being made the third ruler in the kingdom.[651] Different views have been expressed as to the meaning of the phrase 'the third ruler in the

[649] Genouillac, *RA* XXII, p. 79f, advances the view that the Nebuchadrezzar of the fifth chapter of Daniel represents Nabonidus. Genouillac says: "On sait déjà que Nabonide est le Nabukodonosor de Daniel; le prétendu massacre des sages s'expliquerait par les discussion de Nabonide avec les prêtres de Babylone; le songe de Nabukodonosor rappellerait les songes de Nabonide relatés dans ses inscriptions (*VAB* IV, 218); l'histoire de la statue colossale de Nabukodonosor, le culte de la statue de Ḫarrân; la folie du roi répondrait à la maladie de Nabonide et à sa prétendue 'possession du démon' de notre poème-pamphlet; la fuite du roi dément au milieu des animaux du désert serait une transformation populaire du séjour de Nabonide à Téma, au milieu des caravanes; les orgies des fêtes du Nouvel An de 538 (*sic*) seraient le fait dont garderait le souvenir l'histoire du festin de Balthazar." See *BHT* pp. 46, note 1; 50 and note 1; 51. The strongest part of the theory is as follows: Nebuchadrezzar's dream, erection of a great image, and ultimate demented condition with life among the wild beasts represent Nabonidus' dream, erection of a statue of the moon god, demoniacal state and sojourn among the tribesmen of Arabia. Baumgartner in *Zeitschrift für die alttestamentliche Wissenschaft*, XLIV, pp. 45–51, strongly criticises the validity of this interpretation. There can be no doubt as to the extremely hypothetical character of such an explanation of the origin of certain parts of the book of Daniel.

[650] See note 557.

[651] Three statements in the fifth chapter of Daniel refer to this situation. V. 7 provides the following statement: ותלתי במלכותא ישלט, 'and he shall rule as third in the kingdom.' In v. 16 occurs: ותלתא במלכותא תשלט, 'and thou shalt rule as third in the kingdom.' The third statement is in v. 29: די־להוא שליט תלתא במלכותא, 'that he should be the third ruler in the kingdom.'

kingdom.'[652] The most rational procedure is to interpret it in the light of known circumstances. Cuneiform records have demonstrated conclusively that Nabonidus and Belshazzar functioned as two rulers during most of the former's reign, and there is no positive evidence that this political arrangement did not last until the final days of the Neo-Babylonian empire.[653] That the account in Daniel takes cognizance of this, although not mentioning Nabonidus, may be regarded as indicating a true historical basis for the narrative.[654]

(*g*) The *Nabonidus Chronicle* implies that Babylon fell into the hands of the Persians *without a general conflict.*[655] Herodotus and Xenophon describe a surprise attack at night with desultory resistance on the part of the Babylonians.[656] No conclusion can be drawn from the indefinite statement of Berossus.[657] A preponderance of data appears to establish the fact that Cyrus gained possession of Babylon without

[652] See the excellent summary in Montgomery, *A Critical and Exegetical Commentary on the Book of Daniel*, p. 256f. Cf. *JAOS* XLIII, p. 232, for Professor Torrey's view that the three instances of 'third' in the fifth chapter of Daniel refer to the fact that the interpreter of the dream 'shall govern the kingdom as third ruler.'

[653] The writer realizes that the negative data concerning the latter part of Nabonidus' reign cannot be used as definite proof. More positive conclusions can be drawn when additional information has become available.

[654] It is clear that Nabonidus was looked upon as the first ruler in the nation and that Belshazzar was regarded as the second. The interpreter of the dream in the fifth chapter of Daniel was given third place in the kingdom. So far as the writer knows, Hugo Grotius (1583–1645) was the first to suggest this interpretation. See Wintle's commentary, *Daniel*, p. 73. It has been accepted by many since his time. Historical parallels to dual rulership are not wanting. The instance of Cyrus and Cambyses is the most striking because it involves the régime in Babylonia immediately following that of Nabonidus and Belshazzar. See p. 95 and p. 178. The closing prayer in the inscription of Antiochus I Soter refers to Seleucus, his son, as king. See *KB* III, 2, p. 138, line 25; *KA* p. 135, line 25. This suggests that Antiochus and Seleucus were co-regents at the time. Crown prince Nebuchadrezzar exercised a powerful influence in Babylonian affairs as the generalissimo leading the Babylonian army in the war against the Egyptians, although there is no indication that he was granted kingly dignity before the death of Nabopolassar. Esarhaddon before he undertook his campaign against Egypt made his son Ashurbanipal king of Assyria and his son Shamash-shum-ukîn king of Babylon. See Olmstead, *History of Assyria*, pp. 389, 396. Jehoram, the son of Jehoshaphat, acted as co-ruler with his father. See II Kings 8: 16. Cf. Knight, *Nile and Jordan*, pp. 79, 80, 131, 132, 226, 230, 265, 283, for Egyptian examples of father and son ruling together.

[655] See p. 170, lines 15b, 16, of transliterated and translated text.

[656] Herodotus I, 191; *Cyropaedia* VII, 5, 17–32.

[657] See Josephus, *Contra Apionem* I, 20.

a pitched battle. Proof is wanting that the writer of the fifth chapter of Daniel thought that Babylon was captured as the result of vigorous combat involving the full strength of opposing armies. The bare reference to the slaying of Belshazzar is not enough to sustain such an interpretation.[658] It has been shown that cuneiform confirmation of Belshazzar's death in connection with the fall of Babylon cannot be claimed thus far.[659] If there is an inclination to believe that this is an undeniable contradiction of the fifth chapter of Daniel, remembrance of the weakness of argument from silence will prevent final judgment in the matter.

(*h*) *Cyrus was the real conqueror and overlord of Babylon,* but there are cuneiform references to two rulers in Babylonia under him. Cambyses, his son, was king of Babylon early in the reign of Cyrus;[660] Gobryas was governor of Babylon and the District beyond the River.[661] With reference to the authority possessed by Cambyses under Cyrus after the fall of Babylon, it should be noted that it was similar in some respects to that wielded by Belshazzar under Nabonidus.[662] Cyrus was the supreme sovereign of the whole Persian empire; Cambyses was a subordinate king over a limited part of the empire. The parallel is not complete, however, for Belshazzar, so far

[658] Daniel 5: 30.

[659] See p. 173f. It should be noted, however, that Belshazzar disappeared entirely from history. In Tallqvist, *Neubabylonisches Namenbuch*, p. 42, by misreading of signs, a *Bêl-šar-uṣur* is recorded as belonging to the time of Cyrus and Darius. The reading should be *Amurrû-šar-uṣur*. See *StrCyr* 178: 3; 312: 5; *StrDar* 42: 3. In the time of Darius the Great, Nidintu-Bêl and Araḫu attempted to win adherents as pseudo-kings, not by claiming that they were Belshazzar, but by assuming the name of Nebuchadrezzar, another son of Nabonidus. See references in note 236. Cf. Meissner, *Könige Babyloniens und Assyriens*, p. 282. For a further discussion of Belshazzar's career see Baumgartner, *Zeitschrift für die alttestamentliche Wissenschaft* XLIV, pp. 38–56.

[660] See p. 95.

[661] *Klio*, XVIII, pp. 41–58; 226–252.

[662] The high position occupied by Cambyses in connection with Persian control of Babylon is indicated by the fact that he, instead of Cyrus, according to the *Nabonidus Chronicle*, col. III, lines 24–28 (*BHT* pp. 114, 118), presided at the first New Year's festival to be observed after the city's capture. This act of regal significance on the part of Cambyses is significant. Belshazzar, so far as extant cuneiform records reveal, did not celebrate the New Year's festival during the absence of Nabonidus in Arabia, although there is every indication that he performed other royal functions in Babylon, Nabonidus having delegated 'the kingship' to him.

as is known, never bore the title 'king of Babylon.'[663] It may be more correct to assume that Cambyses governed what had been the Neo-Babylonian empire, thus in a sense succeeding both Nabonidus and Belshazzar. Gobryas, on the other hand, never occupied a regal position, although he exercised very high administrative power. Of the two Cambyses was the one whose jurisdiction was extensive enough to warrant the view that he 'received the kingdom'[664] as a viceroy under Cyrus. Nevertheless, the identity of 'Darius the Mede,'[665] remains an enigma, and much more information of authentic origin must be in hand before his historical character can be determined.

(*i*) The foregoing summary of information concerning Belshazzar, when judged in the light of data obtained from the texts discussed in this monograph, indicates that of all non-Babylonian records dealing with the situation at the close of the Neo-Babylonian empire *the*

[663] So far as specific language is concerned, Belshazzar is not referred to as 'the king of Babylon' in the fifth chapter of Daniel. The general title applied to him is 'the king.' The statement in the cuneiform record of the campaign against Têmâ is that Nabonidus entrusted *šarrûtam*, 'the kingship,' not *šarrûtam ša Bâbili*[ki], 'the kingship of Babylon,' to Belshazzar, although the latter is implied. See *BHT* pp. 84, 88, col. II, line 20. In Daniel 5: 30 Belshazzar is called 'the Chaldaean king.' The translation 'the king of the Chaldaeans' is not warranted by the text. Aramaic כשׂדיא is equivalent to Babylonian [amêl]*Kal-da-a-a* (from *Kaš-da-a-a*). It is conceivable that the descriptive title מלכא כשׂדיא could have been applied to Belshazzar as co-regent as well as to Nabonidus himself. In Daniel 7: 1 occurs the phrase 'In the first year of Belshazzar, the king of Babylon,' and in Daniel 8: 1 we find 'In the third year of the reign of Belshazzar, the king.' In both cases the form בלאשׁצר is used. These statements according a royal rôle to Belshazzar need not be regarded as anomalous, inasmuch as Belshazzar was associated with his father on the throne. The cuneiform assertion, quoted above, that Nabonidus entrusted 'the kingship' to Belshazzar carries weight because it is not qualified in any way. The parallel co-regency of Cyrus and Cambyses, in accordance with which documents were dated in the reign of the son during the father's lifetime, cannot be ignored in this connection. See p. 95 and note 311. However, no Babylonian tablet ascribing to Belshazzar the title *šar Bâbili*[ki], 'the king of Babylon,' has been brought to light thus far. For the nature of arguments adduced to disprove the historicity of the fifth chapter of Daniel see Rowley, *The Belshazzar of Daniel and History*, in *The Expositor*, 1924, pp. 182–195, 255–272.

[664] Daniel 5: 31 (= 6: 1 of the Hebrew text).

[665] For recent discussions of the identity of 'Darius the Mede' see Montgomery, *op, cit.*, pp. 63–65; Boutflower, *In and Around the Book of Daniel*, pp. 142–167. It is impossible in this monograph to give references to all that has been written concerning the fifth chapter of Daniel. The reader is referred to the exhaustive bibliography given in Montgomery, *op. cit.*, pp. XV–XXVI.

fifth chapter of Daniel ranks next to cuneiform literature in accuracy so far as outstanding events are concerned. The Scriptural account may be interpreted as excelling because it employs the name Belshazzar, because it attributes royal power to Belshazzar, and because it recognizes that a dual rulership existed in the kindgom. Babylonian cuneiform documents[666] of the sixth century B. C. furnish clear-cut evidence of the correctness of these three basic historical nuclei contained in the Biblical narrative dealing with the fall of Babylon. Cuneiform texts[667] written under Persian influence in the sixth century B. C. have not preserved the name Belshazzar, but his rôle as a crown prince entrusted with royal power during Nabonidus' stay in Arabia is depicted convincingly. Two famous Greek historians[668] of the fifth and fourth centuries B. C. do not mention Belshazzar by name and hint only vaguely at the actual political situation which existed in the time of Nabonidus. Annals[669] in the Greek language ranging from about the beginning of the third century B. C. to the first century B. C. are absolutely silent concerning Belshazzar and the prominence which he had during the last reign of the Neo-Babylonian empire. The total information found in all available chronologically-fixed documents[670] later than the cuneiform texts of the sixth century B. C. and prior to the writings of Josephus of the first century A. D. could not have provided the necessary material for the historical framework of the fifth chapter of Daniel.[671]

[666] See the texts presented and discussed in Chapters IX and X, pp. 93–137.

[667] These texts came into existence at the beginning of the Persian régime. See under *Persian Data*, p. 180f.

[668] For a discussion of obscure references to Belshazzar by Herodotus and Xenophon, see p. 187f.

[669] For a summary of allusions to Nabonidus and Cyrus by Megasthenes, Berossus, and Alexander Polyhistor, with no intimation on their part that they knew anything of Belshazzar, see p. 11f.

[670] The first chapter of Baruch, which synchronizes the lives of Nebuchadrezzar and Belshazzar, cannot be regarded as the norm from which the fifth chapter of Daniel developed. For a brief discussion of the pertinent data of the first chapter of Baruch, see p. 190.

[671] The view that the fifth chapter of Daniel originated in the Maccabaean age is discredited. Biblical critics have pushed back its date to the third century B. C. See Montgomery, *op. cit.*, p. 96, on the dating of Daniel 1–6. However, a narrative characterized by such an accurate historical perspective as Daniel 5 ought to be entitled to a place much nearer in time to the reliable documents which belong to the general epoch with which it deals.

INDEX

wife, 173; impiety ascribed to him in *Cyrus Cylinder*, 176; his bringing of deities to Babylon, 178; represented in unfavorable light, 180; not mentioned in the fifth chapter of Daniel, 195; his dream, 196; supposed demoniacal state, 196; had no share in events connected with the capture of Babylon by Gobryas, 196.
Nabonidus Chronicle, 3, 25, 105, 107, 108, 110, 111, 112, 113, 134, 135, 137, 138, 142, 156, 159, 168, 169, 175, 180, 181, 182, 183, 184, 185, 191, 195, 198.
Nabonidus-Cyrus Chronicle, 3.
Nabonnedus, 8, 12. See Nabonidus.
Nabopalassari, 9. See Nabopolassar.
Nabopolassar, king of Babylon, 1, 19, 44, 45, 47, 48, 53, 54, 55, 59, 75, 79, 197.
Nabopollassar, 9. See Nabopolassar.
Nabû, god, 17, 96, 101, 112, 132, 169.
Nabû-apal-uṣur, 7. See Nabopolassar.
Nabû-balâṭsu-iqbi, the father of Nabonidus, 16–18, 27, 32, 39, 93.
Nabuchodonosor, 9, 10, 12, 189, 190. See Nebuchadrezzar.
Nabucodrosorus, 8. See Nebuchadrezzar.
Nabucolassar, 9. See Nebuchadrezzar.
Nabugdonosor, 13. See Nebuchadrezzar.
Nabukodrosorus, 8. See Nebuchadrezzar.
Nabû-kudurri-uṣur, 7. See Nebuchadrezzar.
Nabû-mukîn-aḫi, the scribe of Belshazzar, 83, 84, 86.
Nabû-nâ'id, the king, 1, *passim*. See Nabonidus.
Nabû-nâ'id, the witness, Aramaean background, 30; prominence, 30; political influence, 31; princely connection, 32; probability that he was Nabonidus, 30, 31, 32, 33.
Nabupalsar, 8. See Nabopolassar.
Nabupalsarus, 8. See Nabopolassar.
Nabû-shar-uṣur, a chief officer of the king, 30, 98, 127, 128, 132, 133, 134.
Nabû-ṣâbit-qâtâ, the steward of Belshazzar, 84, 85, 86.
nadânu, 120, 127, 132.
nakâmu, nakamtu, nakantu, 120.
nakkandu, 120, 124.
Nanâ, goddess, 91, 96, 127, 128.
Naqi'a, one of the consorts of Sennacherib, 43, 56. See Tashmêtum-sharrat.
Narâm-Sin, king of Akkad, 194.
narâm ummišu, 21.
naṣâru, 193.
naš, 100.
našû, 99, 132.
Nebuchadnezzar, 8, 14, 193. See Nebuchadrezzar.
Nebuchadrezzar, king of Babylon, 12, 13, 19, 29, 30, 31, 32, 33, 34, 35, 36, 37, 38, 39, 40, 41, 43, 44, 45, 47, 48, 50, 51, 52, 53, 55, 56, 57, 58, 59, 60, 61, 63, 68, 69, 73, 76, 79, 99, 100, 116, 117, 128, 129, 143, 147, 148, 175, 182, 187, 189, 190, 193, 194, 196, 197.
Necho, king of Egypt, 44, 45, 46, 47, 51, 52, 56, 57, 58, 59, 60, 62.
Neglisar, 9. See Neriglissar.
Neglisarus, 9. See Neriglissar.
Neo-Babylonian empire, 1, 2, 48, 67, 162.
Neo-Babylonian kings, according to cuneiform texts, 7; according to Megasthenes, 8; according to Berossus, 8; according to Polyhistor, 8; according to Ptolemy, 9; according to Saint Jerome, 9; according to Syncellus, 9, 10; summary of chronology, 10; synchronistic table, 45; dynastic table, 79.
Neo-Babylonian Panegyric of Cyrus, 3.
Neo-Babylonian personal names, 47.
Neo-Babylonian texts, their value, 2.
Nergal, god, 101.
Nergal-sharezer, 60. See Neriglissar.
Nergal-šar-uṣur, 7, 14. See Neriglissar.
Nericasolassar, 9. See Neriglissar.
Neriglasarus, 8. See Neriglissar.
Neriglissar, king of Babylon, 1, 14, 19, 35, 45, 53, 60, 61, 67, 68, 69, 70, 73, 74, 75, 76, 77, 78, 79, 128, 146, 147.
Nerogasolasari, 9. See Neriglissar.
New Year's festival, 95, 106, 112, 113, 147, 168, 169, 171, 173, 195, 198.